MY SUNDAYS

WITH HENRY MILLER

a memoir

JEANNE REJAUNIER

Copyright © 2014 Jeanne Rejaunier

All rights reserved.

ISBN-13: 978-1492195726

ISBN-10: 1492195723

DEDICATION

To The Three L's who have influenced my life:

The one and only LEE MERRIN, who played such a special role with Henry and me;

The multi-talented LOUISE CABRAL, a true friend throughout the years;

And the remarkable LEON KATZ, who started me on an untrodden path I'm still treading.

My gratitude and appreciation for all your help and support. Namaste!

CONTENTS

DEDICATION
ACKNOWLEDGMENTS
PREFACE
INTRODUCTION
Chapter One
Chapter Two
Chapter Three
Chapter Four
Chapter Five
Chapter Six
Chapter Seven
Chapter Eight
Chapter Nine
Chapter Ten
Chapter Eleven
Chapter Twelve
Chapter Thirteen
Chapter Fourteen
Chapter Fifteen
Chapter Sixteen
Chapter Seventeen
Chapter Eighteen
Chapter Nineteen
Chapter Twenty
Chapter Twenty-One
AFTERWORD
ABOUT THE AUTHOR
Critics' Reviews - THE BEAUTY TRAP
Other Books by Jeanne Rejaunier
Coming Soon
Watch Jeanne's Hollywood acting performances
Chapter Six: PLANES OF THE HEAVENWORLD
Connect with Jeanne Rejaunier

ACKNOWLEDGMENTS

LITERARY LOS ANGELES, so many of whom are no longer with us, who advised and encouraged me as a writer;

SPIRITUAL /METAPHYSICAL LOS ANGELES, who opened my eyes and inspired me to look beyond;

The heritage of centuries past, without which, as Henry said, where would any of us be?

ACTRESS FRANCINE YORK: "I love to tell the story about how every time Henry came to this friend's house, before he left he would always say, 'May your house be safe from tigers.' Finally the friend asked Henry, 'Every time you come here you always say may your house be safe from tigers. Why do you say that?' Henry replied, 'Have you seen any tigers here lately?' I love that story of Henry's."

####

PREFACE

Email from Jeanne Rejaunier to Lee Merrin:
Hi, Lee, I was wondering if by any chance you might have a copy of the transcript of the Henry Miller/Irving Wallace/Jeanne Rejaunier conversation that Sunday afternoon you arranged between Henry, "Wallace Irving" (as Henry called him) and me at the Wallaces' home? I don't know what happened to my copy. I thought I had it and now can't find it anywhere. It would be so serendipitous if you do have a copy and could email, fax or snail mail it to me. (And let me know any costs involved so I can send you a check). Thanks so much! xxx Jeanne

Email from Lee Merrin to Jeanne Rejaunier:
No costs IF indeed I have a copy at all. My files surprise me at times with hidden treasure so I shall take a look. If I had a transcript I am sure I would have kept it. I remember a reel-to-reel recording I secretly made with the photographer assigned (Don Ornitz of Globe Photos. Did you know that he was a later suicide?). And it was from that recorder stashed unobtrusively behind the bar that I had the conversation taped. The transcription was a gem... I will look, Jeanne. Absolutely great that you're writing about this. Keep me posted. Hugs, Lee M

Email from Jeanne Rejaunier to Lee Merrin:
Thanks so much, Lee. I didn't realize you were the one who taped the conversation! In that case, I bet you must have it somewhere (hope you do!) Yes, I did know that Don Ornitz committed suicide. But Don was the photographer who shot my nude photos in *Playboy*; and it was Ralph Crane who did the 4 page *Life* spread. My fingers are crossed that you have that transcript! xxx Jeanne

Email from Lee to Jeanne, one month later:
No luck but we have a huge garage and several file cabinets. I have not given up yet! So many thanks for the background information below! Love, Lee

Email from Jeanne to Lee:
Lee, I'm trying to piece it all together; I do have some scattered notes, photos, memories... ah, yes, definitely lots of those, some of it a blur, some strong, despite passage of time. The years blend into each other so that it's sometimes hard to remember where one year ended and another began. Many of my personal records were lost with moves. I keep hoping more will turn up. I know exactly what happened to some of my writing and the diaries in general, but specifically don't know what was in each box that has been lost, either in Europe, California, New York, or Florida (flood in the garage destroyed some boxes). But I still have at least 50 or more boxes I haven't been able to access in Florida, and several more in storage in California, and I did find some files, notes, photos, info, so I can go about reconstructing – and of course, those memories persist ... Sundays at the Siegels', invited to Henry's home for dinner on a few occasions, meeting him socially on separate Sunday nights as well, Nicky Blair's informal dinner parties, Eve Bruce and I running into Henry and Joe Grey in restaurants, joining them in interesting table to table conversations. And of course, the memorable afternoon's 4 page shoot for *Life* magazine at the Wallaces' which you so expertly facilitated.

Email from Lee to Jeanne:
Remember what Henry said about you in the *San Francisco Examiner*. "You'll be somebody, I know you will. You have this deep philosophical thing going and this sex thing going also." God bless Henry, wherever he is!

######

JEANNE REJAUNIER

INTRODUCTION

Sunday afternoons beginning in the mid-sixties, author Henry Miller and I were guests of physician Lee E. Siegel, M.D. and his wife, beautiful Hollywood actress Noreen Nash, at their Beverly Hills home on Maple Drive. The Siegels' small private salon was an intimate affair, often attended only by Noreen and Dr. Siegel, Henry, his "boon companion" Joe Grey and me, and sometimes by one or two other guests, some of whom I brought, among others, an international psychic and former Miss Portugal; a former dancer-choreographer card carrying communist, my body movement coach, who had previously introduced me to Anaïs Nin; and a South American actress/activist who fell madly in love with Henry, whose untimely death in her mid-twenties to this day remains a mystery.

The Siegels was a casual literary salon, yet worthy of the adjective glittering thanks to the magnetic and eloquent presence of Henry Miller, his talent as raconteur, his knowledge, erudition and gift of gab, and his unquestionable star power. As an extroverted people lover and great communicator, Henry was invariably the central focus of conversations. Under his guidance, we explored a far ranging assortment of literary, artistic, musical, and metaphysical topics, such as: astrology, reincarnation, life after death, Vedanta, Theosophy, Buddhism, French literature, the lives and works of countless authors, artists and musicians, and much, much more.

In addition to the regular Sundays at the Siegels, I saw Henry at other gatherings during this period, including at actor/restauranteur Nicky Blair's Sunday evening dinner parties; at author Irving Wallace's home on a Sunday, where Henry posed with Irving and me for a four page *Life* magazine spread, and participated in a four hour long taped symposium; for dinners and ping pong with Henry at Henry's home in Pacific Palisades; at two of Henry's favorite restaurants, and at chance meetings elsewhere.

When Henry and I first met, I was acting in film and television and taking writing courses at the UCLA. Extension. Henry encouraged me in my transition from model and actress to writer/author. What follows in this book are some of the recollections of my encounters with Henry, the majority of which took place on a Sunday.

######

CHAPTER ONE

I was living in Italy, having breakfast at the counter of a Roman coffee shop called the California, an American hangout just off the Via Veneto, when singer Eddie Fisher and his burly, large boned bodyguard/ personal assistant/ gopher/companion, came in and sat down next to me.

Pointing at me from his seat on the other side of Eddie, Eddie's sidekick said, "Eddie – M.M.!"

"Absolutely," Eddie agreed, nodding in my direction.

"We'll have to tell Kurt about this, Eddie!"

"Definitely," Eddie agreed, and holding out his hand to me, said, "Hello, I'm Eddie Fisher, and this is my friend Bob Abrams. And you are?" After I introduced myself, Eddie said, "I can tell you're American, Jeanne. What are you doing here in Rome?"

"I live here."

"You must be an actress. You look like an actress."

"That's right, I am."

"Well, we'll have to introduce you to Kurt Frings," Eddie said. "Kurt is my wife's agent."

"Eddie's married to Elizabeth Taylor," Bob Abrams clarified, as if I might not be aware of that internationally publicized fact.

"Kurt Frings is known as the best women's agent in Hollywood," Eddie said. "He's also handles Audrey Hepburn, Eva Marie Saint, Maria Schell, and a bunch of other international stars. He'll definitely want to meet you. You look so much like a girl who was very important in his life."

"Is that the person you were talking about with the initials M.M.?" I asked.

"That's right. Kurt and she had a long term relationship," Eddie replied.

Eddie later confided, "It's sort of a delicate matter. She got pissed off at him, took a pair of scissors and cut up all his designer suits, ruined his entire collection, which ran him thousands of dollars in replacement costs. Kurt loves fine suits. He had to start from scratch building his wardrobe again."

As I was handed a check, Eddie grabbed it, saying, "Let me

get that," then asked, "Are you doing anything for the next hour or so? Why don't you come meet Kurt? He's not far away. He always stays at the Excelsior."

Within the next few minutes, I was heading for the Via Veneto, riding in Eddie's beautifully appointed, nile green chauffeur driven Rolls Royce, a wedding gift from Elizabeth Taylor, on my way to the Excelsior Hotel.

And that was how I met Hollywood super agent Kurt Frings, and ended up spending nearly every evening for the next several weeks together with Kurt, Elizabeth and Eddie, usually at the Taylor/Fisher villa on the Via Appia Antica, which is where I first heard of Kurt's doctor, Lee E. Siegel, who eventually led me to Henry Miller.

Kurt Frings, German born lightweight boxer turned naturalized American Hollywood superagent, was said to be a nephew of Joseph Cardinal Frings of Cologne. Kurt was known for his fastidious grooming, for wearing brown Alpine hats with a jaunty green feather, eating lots of steak tartar, and scheduling high level Hollywood meetings in his sauna. In saunas and elsewhere, Kurt liked to sing, in German, a 1923 tune popularized by Paul Whiteman's band whose English title was "Linger Awhile." He was also known to warble *"Ich bin von Kopf bis Fuss auf Liebe engesteldt,"* made famous by Marlene Dietrich in the movie *The Blue Angel*, the English version which was turned into *Falling in Love Again*. Kurt was considered "old Hollywood" in the best tradition – a handshake sealed a deal and your word was your bond. Two and a half decades earlier, working in France as a ski instructor, Kurt had met the woman who would become his wife, future Broadway playwright and Hollywood screenwriter, Pulitzer Prize winning Ketti Frings *(Look Homeward, Angel, Come Back, Little Sheba)*. Ketti would write their love story in the Academy Award winning film *Hold Back the Dawn*, starring Olivia de Havilland as Ketti and Charles Boyer as Kurt. Their marriage was in the process of unraveling when, meeting Kurt, I experienced an immediate *coup de foudre*.

Elizabeth Taylor, sporting a prominent tracheotomy scar from recent emergency surgery that had saved her life, was in town for the filming of the epic *Cleopatra*. As Kurt's innamorata, night after night, I enjoyed intimate dinners with Kurt and the Fishers, sometimes joined by the Richard Burtons (Richard was married to Sybil then; the Taylor-Burton affair would soon explode); Robert Wagner and future spouse Marion Donen; Elizabeth's lifelong buddy Roddy McDowell, and a host of other Hollywood and Euro stars filming in Rome at the time. After dinner (lots of champagne, which Elizabeth loved), chili flown in from Chasen's Los Angeles restaurant, and cheesecake from Lindy's, New York, Elizabeth, wearing neither diamonds nor makeup, ever gorgeous in a fetching red velour bathrobe, challenged me at endless games of Hearts, her two Siamese cats jumping all over the living room furniture, while Eddie wandered around the villa's spacious rooms, singing loudly, "O, My Papa" and other signature Fisher songs, to Elizabeth's visible annoyance.

We were seated at the long table in the villa's dining room, Elizabeth at the head, Eddie at the foot, I across from Kurt. "Lee Siegel is the best doctor in Hollywood," Kurt pronounced in his oft-imitated and joked about thick German accent. Several guests, Siegel patients themselves, agreed heartily.

A conversation ensued about how wonderful Dr. Siegel was, and about all the great things he'd done for everyone's health and well being. Dialog went back and forth between Elizabeth and Kurt, Elizabeth saying her doctor was Rex Kennamer and she was sticking with him because he'd been so supportive when her second husband, Mike Todd, was killed in a plane crash, Kurt insisting Lee Siegel was the best, bar none, and Elizabeth didn't know what she was missing. I gathered there were only two doctors of worth in the film colony, Siegel and Kennamer.

I took note of Dr. Siegel's name, not knowing then that he would soon become my physician as well, or that he would become my ticket to meeting Henry Miller.

"Why are you wasting your time living in Italy?" Kurt Frings demanded when we were on our way back to the Excelsior Hotel. Kurt had quickly become my mentor as well as *grand'amore* and I found him totally irresistible. Kurt combined continental charm with showmanship. He was dynamic, insightful, trim and fit, always impeccably dressed. I loved his sense of humor. "You shouldn't be here in Rome," he declared. "You need to be in Hollywood." I would love the Hollywood lifestyle, Kurt went on to say. I told him I'd been to Hollywood several times, that I knew it well.

"It's different when you actually settle down and live there," Kurt explained. His best friends, he told me, were film and television star Donna Reed and her husband, producer Tony Owen, that in Hollywood you shared wonderful friendships like that. "Hollywood is a place where individual relationships are important, where home entertaining prevails, friendships are nurtured, deals are made," Kurt said. "And if you're serious about acting, Hollywood is definitely where you belong, not here." In the course of our Roman romance, Kurt and I also discussed possible marriage, after he should obtain a divorce. I loved Kurt, even though I thought he might be a bit old for me in terms of a marital partner. He had told me he was 45.

In early October, October 5, to be exact, Kurt tossed himself a birthday party, inviting a couple of dozen Hollywood glitterati, including Elizabeth and Eddie, Audrey Hepburn and Mel Ferrer, RJ Wagner and Marion, the Burtons, the Kirk Douglases, Cyd Carisse and Tony Martin, Edward G. Robinson and wife Jane (wearing a neck brace due to an auto accident), Barbara Rush and husband, PR man Warren Cowan, Nancy Kwan, Maximilian Schell and others, at a restaurant called Vecchia Budapest. Kurt loved Hungarian food. When the cake came out, Eddie Fisher exclaimed, "Fifty-six candles, Kurt!" to which Kurt replied, "I hate you, I hate you!" The cat was out of the bag. Kurt wasn't 45, he was 56.

Though momentarily taken aback by the obvious lie Kurt had told about his age, I was still entranced, and anyway, Kurt didn't seem that old. The secret of his youth he attributed to two things: daily sessions in his sauna, and the expert care provided by his physician, Lee Siegel.

After several weeks in Rome, Kurt had to fly back to Hollywood. Inside of a few days, I became ill and was hospitalized for the next two months at the Ospedale San Giacomo. Elizabeth and Eddie sent flowers, as of course did Kurt. The diagnosis was hepatitis, which is strange, because years later, a blood test revealed I had no hepatitis antibodies, thus had never had hepatitis. At any rate, I eventually recovered from whatever it was. In the interim came the *Cleopatra* crisis; Elizabeth and Eddie were kaput, as were Sybil and Richard; Elizabeth and Richard were passionately in love and together, an event of international proportions blasted all over the world media.

MY SUNDAYS WITH HENRY MILLER

I left Rome, moved to Hollywood, where a New York actor friend introduced me to Jane Fonda's longtime agent, Dick Clayton at Famous Artists, who wanted to sign me. Dick introduced me to his legendary boss, agent/producer Charlie Feldman, head of Famous Artists, who in turn introduced me to Martin Ransohoff of Filmways, who after testing me, offered me a contract. Charlie decided he wanted to split the contract with Marty, so Famous Artists could not represent me. It was Kurt Frings who then stepped in to negotiate the joint contract with Marty and Charlie.

Shortly after signing, I became violently sick, struck with a bad case of flu. Hearing of my condition, Kurt said, "You need Lee Siegel. I told you he's the best doctor in town. He's my doctor, he's everybody in Hollywood's doctor."

"I can't move, I couldn't get to a doctor," I protested.

"Let me call him for you. Sit tight. You'll hear from him."

Inside of a couple of hours, toward the end of the day, Dr. Siegel, dressed in suit and tie, carrying his black bag, made a house call to the apartment where I was living off Laurel Canyon in the San Fernando Valley. Thus started my long term physician-patient relationship with wonderful Dr. Siegel, a handsome and cultured man, admired and loved by all his patients and the Beverly Hills-Hollywood community.

But Dr. Siegel was more than a family doctor. Lee Siegel, physician to the stars, was the official 20th Century Fox doctor and private personal physician to numerous Hollywood luminaries, including some whose precarious health issues were frequently in the news, such as Judy Garland. Dr. Siegel was always on call by Fox, and was present on the set of at least three Marilyn Monroe films, *The Seven Year Itch, Bus Stop* and *Something's Gotta Give*, where he treated Marilyn for lung infections, stress and depression from the failure of her marriage to Joe DiMaggio.

One evening after my recovery, I was dining at the popular Beverly Hills restaurant La Scala with the suave, worldly and sophisticated Charlie Feldman, who had been squiring me about town, when we were joined by Dr. Siegel and his stunningly gorgeous wife, vivacious, red-haired actress Noreen Nash. What an attractive couple they made. I had been so sick when Dr. Siegel made his house call that I didn't even recognize him socially at first. I soon became one of Dr. Siegel's dedicated patients.

Dr. Siegel's office was in the heart of Beverly Hills, on the Bank of America corner at Wilshire and Beverly Drive. Dr. Siegel's red headed nurse Denise was usually in the room with him when he checked for vital signs and performed other medical exams. The two had a ritual: Dr. Siegel, finding a favorable blood pressure, pulse or heart beat would pronounce, "Bee- you- tee- full!" and Denise would repeat the word. Continuing with pulse taking or checking heart and lungs, Dr. Siegel would declare, "Purr-fect!" and Denise would echo, "Purr-fect!"

Dr. Siegel was always interested in hearing what I was up to. I told him in addition to acting, I had registered for writing courses at the UCLA Extension, and was continuing to work on a book about the modeling business which I had begun writing while living in Rome (which Kurt had read, liked, and encouraged me to keep working on).

Dr. Siegel suggested his teenage son Lee and I would have something in common due to a mutual interest in writing. His son's writing was quite interesting, Dr. Siegel said, very different from the run of the mill. He thought I might enjoy meeting Lee, that as writers, we could read each other's work and exchange ideas.

"I don't know where he comes up with this stuff," Dr. Siegel said, shaking his head. "It's unlike anything I've ever read. I think it's very fine writing, but I'm only his father, so don't take my word for it. You decide. I do think you'll like meeting him, though, and that you'll find his writing interesting. It's different, that's for sure. And I think you two will have a lot in common."

Lee Junior was probably about 18 when we first met. He and I got together several times to read each other's material, to critique each other's work and share ideas. Young Lee was a remarkable writer and person, very mature for his years. His initial promise was more than realized; he went on to author over a dozen books. His 1999 novel, *Love is a Dead Language*, was a New York Times Notable Book of the Year and was nominated for a Pulitzer Prize.

Over the years as my physician, Dr. Siegel gave me yearly physicals, treated me for low blood sugar and low blood pressure, allergic rhinitis, a urinary tract infection, various injuries, infections, and other problems, as well as giving me all the shots I needed to travel to Asia and the Middle East. One time he gave me a cortisone shot that relieved neck pain from a whip lash. He also performed my EKGs and EEGs. Those were the days when family doctors did everything.

Ever since college, I had wanted to have my ears pierced, but never knew where to go for it. I asked Dr. Siegel if he could do it for me and he said sure, he'd be glad to. He performed the task, then stepped back to survey his work

"What do you think, Denise?" he asked

"Bee-you-ti-ful!" Denise exclaimed.

"I think we may have gotten the right one a little low ... Denise?"

"I think it looks purr-fect."

"Purr - fect," Dr. Siegel decided, satisfied with his handiwork. "Purr-fect!"

Right after that, seeming to come from left field, was an invitation to meet Henry Miller. "Since you're so interested in writing, you should meet Henry Miller," Dr. Siegel began. "Why don't you stop by our house Sunday afternoon and say hello to him?"

Say hello to Henry Miller?! "Henry Miller? You know Henry Miller? Henry Miller is here in town?"

"Henry lives here. Moved here not too long ago. He comes to our house every Sunday afternoon. You should drop by. I know you'd enjoy Henry."

"I'd love to meet Henry Miller!"

"Jean Renoir, sometimes his wife too, were also joining us Sundays, only they've been ill lately and haven't been able to make it, or you could have met them too. But Henry comes every week without fail."

"I'll certainly be there! What time should I come?"

"Come any time after lunch and stay for the afternoon."

And that's how my Sundays at the Siegels began.

Only later did I discover I was Dr. Siegel's first ear piercing job.

CHAPTER TWO

I was conditioned early in life to believe that Henry Miller was a nothing but an immoral, creepy, cheesy pornographer and smutmeister who had been forcibly exiled to France because of his filthy writings. As a child, I even lost a fingernail because of Henry – or rather because of my curiosity about Henry's forbidden, salacious writing.

My first experience of Henry happened when I was around ten years old. A group of boys in my classroom at school were tittering in the cloakroom over some mimeographed sheets they were sneakily sharing with one other. Curious, I wanted to find out what this was all about, but the boys refused to let me in on the secret. I did pick up from their whispers that what was contained in the mimeo sheets were printouts of the raunchiest parts of a scandalous dirty book by a notorious writer barred from the United States, banished to Paris (a city which had a reputation for naughtiness), named Henry Miller. As I persisted trying to learn more, I ended up physically struggling with a classmate named John Woodburn, a boy I had disliked since kindergarten, when he sneered about a crayon drawing I created, "That stinks!"

What was so intriguing in these Henry Miller dirty book pages? Since I really wanted to know, I continued fighting with the despised John, until at one point my thumb got caught in the locker John was trying to shove the expurgated Miller pages into. I screamed in pain, the teacher came running from the front of the room, and a huge scandal over Henry Miller and his prurient output erupted throughout Garden City's Stewart School. My thumbnail subsequently turned every shade of black, blue, yellow and green, and inside of a few days, fell off entirely. When it grew back, it came in ugly and crooked. For years, I had a deformed right thumbnail that made me think of Henry Miller every time I looked at it.

Henry popped up in my life again when I was around fifteen or sixteen, at Jones Beach, Long Island. I was basking in the sun, and once again, on the next blanket over, the scene involved a group of snickering boys, teens this time, who would not let me in on the written material they harbored, again in mimeographed sheets containing the most lurid parts of both Henry Miller and Frank Harris. Henry's reputation preceded him. Miller was a man with dangerous, pathological sexual predilections who wrote disgustingly depraved sex scenes, whose material was so incredibly scatological and shocking that girls must not be exposed to it, the smutty material being fit for boys' minds only, we girls were told. Henry Miller's writing was banned in order to keep its graphic sexual content out of reach, so as not to corrupt the purity of readers like me. I have no idea how those mimeographed sheets originated; I did manage to see that the pages were dog eared, printed in purple ink and looked like someone had spilled coffee all over them during a hurricane. What a horrible dirty old roué this crude, vulgar lech Henry Miller must be.

My next experience of Henry occurred in Italy. During my two years living in Rome, I had been seeing a lot of a Frenchman named Émile who had changed his name to James, because he thought the Anglo-Saxon name had more class than Émile. You still couldn't get Henry's books in the United States; the ban was yet another couple of years from being lifted, but his titles were freely available in Europe. Having been indoctrinated that Henry was a gross pornographer, the lowest of the low, the kind of sociopath who was a menace to society, I was surprised to hear James praising him as a big Henry Miller fan.

In France, James said, Henry was revered; he was a cultural icon, a legend, a folk hero, considered a serious writer. Sartre, Gide and Camus had all praised his writing. It was because of the thrust and energy of Henry's prose, its stream of consciousness, its honesty and freshness, Henry's love of humanity, his rhythms and pulse, his lyricism juxtaposed with unabashed reality, the liberation of his soul that shone through his prose, his sentimentality and romanticism, plus Henry's enthusiasm for French culture, the fact that he created a wholly new genre and yes, had the guts to write about sex realistically, that made James a devoté. James did not find either the seedy characters Henry wrote about nor his scabrous descriptions in the least offensive. Henry's writing had changed his life, James declared. Henry was in the literary vanguard, breaking traditions. His genius, so well appreciated by Europeans, should be recognized in the United States, but James was convinced the American ban on Henry's work centered on our prudishness, on the Puritanism of the American public.

Given my own preconceived, false opinion of Henry's writing, remembering my childhood and teenage Henry-related experiences, I was initially skeptical of James' assessment, but nevertheless curious, because I respected James's views. So I bought *The Tropic of Cancer, The Tropic of Capricorn, Black Spring,* and *The Colossus of Maroussi*, at a bookstore on the Via Veneto near the Piazza Barberini, and soon became a Henry Miller aficionado myself.

The famous American expatriot jazz era performer Bricktop, discoverer of Duke Ellington, Josephine Baker, and Mabel Mercer, for whom Cole Porter composed *Miss Otis Regrets*, had owned a celebrated nightclub in Paris during the time Henry lived there. After the war, Bricktop moved to Rome to operate a club on the Via Veneto, which I had frequented one summer as a college student, when the place was alive with tourists. Together, James and I revisited Bricktop's establishment, which was now virtually deserted, dark inside and in the process of closing. I imagined Henry at Bricktop's in Paris. James and I talked about how Henry certainly would have known about Bricktop's Paris club, and speculated whether, given Henry's poverty in those days, he would have ever gone there, but even so, we were sure he would have wanted to and would definitely have been a Bricktop fan. It was a positive tie to Henry, a feeling of oneness with him.

So Henry Miller was a part of me before I ever met him. Reading his works, Henry's tastes became mine. It was because of Henry that I started reading Louis-Ferdinand Céline, Lawrence Durell, Romain Rolland, Blaise Cendrars, Knut Hamsun, and others of Henry's favorite writers. Some of the books I read I probably never would have, had it not been for Henry's piquing my interest. Leaving Rome, I left most of my belongings behind with someone whose name I have long ago forgotten whom I never saw again. But Henry's books were among the few things I brought with me when I moved back to the United States.

CHAPTER THREE

Before I met Henry, I met Anaïs Nin, who had figured so prominently in Henry's life in the 30's in Paris. As part of being under contract to Filmways, I was sent to acting and body movement coaches Jeff Corey and Jacobina Caro. It was Jacobina who introduced me to Anaïs.

Immediately taking me under her wing, Jacobina became like a second mother to me. Jake was a thoroughly delightful woman, lighthearted, insightful, with enormous understanding and joie de vivre, always full of sensible, intuitive, caring advice. She loved to cook and frequently invited me to healthy, delicious meals at her home on Fuller Street in Hollywood. She taught me how to grow plants from sprouted potatoes and avocado pits, blooms from which decorated her kitchen, making it look like a florist shop. We traveled up and down the California coast together. She shared with me the pleasures of collecting shells, stones and bits of colored glass from beach walks we took together. Later, Sharon Tate, the second actress signed by Marty Ransohoff, who was also coached by Jacobina, often came with us. Jacobina introduced me to L.A.'s health food restaurants, to cats, sweet oil of almonds as a beauty treatment, beachcombing, and later, to the man I married.

One evening at her house, I met Timothy Leary and Richard Alpert (later rechristened Ram Dass). Leary and Alpert were just beginning to publicize their LSD experiments with what later became known as "acid," and had as yet received virtually no media attention. So impressive and persuasive were these two Harvard scientists that I was convinced I wanted to follow them to Mexico to "tune in, turn on, and drop out." LSD would become a major topic of conversation with Anaïs.

"I met a fascinating woman a few days ago," Jacobina said, as she was serving me one of her famous Saturday morning banana omelettes. "You'll be interested, because she's had LSD. She invited me to lunch the other day. She's a writer who lived in Paris before the war and was very close to Henry Miller. Her name is Anaïs Nin."

"Anaïs Nin!" I exclaimed, barely able to contain my astonishment. "My God! Anaïs Nin wrote the introduction to *Tropic of Cancer.* She's a wonderful writer. I love her writing! She's here? In Los Angeles?"

"You know who she is? I'll have to tell her you like her writing – she'll be happy to hear that."

"How long will she be here? Is she visiting a particular reason?"

"She lives here."

Anaïs Nin living in Los Angeles? What an unlikely place for such a woman. Knowing very little about her life, Anaïs Nin to me was a mysterious figure whom I thought of as a perpetual Paris resident. Ever since seeing the name Anaïs Nin in print, I had wondered about her. Who was she? I was enchanted with her magical, evocative name, one I had never heard before. I fell in love not only with that name, but with Anaïs's writing, as exhibited in the forward to *Tropic.* I knew she was an artist of sensibility and discernment who thought highly of Henry, given the praise she heaped upon him in her preface. But I had no idea how entwined their lives had once been or that Anaïs was Tania in *Tropic.* All I knew was she was an exotic creature with a memorable name whose writing I had truly appreciated. And now, this legendary woman, so European, so associated with Paris in the thirties, was here? It seemed out of time and space. How, why did she end up in L.A. in the sixties? What a stunning change of fortune. Did anyone suspect such an iconic figure was among us?

"I can't believe Anaïs Nin actually lives here," I said. "How did she happen to come here?"

"I believe it's because her husband's roots are here," Jacobina answered. "He grew up in L.A. His mother is married to Lloyd Wright, the son of Frank Lloyd Wright."

Briefing me further on the story of Anaïs, Jacobina said, "Anaïs's husband, Rupert Pole, is 16 years younger than she, and is totally devoted to her. They met in an elevator. They left New York together, and Rupert became a forest ranger. They lived in a cabin in the Sierra Madre during that period, then decided to move here. Frank Lloyd Wright's son is Rupert's stepfather. Rupert is related to actress Anne Baxter – she's Frank Lloyd Wright's granddaughter. Rupert's half brother, Eric Lloyd Wright, like his father and grandfather, is an architect. He designed and built Anaïs and Rupert's house. The house is an absolutely mystical experience. It has a

Japanese quality. It's so serene. Just like Anaïs."

"What is she like?" I asked

"Deep and wise. A mystic, a visionary with the soul of a poet. Anaïs exudes a subtle, seductive charm, elegance, tact, sensitivity. She's delicate but strong; mysterious and romantic. Extremely cultured, cultivated, well-read. She's a perfect fusion of contrasts – both a child-woman, a sophisticate and a femme fatale She's caring and intuitive. She leads a harmonious and peaceful lifestyle together with an intense inner life. She was once a model, a Spanish dancer, and assistant to a famous psychoanalyst, Otto Rank.

"Anaïs wrote a book about D.H. Lawrence when she was young. She printed her books herself on her own printing press. Her father deserted the family and she was reunited with him as an adult, a traumatic experience. There are her diaries – which she's been writing since the age of 11. And as I mentioned before, she's taken LSD."

The very next day, Jacobina phoned to say, "Anaïs has invited us to lunch. She wants to meet you."

"Anaïs Nin wants to meet me?"

"I told her about you, how you love her writing, that you're interested in writing, too. I told her you're a Vassar graduate, that you speak fluent French, that you met Timothy Leary and Richard Alpert at my house, and you're interested in having LSD with them. Anaïs wants to talk to you about that. She's looking forward to meeting you."

Jacobina spoke of her previous lunch at Anaïs's, about Anaïs's unusually lovely hands, how she prepared food with "fairy hands," in dainty, delicate gestures, "as if fairies were making the food for her." Of Rupert Pole, Jacobina said, "They obviously have a relationship which few women are lucky enough to find in life.

"One thing: I said Rupert and she are married, which apparently they definitely are, but the scuttlebutt is that Anaïs never bothered to get a divorce from her first husband, a banker and experimental filmmaker who lives back in New York."

"Wouldn't that make her a bigamist?"

"More or less ... yes."

It was a beautiful, warm autumn day, the kind of late

summer/early fall weather Los Angeles is famous for. Driving from Hollywood on the way to Anaïs's home, Jacobina said, "You'll adore Anaïs. She is utterly lovely. She gives the impression of harboring a beautiful secret." She then told me more about Anaïs's beloved Rupert:

"The Broadway run of *The Duchess of Malfi*, in which Rupert was appearing, had just ended when they met in that elevator. Rupert is a very talented man, he has a degree in music from Harvard, he plays the violin, the viola, and the guitar. You'll see his instruments on display in the living room, under the piano. He's a junior high school science teacher now. Rupert's father, Reginald Pole, was a highly regarded Shakespearean actor, director, musician and writer who worked with John Barrymore. He and Rupert Brooke founded the Marlowe Society. Rupert Pole was named for poet Rupert Brooke, by the way."

Anaïs and Rupert lived on Hildalgo Avenue in the Silver Lake section of Los Angeles in a home overlooking the Silver Lake reservoir. We parked the car and walked down a long and winding driveway. Pine trees lined the path to the front door. The home was Eric Lloyd Wright's first solo project, I learned, only completed the previous year, 1962. I didn't know at the time that Anaïs and Rupert had only recently moved into the house; there was such a feeling of permanence, as if they had always lived there. It was, as Jacobina had previewed, a serene setting, a small but very open house that gave the impression of spaciousness. The 1,400-square-foot, one-bedroom dwelling had been designed with the couple's requests in mind. From the living room and patio, Anaïs and Rupert wanted views of the pool, the Silver Lake reservoir, the sunset, and a willow tree at pool's edge. To capture these views, the living room and dining areas had long walls of windows and sliding glass doors that opened onto the small pool. The home's spaciousness despite its small square footage, struck me immediately. Dangling wind chimes and a mobile clinked together softly.

In the sixth volume of her *Diary* (1955-1966), Anaïs wrote about her life in Los Angeles, describing her Silver Lake home as one large studio with no separate, small partitions. "It had the sense of space of Japanese houses; it had the vista of a Japanese screen, all sky, mountains, lake, as if one lived out of doors," Anaïs wrote. "Yet the roof, held by its heavy beams, gave a feeling of protection, while the big windows which separated the roof from the studio, framed the flight of birds, the sailing of clouds."

In this dreamlike atmosphere, Anaïs greeted us warmly. A woman of a certain age, she had retained her youthful charm and grace, her remarkable dancer's sinuous body, slim, erect posture and flowing movements, her "sense of self," to use a phrase Jacobina often spoke of. She was a timeless beauty with a distinguished heart shaped face, translucent complexion and unusual, distinctive features.

Her coppery/reddish gold/ hair was parted in the middle in an upsweep do. She wore a purple (her favorite color) dress in a rich, clinging fabric that flattered her cornflower blue eyes and showed off her trim, feminine figure, emphasizing her rounded, firm breasts. Circling her neck was a choker of violet beads. Kohl ringed eyes, heavily beaded mascara and eyelids smudged with lavender eye shadow complemented the purple dress. The harshness of pronounced black lines on both upper and lower eyelids contrasted with the quality of feminine softness she radiated. The eyebrows were a throwback to her 30's epoch, when women plucked or shaved their brows down to the minimum. Anaïs had retained that look, while her lips had assumed their natural contours, as opposed to the look in decades old photos of her with fashionable bee stung lips of an earlier era. Strength and fragility, vulnerability and toughness, an incisive mind, a brilliant woman, I soon decided. Unassuming yet unmistakably strong, she radiated sensuality. Her English was fluent, spoken with a slight, melodious accent that was hard to identify, definitely neither French nor Spanish, but something unique, which added to her mystery and fascination.

She made her guests feel at home immediately, even as Jacobina and I followed her to the kitchen and watched her prepare lunch. In my mind's eye, I can still see Anaïs tossing the salad on a counter not far from the sink, with slim, delicate fingers, her "fairy hands" moving gracefully, just as Jacobina had described. She seemed very familiar with such movements, as if she often practiced them, and seemed at one and the same time both suited and unsuited to them. She had mastered them, as she had mastered so many other things in life, but she was otherwise. I thought of her at age 11, fatherless, incongruously living in Queens, New York, of all places, starting her diary. I thought of her printing her books on her own printing press.

We relished a beautifully presented lunch – grilled salmon with fresh veggies and salad greens. The mouthwatering dessert was a delicate custardy concoction served with delicious fresh strawberries. We ate at a long table. The house was open, its Eastern inspired minimalist décor with Asian accents reflecting the simplicity of Anaïs's taste fully in view. Anaïs occupied the head of the table, I was opposite her at the foot, with Jake between us to Anaïs's left.

Anaïs told me she loved the way I pronounced her name, that almost no one in Los Angeles got it right. We spoke a little French together. She complimented me on my accent, commenting that just as in English today, so many people were careless about how they spoke French, which was a shame, because French was such a beautiful language. I told her I thought my French diction had benefitted from having, in my seventh grade French classes, practiced daily *"La Triangle Vocalique,"* an ingenious, wonderful way of perfecting one's French pronunciation.

I brought up her relationship with Henry, but Anaïs seemed reluctant to talk about him except in the most detached of terms. In instances where his name arose, she artfully diverted the conversation to other topics. When asked pointed questions about him, her guarded reply was it had been a while since they'd seen one another. Since she made no mention of his whereabouts, I assumed he was still up in Big Sur. Henry may not yet have moved to L.A., or if he had, Anaïs either didn't know he was here, or she simply chose not to divulge his location. In any case, Henry's current dwelling was never mentioned. Whenever he was referenced, it was invariably in connection with the long ago Paris years, part of the distant past. Her reticence regarding Henry actually spoke volumes, alerting one to the fact something might be remiss in their current relationship. I couldn't put my finger on it, but later learned they were estranged, though I had no idea why.

Anaïs kept it impersonal regarding Henry: "Henry always had his important literary defenders, but it's taken a long time for him to start becoming mainstream. It should have happened a long time ago," she said.

"Who were his literary defenders?" Jacobina asked.

"Oh, there's quite a number. William Carlos Williams, Aldous Huxley, John Dos Passos, Edmund Wilson ... Samuel Beckett calls *Tropic* a momentous event in the history of modern writing. Ezra

Pound praises Henry for having out-Ulysses Joyce and written 'a dirty book worth reading.' George Orwell calls Henry the only imaginative prose writer of the slightest value in the English-speaking world, and recognizes *Tropic* as the work of a remarkable literary stylist. He says Henry is a prose writer with the expansive rhythms of Whitman's free verse. To Larry Durrell, Henry is a literary master. When he compared *Tropic* to *Lady Chatterley's Lover*, T.S. Eliot declared *Tropic* to be unquestionably better. Blaise Cendrars, one of Henry's literary heroes, saw Henry's work as being in the great moral tradition of French writing. H.L. Mencken congratulated Henry on his excellent work. For Havelock Ellis, *Tropic of Cancer* possesses great psychological truth. Sartre, Gide, Camus, and many other French literary figures revere Henry. The great Welshman John Cowper Powys, an idol of Henry's, said Henry's writing reaches a point of perception that is almost Shakespearian. And I could go on."

Anaïs preferred to focus on topics other than Henry, such as the inner conflicts she herself experienced in the struggle to get her work published. We talked about her first book, the one on D.H. Lawrence, which she wrote in her twenties and which she published herself, running off 500 copies on a second hand printing press, in the great American tradition of self-publishing. She was in good company, listing important writers who had also self-published their works – Tom Paine, Benjamin Franklin, Walt Whitman, Mark Twain, Zane Grey, Upton Sinclair, Carl Sandburg, Edgar Rice Burroughs, Edgar Allan Poe, Henry David Thoreau. Britain too, had its self-published authors, including Kipling, George Bernard Shaw and Lewis Carroll.

The atmosphere was meditative, calm. Anaïs mesmerized us with her lilting voice and its unusual cadence, its hard to pigeonhole accent that lingers in memory. The focus shifted to astrology, one of Anaïs's interests. She was a Pisces, and her Venus was in Pisces, as is mine. Upon discovering we had that astrological aspect in common, Anaïs remarked, "Ah, then we two share a bottomless depth of love and feeling. We are alike, you and I. We are both full of passion and compassion. We are romantics! We are both gifted with rich imagination!"

We spoke of French literature – Proust, George Sand, Colette, Villon, Ronsard, Baudelaire, Rimbaud; current French culture, of the inspiration Anaïs had felt in her house in France that had once been owned by Madame DuBarry, her "laboratory of the soul," in the historic town of Louveciennes, She touched on British writer Lesley Blanch: "A scholarly romantic, traveling about remote regions. Blanch started out as an artist. She did book jackets for T. S. Eliot. She married Romain Gary. Gary left her for Jean Seberg." Blanch had written *The Wilder Shores of Love*. "It's about four women: Isabel Burton, Lady Jane Digby, Aimée du Buc de Rivéry, a cousin of Josephine Bonaparte, and Isabelle Eberhardt – no, not Ogden Nash's daughter, but a Swiss explorer of the same name who lived and traveled extensively in North Africa and embraced Islam. Blanch's book pioneers a new kind of group biography focusing on women leading unconventional lives." By coincidence, I had that same book on my shelves, having spotted it on a Pickwick Bookshop remaindered counter, but not yet having read it.

We adjourned to the airy, uncluttered living area that was sparsely furnished with rich violets and brilliant magentas, a touch of turquoise here and there, soft nile greens and marine blues, with scattered pillows in shades of Anaïs's favorite colors.

I was most interested to hear what Anaïs would have to say regarding LSD. She spoke about her experience with Dr. Oscar Janiger, who had administered the drug to her and a number of other artists, writers and Hollywood film stars, among them Alan Watts, Aldous Huxley, and Cary Grant, the latter who had over seventy LSD sessions with "Oz," as he was called. Janiger, incidentally, was Allen Ginsberg's cousin, Anaïs said. He prescribed two micrograms per pound of body weight, which produced an ephemeral flow of kaleidoscopic sensations, marked interior rhythms, a poetry of the soul.

"I'm sure it can be useful for some," Anaïs conceded, "but as for me, I would not continue with it, I have no plans to take it again."

"Why not?" I asked, feeling a bit deflated by her dismissive verdict.

"Because I don't need it to break through as an artist. What LSD offers, I do myself, without outside help."

As I pursued the issue further, Anaïs elaborated, "I am able to have that level of experience without the help of hallucinongens. I need no external method to be in touch with my subconscious, my creative self. My inner life is accessible to me. At will, I experience the same kind of dreams and visions, I feel profound related emotions, I reach an exalted poetic state which is the same experience LSD affords. LSD, I believe, is a method for those who need to open up to life, to reach their inner core. That is not my situation."

I was marveling that Anaïs had achieved such results on her own, unaided by what was said to be incredible breakthroughs available through LSD, when Anaïs asked, "Do you know the writer Henri Michaux?"

"By name, yes," I answered, "but I haven't read his work."

"He wrote a remarkable book on his experiences with mescaline," Anaïs said, "*Misérable Miracle*. Michaux is a highly original artist as well as writer. His drawings are inspired by orientalism, which is one of his biggest influences – oriental culture, Buddhism and calligraphy. He has written poetry, travelogues, art criticism.

"Michaux's ego was certainly shattered from his mescaline experiences," Anaïs continued. "Afterwards, it took him several months to return to a normal state. At one point, he said, 'I'm getting farther away from this drug, which is not the drug for me. My drug is myself, which mescaline banishes.' This describes my own feelings about LSD. I share his thought that it's not the drug for me. Michaux said this after having some negative effects. I personally had no negative effects; my only judgment is that I have no need of the drug."

At times her directness was disconcerting, at other times she would revert to a private, unknowable self. With respect to her own work, she said, "There is no separation between my life and my craft, my work. The form of art is the form of art of my life, and my life is the form of the art. I refuse artificial patterns – my life and my work are inseparable. My life is my art, my art, my life."

Jacobina, who was reading *The Tibetan Book of the Dead*, popularized by Tim Leary, said, "When a deceased person awakens in the bardo, he's confused and doesn't know where he is. The deceased realizes his changed condition when he walks in the sand or in the snow and see that there is no footprint or he doesn't cast a shadow when walking in the sunlight."

Anaïs said, "The consciousness of a dead person is seven times clearer than that of a living person. The deceased can be introduced to the luminous nature of the mind and thus be liberated."

Later Anaïs would write: "Huxley reminded me that drugs are beneficial if they provide the only access to our nightlife. I realized that the expression 'blow my mind' was born of the fact that America had cemented access to imagination and fantasy and that it would take dynamite to remove this block! I believed Leary's emphasis on the fact we use only one percent of our mind or potential, that everything in our education conspires to restrict and constrict us. I only wished people had time to study drugs as they studied religion or philosophy and to adapt to this chemical alteration of our bodies. LSD's value is in being a shortcut to the unconscious, so that one enters the realm of intuition unhampered, pure as it is in children, of direct emotional reaction to nature, to other human beings. In a sense it is the return to the spontaneity and freshness of childhood vision which makes every child able to paint or sing."

Rupert Pole arrived later in the afternoon and we were introduced. He was a quite tall and unusually handsome man. I was taken by the brilliance of his blue eyes, his strength of character and soft-spoken manner. One immediately noticed Rupert's solicitousness, his gentle protectiveness of Anaïs. Despite being a good deal younger than she, to me, they seemed the same age and, as Jacobina had remarked, he was indeed utterly devoted to her. He soon disappeared, leaving us three women to continue our talks in an atmosphere of intimacy and harmony.

Reluctant to leave, Jacobina and I lingered at Anaïs's for several hours. At the end of the afternoon, Anaïs gave me a collection of her books, *Winter of Artifice, Cities of the Interior, Ladders to Fire, Under a Glass Bell*, and autographed each with personal messages. In one, she paid me the lovely tribute in French of: "*À Jeanne Rejaunier, belle dehors, belle dedans.*" As I eagerly read these remarkable books, I delighted in discovering a previously unknown universe by a wonderfully unique voice.

Luxe, calme et volupté, a line from the Baudelaire poem which Henri Duparc set to music and which inspired the Matisse painting of the same name – this line captured perfectly the atmosphere of Anaïs' home and the feeling of being in her magical presence.

After that, Anaïs and I began a correspondence, usually in French.

November 22, 1963, Anaïs and Rupert were coming to my home to dinner, along with Jacobina and one or two others. I was shopping for groceries at a small mini mart on Sunset Boulevard just off Larrabee, the West Hollywood street where I lived, when the first news of President Kennedy having been shot in Dallas came on the overhead TV.

Always thoughtful and generous, Anaïs brought another book with her that evening. It was the one she had spoken of at lunch, the book written in French about mescaline by Henri Michaux, *Misérable Miracle*. Both Anaïs and Jacobina were distraught by Kennedy's assassination, especially, they lamented, because he was so young to die. In fact, Anaïs was so upset she couldn't eat even a bite of the coquilles St. Jacques à la vodka I'd cooked. Jacobina was heartsick because it reminded her of the death of her third husband, a promising young man, father of her only child, Hollywood writer Bob Meltzer, who had been killed in World War II. Anaïs later immortalized the dinner at my home in Volume 6 of her *Diary*.

The entire evening, Rupert showed great concern for Anaïs; his total adoration and admiration of her being always in evidence. Their loving interaction spoke of how and why Anaïs and Rupert had come together and of their complete devotion to one another.

After Anaïs and Rupert had left, Jacobina commented, "Anaïs was clearly very upset tonight, deeply affected by Kennedy's death. Yet despite that, she made the effort to come here to your dinner party. I think that says a great deal about what kind of person she is."

"Yes, it certainly does."

"And she even thought to bring you a book. Such a gracious and thoughtful lady."

Shortly after the television airing of the episode of *Combat!* in which I played the part of a French nun entirely in French, demonstrating once again her enormous warmth and kindness, Anaïs wrote, complimenting me on my performance and on my French.

CHAPTER FOUR

Henry Miller and Anaïs Nin, two Paris literary immortals, both now living in Los Angeles – it was incredible. I had met Anaïs, and now I was going to meet Henry!

What was he doing here? As written about in his *The Oranges of Hieronymus Bosch* and other Miller offerings, as well as being depicted in the press, Big Sur had become as much a part of Henry in the post war years as Paris had been in the 30's. So what was the story of Miller being in Los Angeles? When had he come here and why? What would this city have to offer this extraordinary man?

I arrived at the Siegels just minutes ahead of Henry, and awaited his entrance with eager if nervous anticipation, seated on a chair on the left rear side of the living room. And there he was, the famous Henry Miller himself, coming through the front door, wearing a grey tweed tam o'shanter/ newsboy cap, a plaid shirt with V neck sweater vest and a tweed sports jacket, his musical Brooklyn-accented voice talking about some experience that happened on the way over. Henry was accompanied by his boon companion, bit actor and stunt man Joe Grey, who, when he removed his modified fedora/ rain hat (the type worn by Carl Reiner in the *Oceans* movies), displayed a great head of wavy brown hair, a contrast to a nearly bald Henry, with his sprinkling of baby thin white peach fuzz. Henry was slim of build, around 5 foot 8, with a slightly bent posture and caved in torso. He was in his early seventies at the time.

Although everyone has a stronger side of the face and body and none of us is symmetrical, I noted Henry's face seemed even less so, having distinctly different right and left sides and a predominant Chinese look about him, as if in the distant past, he must have had Asian ancestors whose genes persisted alongside his German DNA. Slanty, receding eyes, one of them more so than the other, added to Henry's oriental demeanor. He had very expressive arms and hands, which he frequently waved when making statements. I immediately liked Henry, and identified with the nice, neat way he dressed, as befitting a man of his age and point in time, reminding me so much of the older men in my family.

"I'm sorry the Renoirs couldn't be here. I shall miss them,

and, Noreen, please do tell them I hope their health improves, and send them my very best when you speak to them," Henry said, as he headed over to a chair near me by a window that overlooked the quiet street. Noreen Nash had starred in Renoir's *The Southerner*, a film about Texas sharecroppers which is considered the best film Jean Renoir made in the United States, for which he was nominated for an Academy Award as Best Director.

No sooner was he seated than Henry lit a cigarette, one of hundreds he would light in the times I was in his presence. Such a mystique surrounded Henry. In the short space of a couple of years, since the ban on his books was lifted by the courts, Henry's status had catapulted from cult figure to star attraction. I don't know what I was expecting, but I think Henry was friendlier and more down to earth than I had imagined. I was unprepared for his outgoing, unassuming nature, his exuberant personality. In short order, I would see that without ever hogging the floor, he had something unique and vitally interesting to say about every subject under the sun. One sensed his graciousness immediately in the way he sought to include the entire room in conversations.

Henry frequently punctuated remarks in his pronounced Brooklynese with pet phrases: "ya see," "don't ya see?" "do you see?" "doncha know," "do you know?" "ya know," "sure, sure;" "you might say;" "shall I say?" "I have to say," "in a manner of speaking," "so to speak," "if you will," "isn't that right?" "yas, yaz . . . hmmm . . . hmmmm . . . yas ..." Other Henryisms: "lez" instead of "let's;" "woik, woid, woild," instead of "work, word and world."

I was a bit shy and awestruck at first, but it didn't take much for Henry to put me at ease. He was so easy to talk to. Conversation flowed from one topic to the next, propelled by Henry's genial, gregarious, extroverted nature.

Interested in everything, Henry immediately wanted to hear all about me. In one of our first encounters, I alluded to James, who had introduced me to Henry's work, as *mon minet*. "You're much too young to have a *minet*," Henry said, and laughed when I told him James was only two years younger than I. "In France, a *minet* is the equivalent of a gigolo, a young man in a relationship with an older woman," Henry explained to the others.

Henry said he was not writing at this time due to a problem with his eyes, and that he was easing up on reading, trying to pace himself in order to keep up with his extensive correspondence and other eye-intensive activities. But he was painting every day. I had read about Henry's painting in his book *To Paint is to Love Again*. I could only wonder what the reading world was missing out on, Henry having laid his pen aside, at least temporarily... so to speak.

"So you know Anaïs," Henry said. His voice, though hoarse, nasal, scratchy, gravelly and raspy, was nevertheless pleasing, at once mellow and musical.

"Yes, we were introduced by my body movement teacher, Jacobina Caro," I replied, and expounded on my meetings with Anaïs, about our correspondence, the books she had given me. "When we spoke about LSD, Anaïs said she didn't need it, she has visions and inspirational connections without it – she has the same experiences without taking the drug."

Henry nodded. "That sounds like Anaïs, sure, sure, that's something she would say." Echoing Anaïs, Henry indicated they had seen little of one another recently. By now, I had gathered they were in effect estranged, but out of respect for privacy, made no inquiries about it.

I told Henry about Anaïs and Rupert having gone to my home the night Kennedy died. I said, "I cooked coquilles St. Jacques à la vodka, but Anaïs couldn't eat a thing, she was so upset."

"That must have been disappointing, such a traumatic event the day of your dinner party."

Since I believed in reincarnation and life after death, perhaps I wasn't as affected by Kennedy's death as many people were, I said. I found out Henry too was a believer in reincarnation. This prompted him to ask, "Have you ever read any books by Marie Corelli?" Indeed I had. As a big fan of Corelli, I owned several of her works, and listed them for Henry: "*A Romance of Two Worlds, The Soul of Lilith, The Sorrows of Satan, Life Everlasting, Wormwood, Thelma, Ardath* ..."

"All those? Her books are out of print, you know. Where did you find them? At the library?"

"No, at Larsen's Bookshop."

Henry knew Larsen's, he said; he had been there. Larsen's was located either on Hollywood Boulevard or Sunset, I forget which, not far from Western Avenue in a shabby démodé section of Hollywood. Widowed Mrs. Larsen, the owner, was phasing out her late husband's business, preparing to close it. The store was fantastic, with a huge, predominantly metaphysical and occult inventory you would never find anywhere else on the planet. Plump Mrs. Larsen had a harsh shade of dyed red hair that evoked an aging Parisian streetwalker. She would perch on an elevated seat resembling a bar stool at the checkout counter facing the street, always quietly immersed in a book, scarcely looking up at her customers until they came to the cash register with their found bargain treasures. It was a loss of a great store when Larsen's finally closed. Larsen's was where I had found not only all my Marie Corellis, but so many other obscure and hard to find books with a spiritual slant.

Henry told the group, "Marie Corelli was a British novelist who enjoyed enormous literary success dating from the latter part of the 19th century till World War I. She was a contemporary of Oscar Wilde, and the most widely read author of fiction of her day. Her novels sold more copies than the combined sales of her contemporaries Sir Arthur Conan Doyle, H. G. Wells, and Rudyard Kipling. Although critics often derided her work as fare for the hoi paloi, she was Queen Victoria's favorite writer, and her works were collected by Winston Churchill and members of the British royal family. Sadly, unjustly, today very few people read her or even know who she is.

"The curious thing is she wrote these absolutely beautiful books, so pure, so idealistic, no sex in them at all. In fact, she had no great known love affairs. She may have been one of those who rise above sex. Or she may have had one great love; there are rumors of that. On the other hand, she did live with a female companion for a number of years. But who knows? She gave the impression of purity, and her books certainly reflect this, with her themes of melding Christianity with reincarnation, astral projection, soul travel, and other mystical ideas."

Temporarily without a cigarette to puff on, Henry stroked his bottom lip with a long index finger. Asked several questions about Corelli, he elaborated with a soft shake of his head. "She was the illegitimate daughter of Scottish poet and his servant girl. She was educated at a convent in Paris. She began her career as a musician, adopting the name Marie Corelli. Her first novel, *A Romance of Two Worlds* was a sensation. Corelli was one of the first writers to become a star. There were several film adaptations of her works – *Vendetta, Thelma, Wormwood, The Sorrows of Satan*. She would float down the

Avon in a gondola, complete with a gondolier that she brought over from Venice."

It soon became apparent that Henry was an honored and respected mentor to his good friend Joe Grey, having introduced Joe to many cultural ideas, books, writers, artists and musicians Joe might not have encountered otherwise. It didn't take long to hear what Joe's tastes were: Ravel, Debussy, Proust, James Joyce, Hesse, particularly *Siddhartha*; Céline. Alan Watts, Élie Faure, Thomas Mann, and yes, Marie Corelli, among others. Joe always carried two or three books with him, including a notebook in which he copied passages from books he liked, and jotted observations about his favorites. Sometimes he would read them aloud and other times spout them off the top of his head. Now Joe read us some of his Marie Corelli entries:

"'What can you really call your own? Everything is lent you, every talent you have, every breath you draw, every drop of blood flowing in your veins is lent to you only; you must pay it all back.'

"'What we want doesn't count. Our ego has to be completely broken, the small self for the larger self. This is a sacrifice we agreed to – to be apart to grow better together.'

"'Doubt is the destroyer, the curse mankind has brought on itself. Believe in the miraculous. Know that every wonderful thing is possible.'

"'Has the universe been set in motion for nothing?'

"'Become acquainted with that place that is your future home, become acquainted with your own heart, which is your spiritual home.'"

Henry nodded approvingly, lit another cigarette, then continued talking about Corelli. "Marie Corelli said many interesting things about death. Death is a triumph; death is a parting, but not a finality; nothing can ever really separate us, not even death; there is no death, there is only a temporary parting."

"I'm sure Kennedy will return in another incarnation," I said.

Henry agreed, "As we all will. Death is a part of life, in a manner of speaking. It's the other side of life. I have no fear of death. Death is a natural process. We're all meant to die, so there's certainly something natural about it, doncha know. The hard part is living! Living is the true art."

The subject of *Misérable Miracle*, the book Anaïs had given me, arose. "Michaux was Belgian before becoming a naturalized French citizen, doncha know," Henry said. "He was studying medicine, but quit to become a stoker on a French merchant marine ship."

"What's a stoker?"

"It's someone who shovels coal to power the ship. Blaise Cendrars did the same thing when he left home and ran off to see the world when he was a kid of fifteen or so. That's a job that no longer exists."

"Cendrars is Henry's literary idol," Joe informed us. "One of them, anyway."

Henry said, "Like Cendrars, Michaux was widely traveled – all through South America, Africa and Asia, which inspired the travel books he wrote, so to speak, especially on Ecuador and Asia. He lived in Brazil for a while, too, ya know. Cendrars and Michaux had that in common, travels to faraway places. It takes guts to leave home as a youngster, get out on your own, see the world as they did."

I said, "When I saw Michaux's picture, I was surprised, because I wouldn't have imagined him to look like he does."

"You saw his picture? His face? Well, that's interesting," Henry said. "Doncha know, for years the only photograph of himself Michaux allowed to circulate was one of just his hand holding a pen over a sheet of paper on a messy desk, taken by my Paris friend Brassaï... hmmm ... hmmm ... Brassaï actually did photograph more of Michaux than his hand, and eventually, those photos were released. So how did you visualize him?"

"Pudgy with lots of hair, not bald and effete as he looks in the photo I saw of him."

"It's strange the way the mind conjures images, isn't that so? Sometimes we get it right, d'ya know, sometimes we're way off base." Henry turned to the group and said, "A horrible accident happened to Michaux's wife – her nightgown caught fire and she burned to death. After that, he started experimenting with hallucinogens, which resulted in the book *Misérable Miracle*, in which he describes his experiences with mescaline. The book is an absolutely riveting, breathtaking vision of interior space; it's fabulous writing. And the book includes many of his drawings that provide insight into Michaux's mind under mescaline, so to speak. But even though there were decidedly positive results from his experiments, d'ya know, at a certain point, Michaux said, 'I'm getting farther away from this drug, which is not the drug for me. My drug is myself, which mescaline banishes.'"

"That's similar to Anaïs's opinion of LSD."

"Yas, yas, that's right, hmmm ... hmmmm," Henry trailed off, momentarily sinking into his own thoughts.

A couple of years later, we would speak about Michaux again, when the Grand Prix National des Lettres was awarded to Michaux by the French and he refused to accept it. Henry, commenting, said Michaux was not the first in the French tradition of refusing coveted literary honors: Cendrars had done so as well, and Sartre had even refused the Nobel Prize. "When Sartre was awarded the Nobel Prize in Literature," Henry said, "in declining it, he stated that 'a writer must refuse to allow himself to be transformed into an institution, even if it takes place in the most honorable form. It is not the same thing if I sign Jean-Paul Sartre or if I sign Jean-Paul Sartre, Nobel Prize winner.'

"Well, that's one way of looking at it," Henry concluded with a chuckle, "but let me go on record right now for saying that if they offer the Nobel Prize to me, I will not turn it down – and you can quote me on that."

"Henry," Joe declared, "it's not a question of if – but when."

CHAPTER FIVE

Henry briefly switched a lit cigarette from one hand to the other, then moved it back again. There was something graceful about the way his hand held the burning cigarette. He had the hands of an artist, a pianist, both of which he assuredly was.

Henry and I shared a common heritage, both Henry's parents and my paternal grandmother being children of German immigrants. Henry's grandfather deserted the German army in the Franco-Prussian War, Henry said, and was forced to emigrate. Henry was born in the Yorkville section of Manhattan on East 85th Street. Today, little if anything remains there of anything German; the German stores, restaurants and biergartens are mostly all a thing of the past. When I graduated from Vassar, I moved into an apartment in Henry's old neighborhood on East 89th Street, right near Gracie Mansion, but of course, Henry was long gone, his family having moved to Brooklyn when he was a year old.

Clothing, specifically tailoring, was a family tradition Henry and I shared. Henry had acquired a taste for fine suits from his father, who ran a tailoring business from their Brooklyn home and also worked as a Fifth Avenue tailor. My French great-grandfather, Edward C.C. Rejaunier, was a partner with his sister and brother-in-law, the Texiers, in a Fifth Avenue clothing establishment in the early part of the 20th century. One of my dad's fondest boyhood memories was of the Texiers' twice yearly pilgrimages from Paris to New York, their little daughter Marie-Louise in tow, in which they would always take my dad and his family to dinners at fashionable Manhattan restaurants. Even more distant Rejaunier ancestors, led by Charles Rejaunier, had created wardrobes for the Bonapartes and other French notables in the 19th century. I still treasure the Limoges china the Texiers sent as a wedding gift to my parents.

Henry said he had sometimes gone into Manhattan with his father, "who once beat up a Frenchman who was in the clothing business. I hope it wasn't your great-grandfather."

Like Henry, I too had family roots in Brooklyn. My maternal grandmother, Sadie Allyn Wright, was born and raised in Williamsburg.

"I lived in Williamsburg as a child," Henry said. "I loved it. I hated to leave when we moved to another part of Brooklyn."

"My grandmother lived there back when Brooklyn was a city, not a borough."

"I too," Henry said. "Most people don't know Brooklyn was once an independent city; they think it was always a borough. It was only annexed by New York City in 1898."

I told Henry that my ancestors were the first twins born in the city of Brooklyn, for which they were given free passage on the Staten Island ferry for life.

Henry and I shared a mutual love of French language and culture, I with French ancestry on the Rejaunier side of the family as well. Henry and I would sometimes pepper our conversations with French as a natural way of describing something unique and particular to both of us. Henry's French was fluent, albeit spoken with that characteristic, unshakeable Brooklyn accent.

Henry wanted to know more about my French ancestry. "The name Rejaunier is not a common one even in France," I answered. "My family is the only one with the name Rejaunier in the entire United States, and in France there are only about twelve Rejaunier families."

"How does it happen you speak such good French?" Henry wanted to know. "With your French name, did you grow up in a bilingual home? Did your father speak the language with you?"

"No, my dad never learned much French. His grandfather spoke it fluently, but I never knew him. I started teaching myself languages when I was seven, using opera libretti. You know, on one side is the English translation, on the other, the original French, Italian or German. My great aunt Marie, who lived with us and was an avid operagoer, had a huge collection of these libretti. In school, I began French in seventh grade, and continued it all through college."

Henry, as the product of two German strains, had grown up in a German speaking family. I too had the German language in my background. As I told Henry, "Aunt Marie spoke German at home with me, then I had three years of high school German and a year at the Goetheschule in Rome."

"And you speak Italian too?"

"I studied Italian at Vassar, took summer courses at the University of Florence and at the Scuola per Stranieri in Viareggio, which is part of the University of Pisa – and lived two years in Rome."

"What was it like, living in Italy?"

"Fantastic! I loved it."

"What were you doing there?"

"Acting, modeling, writing, studying, socializing; I made a couple of films, enjoyed the dolce vita, dated interesting men, met the intelligentsia – artists, writers, film directors, producers, stars; attended the Cannes and Venice Film Festivals, traveled all over Italy and neighboring countries, and began a novel I'm still working on."

Music was another bond between Henry and me. I was a classically trained singer and Henry had studied piano for several years. He said, "Originally, doncha know, music, piano was the big thing with me. For a time, I thought about making a professional career in it, but I really didn't have what it takes. Nevertheless, today, after all these years, music is actually more important to me than writing or painting. It's always there, a part of me that never leaves me. It's there all the time. Music was the most important influence in my life."

Henry had heard many of the same operas as my Aunt Marie during the Met's so-called Silver Age under the celebrated Metropolitan Opera General Manager Giulio Gatti-Casazza. Henry would stand in line to purchase opera tickets and would go without meals to afford them, he said. Then he had the good fortune to meet a man who could provide free tickets to the opera, ballet, and Broadway musicals.

"My Aunt Marie was a pianist and singer, a contralto," I said. "She taught school on the lower east side. She attended the opera every week for decades, where she always sat in the Family Circle." I was familiar with the voices of the great singers whose performances Henry heard because of Aunt Marie's extensive collection of Victor Talking Machine recordings – stars who sang before and after World War I. Henry and I exchanged our lists of them, including Geraldine Farrar, Ernestine Schuman-Heink, Alma Gluck, Gigli, Caruso, Mary Garden, Galli-Curci, Emma Eames, the Ponselle sisters, Rosa and Carmela, Giuseppe de Luca, Giovanni Martinelli, Lawrence Tibbett, Claudia Muzio, Luisa Tetrazzini, Frances Alda, Elisabeth Rethberg, Lucrezia Bori, Chaliapin, Antonio Scotti, Olive Fremstad, Louise Homer, Pasquale Amato, Leo Slezak, John McCormack, Florence

Easton, Herbert Witherspoon, Nellie Melba, Emmy Destinn, Flagstad, Melchior, Richard Crooks and scores of others.

Although I too had studied piano as well as violin, my chief interest had always lain in the vocal area, and like Henry, I also had at one time entertained the desire for a musical career, in my case as an opera singer. In fact, at the time, I was currently studying with an outstanding opera coach in Monterrey Park, the fabulous Maria Martino. Henry expressed interest in my vocal studies, said he wanted to hear me sing (he never did). He asked, "Are you still planning a career as a singer?"

"Not anymore. Like you, Henry, I once dreamed of it, but I became sidetracked with modeling and acting, and it got too late for that ... although my teacher says it isn't, but she's thinking it's not too late for a local career."

"And you don't want that?"

"No, I'd want the chance for an international career if I were going to do it."

"So now instead of looking toward a musical career, you're writing."

Henry and I shared something even more deeply personal in common, something that had indelibly shaped both our lives: both of us had siblings who were what is now referred to as "mentally challenged" or "special needs," but at that time was called "retarded." Henry's was a sister named Lauretta, mine a brother, Billy. Coincidentally, each of our siblings was four years younger than we, Henry's sister having been born on July 11, my brother on July 12.

"Two adversely aspected Cancers," Henry observed wryly, shaking his head, which said volumes about the effects of mental retardation on the afflicted and their families. Neither Lauretta nor Billy could attend school; no school would accept them. The children were burdens for both Henry's mother and mine, a cross to carry for Henry and me as well. Lauretta's mentality, Henry estimated, was at moron level, between ages 8-10. Billy's was even worse; I would say around age 2 or 3 at most.

Henry spoke of Lauretta as being "a great burden in my life. I had to defend her against other kids ridiculing and bullying all the time and trying to beat her up. My mother beat my sister, too. She was always asking me, just a youngster myself, what did I do to deserve this child? Since Lauretta couldn't go to school, my mother tried to teach her, but the task was beyond her capabilities."

Henry asked about Billy, how his mental retardation manifested and how it was handled by the family. I said, "As an infant, Billy would bang his head against his crib for hours at a time. He didn't walk till he was two or learn to talk, albeit poorly, till he was five. As he got older, instead of banging his head on the crib, he constantly banged it with his fist, alternating that by clapping his hands in monotonous rhythm. His only interest was the weather. He would ask over and over, 'Gonna wain today? Gonna wain, gonna wain, gonna wain?' He lived at home till one day, when I was living in Italy, he attacked my mother, was put in a straightjacket and institutionalized, where he's been ever since."

Henry noted, with irony, "My mother tried to beat brains into my sister, and your brother tried to beat brains into himself."

Changing direction, seizing on the subject of eating, Henry said, "I used to hate it when my mother insisted I finish everything on my plate. To this date, I delight in not finishing everything in front of me, and in throwing out food, which my mother would never do; she had that German frugality, saving bits of everything for later use. Sort of gives me the feeling of having outwitted my mother when I get to toss food in the garbage can, doncha know. When my mother told me to clean my plate, to 'lick the platter clean,' she'd sometimes say, I had an image of licking the remains like a dog and I never wanted to do it, doncha know."

It was no secret that Henry bore the scars of having been severely handicapped in not having a loving relationship with his mother, or by the fact that he outright hated his mother. He made no bones about it, emphasizing what a huge, still unresolved issue his relationship with his mother was. He described her as exacting, orderly, and demanding, identifying these as typically German characteristics which his mother possessed in the extreme. He recalled how he was "struggling to set myself free from German conventionality, punctuality, and super-cleanliness. I hated what seemed to be the most important part of my mother's existence – cleanliness and sterility."

I said, "My mother is a lovely person who in no way resembles yours, Henry, but nevertheless, 'demanding, exacting, punctual, emphasizing super-cleanliness, or as my mother calls it, immaculateness' – my mother tried to instill those traits in me, too, yet she has no German ancestry ... she's a Mayflower descendant, a Colonial Dame, Daughter of the American Revolution. I didn't go for the neatness and super-cleanliness part, but I'll say one thing that did register that I wholeheartedly embraced, that is, being punctual."

"Hmmm ... hmmm ... that's because you're an Aries," Henry observed. "Aries people are always on time – usually even early, doncha know. They're the most punctual people in the zodiac ... great believers in the early bird catches the worm. Isn't that right, Noreen?"

Noreen Siegel, an Aries like myself, was not only absolutely gorgeous, but a sweet and gracious woman as well. In addition to the Jean Renoir film, under her acting name, Noreen Nash, she played a series of film and television roles, including in George Stevens' epic *Giant*, starring Elizabeth Taylor, Rock Hudson and James Dean. She had married Dr. Siegel when very young. After having two children and retiring from show business, she enrolled in UCLA for a bachelor's degree in French literature. Later, Noreen would begin a career as a historical novelist – no doubt encouraged by Henry, who was extremely fond of her.

Henry told us that due to a particular placement of Aries in his astrological chart, his Aries rising coupled with other Aries-related aspects, he had a weakness for Aries women, and he had two of us in Noreen and me.

Henry didn't drive and didn't own a car, so he was driven everywhere. It was always his constant companion Joe Grey whose wheels brought them to the Siegels' and elsewhere. Joe was very solicitous of Henry. He was almost young enough to be Henry's son; they were 21 years apart in age. The two were unusually close, sometimes seeming almost co-dependent. Joe was a New Yorker, I believe from Brooklyn, like Henry; the two shared a similar New York/Brooklyn accent. A common heritage and love of reading drew them together.

Joe had been in Hollywood since the late 1930's, and in addition to his devoted friendship with Henry, had also become close friends with Aldous Huxley and George Raft. Joe used to talk about taking Huxley many times to the UCLA campus, because Huxley liked to watch the "little girls" there, undergraduates whom he referred to as "cunt-lets" (perhaps alternatively spelled "cuntlettes"?). Huxley had recently died on the same day President Kennedy was assassinated, but Raft was still alive and well. Joe liked to tell the story of how George Raft could have been a bigger star than Bogart, had he not turned down *The Maltese Falcon* and *Casablanca*. He also mentioned that the secret of George Raft's youth was having sex with a different woman every night. I wondered how George managed to pull this off year in, year out. How was he able to meet that many available women, and did he ever trip up and repeat one, without remembering he had already slept with her? But I never asked.

Over the past couple of decades, Joe had worked in dozens of movies, probably more than 100, several in which his good buddies Frank Sinatra and Dean Martin starred, among them *Von Ryan's Express, Robin and the 7 Hoods,* and *Ocean's Eleven*. Other high profile films in which Joe appeared included *Irma la Douce, Bye Bye Birdie, Breakfast at Tiffany's, Some Like It Hot*, and *Guys and Dolls*. Apart from his acting roles, an ex-pugalist, Joe was in demand as technical consultant on films in which stars John Garfield, Elvis Presley, Jeff Chandler, James Cagney, George Raft, Tony Curtis and Kirk Douglas, among others, played boxers. Additionally, Joe was a talented stunt man and functioned as Dean Martin's stand-in on all of Dean's pictures. I think he appeared in about thirty of Frank Sinatra's films. He had a well-connected older brother, Mack Grey, who like Joe, was something of a Hollywood fable.

Having heard about my body movement coach Jacobina Caro in connection with Anaïs, Henry wanted to meet Jake. I considered Henry and Jacobina to be roughly of the same generation, though Jake was some dozen years younger than Henry, having been born early in the 20th century, the same year as Anaïs (1903). Both Henry and Jake were Capricorns of similar temperament, both lively, entertaining, and always in jolly good humor.

I knew Henry and Jacobina would find common ground. Jake had led a fascinating life, she knew the proverbial "everyone" in Hollywood of past and present eras. Among her contemporaries and friends were the European artist and writer emigrés who left Europe at the beginning of the war – Heinrich and Thomas Mann, Marta and Lion Feuchtwänger, Fritz Lang, Billy Wilder, Peter Lorre. She was an intimate of Orson Welles, Christopher Isherwood, Gerald Heard, Alan Watts, Laura and Aldous Huxley, and many other major literary figures, actors, producers, and directors. She knew the blacklisted Hollywood Ten, and as a registered, card carrying Communist herself, she (and two of her four husbands) had also been blacklisted. Beginning her career as a flame-haired New York dancer and choreographer, Jake migrated to Hollywood, where over the decades, she morphed into a highly respected, now grey-haired acting and body movement coach. She had been a teacher at the Actors Lab, worked with drug addicts at Daytop, and taught some of Hollywood's biggest stars.

Henry was particularly interested in hearing Jake's experiences with the Hollywood blacklist. After covering that subject, the conversation moved to Anaïs. Jacobina told Henry how watching Anaïs prepare food fascinated her. "She has the most delicate hands. Like fairy hands. Dainty, magical hands. They move in a lovely rhythm and before you know it, the meal is ready, as if by magic."

Henry said, "I always admired those hands, in ways you mention and more. And many other aspects of her too, of course. Hmmm ... hmmm ...a complex, intriguing woman, a woman of mystery to many, and I think she likes it that way."

Jacobina spoke of Anaïs's artful, elusive, feminine manner, and added, "Anaïs has the remarkable faculty of making people feel wonderful in her presence."

"Yas, yaz," Henry nodded agreement, exhaling a cloud of smoke.

"She seems very happy with Rupert," I joined in. "Perfectly matched."

Jacobina said, "I love the way they met. In an elevator! It was fated, it was meant to be."

I said, "Rupert is such a handsome man. Yet he's not a pretty boy; he's very masculine."

"And self-effacing," Jacobina added. "Amazingly sensitive. He's very interested in Eastern philosophy."

"Yas, yas, hmmm hmmm," Henry said.

"Anaïs is his life, everything radiates around her," Jacobina said, "and Rupert is so supportive."

I added, "He seems like the ideal mate for her, a man who respects and admires her, is very protective of her, and does everything to nurture her artistic creativity. He's much younger than she, yet they don't seem that far apart in years at all."

"Yaz, yas," Henry said, adding, "Those Candida-Marchbanks relationships do well, doncha know. Hmmm ... hmmm ... women seem to thrive on being with younger men, if I may say so. I'm all for it. And the reverse is true, of course – older men, younger women. It works out well."

"My third husband, Bob Meltzer, was twelve years younger than I," Jacobina said. "He died in the war. He was the only man I ever truly loved."

"I'm sorry about that," Henry said. "But as to older women and younger men, I'm sure nature intended things that way, and it's only society that screwed things up by frowning upon it, doncha know."

Henry and Jacobina discovered they knew Man Ray in common. "Man Ray lived on Vine Street," Jacobina said, "not far from where I was working during the war at the Larry Edmunds Bookshop on Cahuenga. The store has since moved to Hollywood Boulevard."

Henry said, "Larry Edmunds, hmmm... hmmm – great bookstore. I might have seen you there back in the 40's, ya know?"

"Henry knew Man Ray in Los Angeles," Joe put in, "right, Henry?"

"Indeed I did," Henry returned, crushing his cigarette into an ashtray. He was soon lighting another. "When I was living up Beverly Glen, we used to get together often, and when we were apart, we corresponded on a frequent basis. We were introduced by Margaret and Gilbert Neiman. The Neimans moved to Colorado for a while, and eventually came to live in Big Sur. Gilbert knew Spanish quite well, well enough to have translated Garcia Lorca's *Blood Wedding*. Lepska and I stayed with the Neimans in Colorado. Gilbert and Margaret were witnesses at my wedding to Lepska."

"Man Ray photographed you, too," Joe prompted.

"Several times."

"Man Ray did two very famous photos of Henry," Joe explained to the group. "Henry's dressed in a shirt, suspenders and tie, he's posed in front of Margaret Neiman. Margaret is naked, her face is decorated with leafy designs. And there's also another famous Man Ray photo of Henry in which Man Ray's wife, Juliet, appears alongside Margaret, the two of them behind Henry, both naked with leafy masks covering their faces."

Henry said, "Gilbert Neiman became the editor of an international magazine published in Puerto Rico, to which Man and I both contributed, along with Marcel Duchamp, Herman Hesse, my good friend Alfred Perlès, and several others of us."

Jacobina said, "I remember Man Ray as a rather short man who resembled Mr. Peepers. He spoke with a Brooklyn accent."

"Man spent most of his career in Paris, but he lived in L.A. for at least ten years, particularly during the war years. Man's father was a garment factory worker who also ran a small tailoring business out of the family home in Brooklyn, and enlisted his children to help out. I suppose you would say we have something in common there," Henry said.

Henry puffed on his cigarette. "What else did you ladies talk about at Anaïs' luncheon?" he wanted to know.

"We talked about Proust, Colette, Rimbaud, D.H. Lawrence," Jacobina began, "among others."

"D.H. Lawrence," Henry seized upon the name. "He interested me, too. I started to write a book on him. It remains unfinished; I just never got a handle on it, I was going in circles. Perhaps some day I'll take it up again. I never met Lawrence, but I did meet Frieda. She spent a winter in Big Sur with us. A wonderful woman – very much the earth mother, doncha know."

"Anaïs wrote a book on Lawrence," I said

"Yes," Jacobina said, "her first book."

Henry said, "Sure, sure, and I don't believe her Lawrence book was ever finished, either."

"But she did finish it, Henry. She published it," I said.

"Hmmm ... hmmmm – in one sense yes, the book has a beginning, middle and end, and so indeed it was a fait accompli, especially because she did run off a few hundred copies of it herself. But I don't think she was ever satisfied with it, in a manner of speaking. Not to the degree she was with her other books. She never pursued it after that initial run. But admittedly, she got farther on the subject than I did."

Henry frequently mentioned two authors who had greatly influenced him, Lawrence Durrell and Blaise Cendrars. He said, "Cendrars said, go take a walk through the Bibliothèque Nationale and you'll see where that route leads: to a cemetery, a submerged continent. Millions of volumes delivered over to the worms. No one knows any longer whose they are. No one ever asks. Terra incognita. It's rather discouraging."

In the course of our Sundays at the Siegels' get togethers, several examples of undeservedly forgotten authors arose whom Henry always wanted to bring alive for us again, Marie Corelli, Romain Rolland, the recently deceased John Cowper Powys, Alfred de Vigny, Lord Bulwer-Lytton, and Konrad Bercovici, to mention a few. Other categories Henry liked to talk about were literary figures who as teenagers left home to seek adventure; prominent writers and artists who died tragically young; and writers and musicians who lost their hearing. Henry often spoke of the "years of misery," and the loneliness of the tortured spirits of the 19th century.

In the category of young deaths was one of Joe's heroes, John Garfield, the New York actor and member of the Group Theater who moved to Hollywood and became a major star. Called to testify before the U.S. Congressional House Committee on Un-American Activities (HUAC), Garfield denied Communist affiliation and refused to "name names," effectively ending his film career. Some claimed the stress of this incident led to his premature death at 39 from a heart attack. Jacobina had known Garfield at the Actors' Lab.

"Men who left home young," Henry was saying, "Cendrars, Frank Harris, Rimbaud, and you might include Raymond Radiguet in that category, since he left school at 15 to dedicate himself to writing."

"What about you, Henry?" Joe asked. "You left home to travel through the West, you worked as a ranch hand to break away from city life."

"Sure, sure, but I was no teenager; I was over 21 at the time. That was around 1913 or so."

"That must have been around the same time you met Emma Goldman, the anarchist," Joe said.

"Yas, yaz," Henry replied. "A turning point in my life, doncha know."

Hearing of Jacobina's early career as a dancer and choreographer, Henry asked, "Did you ever know George Raft back in New York? He was quite the dancer, ya know."

"He was a wonderful dancer," Jacobina agreed. "I didn't know him in New York, I only met him here in Hollywood."

"George Raft is a great friend of Joe's," Henry said.

Joe said, "George got his start dancing at Texas Guinan's speakeasy. That must have been around the same time you and June were running your own speakeasy in Greenwich Village, Henry, when you were working for the Queens Parks Department."

I jumped into the conversation. "Before they were married, when they were dating, my parents used to go to speakeasies in the city. They went to Texas Guinan's, to the 21 Club, which used to be a speakeasy, and to Sherman Billingsley's," I said. "Maybe they even went to your speakeasy, Henry. My grandmother always insisted they be chaperoned."

"Chaperoned to a speakeasy?" Henry guffawed. "That's a new one on me!"

CHAPTER SIX

As I knew he would, Henry found Jacobina charming, wise, fun, and funny. When I came alone to the Siegels the following week, he commented, "Your friend has an interesting background. She must have had a fascinating life. A woman of experience, isn't that so? ... hmmm ... hmmm ... I can tell she's a born teacher. She's got that inner wisdom. Still has a trace of Boston in her, you could say. She's a part of a slice of controversial history. I always enjoy meeting such people."

I told Henry that Jacobina had introduced me to the joys of cat companionship. "Her black cat Sam is amazing," I said. "Jacobina's house in Laurel Canyon burned down a few years ago when she was away in New York. She came back to a pile of cinders. Everything was destroyed. Sam was gone. But four years later, Sam found her at the new address where she was living in Hollywood. One day she heard a meow, opened the back door, and there was Sam.

"I had always had dogs, never cats," I said, "because my mother objected to cats." I told Henry I would always be grateful to Jacobina for encouraging me to acquire my first cat, a beautiful, sweet natured calico I named Kimetha, called Kimmy, who soon produced a litter of four daughters, Sabrina, Esmeralda, Phoebe Ann and Claire, each of whom was given a good home, including one who went to a Las Vegas mobster's girlfriend. Kimmy's next litter produced one cat only, another calico I named Tabitha and kept.

Henry took note of my love of cats and mentioned it often during our conversations. He said that many well known people were cat lovers: "Louis XV, Marie Antoinette, the Brontë sisters, Lord Byron, who incidentally is Joe's favorite writer," he began; "Cocteau dedicated a book to his cat; Winston Churchill, Dickens, Einstein; of course T.S. Eliot, with his wonderful *Old Possum's Book of Practical Cats*; Hemingway, who kept thirty cats in Key West; Florida; Nostradamus, one of Cendrars's favorite authors and mine too; Queen Victoria, Nikola Tesla, Albert Schweitzer, and there's a whole bunch more of you cat people, ya know. Are you familiar with Baudelaire's poem *Les Chats*?"

"Of course! I have a wonderful recording of it – an album of Eva Le Gallienne and Louis Jourdan reading all of Baudelaire's most famous poems." In unison, Henry and I quoted the opening lines of *Les Chats*. Then, changing the subject, Henry asked, "When you were living in Rome, did you ever meet Caresse Crosby?"

"I'm sorry I never did. I knew people who knew her and I could have met her. I was invited to meet her a couple of times but didn't go. I don't know why I didn't. I wish I had."

Henry was interested in the mafia in Italy, both the Italian and American mafiosi who had been deported. One such was Lucky Luciano. An American actor friend then living in Rome, Vince Barbi, was a friend of Luciano's and offered to introduce me. "It was arranged, it was all set – I was going to meet him."

"What happened?"

"I ended up in the hospital, so the meeting was postponed. Then I came back to the U.S., and only a few weeks after that, Charlie Lucky died. Vince left Italy, moved here, and recently, we worked for a couple of months in a film together, Blake Edwards's *What Did You Do in the War, Daddy?* in which I play a German-speaking Italian prostitute.

"Ezra Pound is another person I had the opportunity to meet but didn't. My Vassar College Italian teacher Lina Manca and her daughter Mietta did a lot of traveling all over Italy with Pound and knew him well. Why did I not go with them? I could have. I should have. So many things I think about in retrospect where I made the wrong choice."

"We all have these missed opportunities or imagined ones. You have to look at it this way, that everything that happens to us, good or bad, is a learning experience. Missed opportunities are unavoidable, so we can't dwell on them, doncha know," Henry said. He straightened a bit and leaned in. "Ya know, John Dos Passos was a yardstick in a way, toward my thinking of what I was, what I wasn't, what I thought I should be, what I was afraid I might not be, what I was sure I could be – but why wasn't I yet? Same age, same era, he made it early and I didn't. I always thought I could do that, do what he did, but I never did it. I didn't have the confidence to start writing ... so I made a lot of handwritten charts, outlining ideas, characters, arcs, scenes, that kind of thing. I used to berate myself that I missed years of opportunities by not taking the bull by the horns. Again, I just didn't have the confidence, doncha know. I drew up all these plans, I had all these ideas, but I didn't really get up the courage to do what I needed to do. Paris changed that."

Henry never tired of hearing about my life in Italy. He asked, "How did you end up living there for two years? What led you to go there in the first place?"

"Complicated reasons, but the main impetus was I was running from an advertising man I was involved with, trying to end it with him, but always getting back together. I needed to break the pattern, so I decided to put an ocean between us. And I thought Hollywood on the Tiber would be an interesting place to be."

"And you already spoke Italian."

"Right, I had a solid literary background in it. My senior seminar in Italian at Vassar was an entire year reading Dante's *La Divina Commedia*, and I was so saturated with medieval Italian literature and culture that when I started living in Italy, I was told, 'Signorina, you speak delicious 13th century Italian.' I had to modernize my vocabulary."

Henry chucked at that. Returning to Caresse Crosby, he said, "Caresse is part of the Roman scene, in a manner of speaking, doncha know. She's been around there for the past several years. Sooner of later, everyone in Rome runs across her. She bought this dilapidated 15th century castle, Castello di Rocca Sinibalda, that was built for a cardinal, which she runs as an artists' colony. She calls it the Center for Creative Arts and Humanist Living. She uses it to support artists and give seminars. It's located some fifty or sixty kilometers north of Rome in the Abruzzi, which is considered the Mezzogiorno, southern Italy, even though it's actually central Italy, ya know. That's because of its association with the Kingdom of the Two Sicilys.

"Caresse got the joint for a song. It came with the Papal title of Principessa, so she's technically a princess, even though Italy no longer has royalty."

"Even so, people still use titles."

"Even flaunt them – sure, sure. The castle has around 200 rooms, I think, some with 20 foot high ceilings; some rooms are decorated with 16th century frescoes, ya know. The place is a cavern, impossible to heat. Caresse said she wouldn't live there if you paid her.

"Not long ago, there was a documentary made about Caresee and her castle, called *Always Yes, Caresse*," Henry continued. "At one point in the film, Caresse pulls her blouse up to reveal her breasts, which are quite large specimens, if I do say. Of course, one of her great claims to fame is that she designed and got the patent for the first backless brassiere, doncha know."

I said, "I know the castle; I've actually been there. I did a foto romanzo for the fumetto *Sogno*, called *La Valle dei Sogni Perduti*, (The Valley of Lost Dreams) with Rosanna Galli, a former Miss Italy. We filmed it in wintertime at Caresse Crosby's castle, and it was absolutely freezing there. When we had to remove our outerwear for the shots, it was pretty hard not to look frozen for the camera."

"That's why Caresse won't live there, and certainly not in winter. I don't know how the people who lived in the 15th century tolerated it. They were made of tougher stuff than we are, you might say."

Henry elaborated on the celebrated Caresse. "She came from a wealthy blue stocking background, with colonial American antecedents – she was even presented to the King of England, ya know. A woman of sizeable social standing, I must say. Harry Crosby was her second husband, a man several years younger than she. You women and your younger men!

"Caresse and Harry ran the Black Sun Press and were instrumental in publishing the works of so many struggling writers who went on to become established, doncha know." And Henry named them: James Joyce, Kay Boyle, Hemingway and Faulkner, Hart Crane, D. H. Lawrence, T. S. Eliot, Ezra Pound, Archibald MacLeish, Dorothy Parker, Saint-Exupéry, "and so on and on and on. Every endeavor Caresse headed, she always secured contributions from well-known artists and writers – Sartre, Robert Lowell, Camus, Picasso, Matisse, Cartier-Bresson, Louis Aragon, Jean Genet, George Grosz, Max Ernst, Jung, Anaïs ...

"I owe Caresse a debt of gratitude, and I'm hardly alone in that respect; so many others do as well. I personally owe her both as a writer, as an artist, and as a human being for coming to my rescue on more than one occasion. At times in my life when I most needed a helping hand, Caresse was there."

Joe asked, "How about the time you and Anaïs were writing erotica for the oil baron? Isn't that one of the times you're referring to, Henry?"

"That was one of them, yes," Henry acknowledged, taking a long drag on his cigarette. "What Joe brings up, a story that's been told and retold – I was grinding out erotica at a dollar a page for the aforesaid oil baron, but after two 100-page stories for which I earned $200, I just couldn't keep on with it. I was itching to tour the United States and write about it. I was all ready to go, but hadn't provided all I'd promised to the oil man. So Caresse stepped in. She was a member of Anaïs's New York City smut club for the fun of it, not for the money, of course – money she was swimming in. Anyway, she took over for me, which freed me to drive through the country and end up in California.

"Caresse had also invited me to stay in her New York apartment on East 54th Street when I returned from Paris in 1940. Later, in Washington, when she was opening the Caresse Crosby Modern Art Gallery, she wrote me, asking if I'd be interested in exhibiting my paintings there. That was my first one-man art show, thanks to Caresse.

"Caresse isn't her real name, doncha know, it was Polly – actually Mary, and they nicknamed her Polly, until Harry Crosby came along and gave her the name Caresse, which actually suits her quite well. Ya know, her good friend Hemingway offered her a choice of *The Torrents of Spring* or *The Sun Also Rises* as their first effort together. Caresse picked the former, which was the less well received of the two."

I asked Henry why he had returned to the US after a decade in France.

"I had little choice; Americans were told we had to leave," he answered. "Everybody wanted to get out. The Nazis took over."

"But many people stayed."

"Not if they knew what was good for them, they didn't."

"Gertrude Stein and Alice B. Toklas spent the entire war in France."

"They had connections, they were protected."

"In spite of being Jewish?"

"That's right. They had friends in high places."

"Like who?"

"Well, there's no getting away from it. Stein was a Vichy propagandist and collaborationist, as implausible as may seem, ya know. She was very pro-Vichy and had the protection of a powerful Vichy government official, Bernard Faÿ."

"You actually call her a collaborationist?"

"Put it this way: Stein translated some 200 pages of contemporary speeches given by Marshal Pétain, the 'Victor of Verdun,' as he became known during the First World War, whom she continued to praise well after World War II ended, even when Pétain was sentenced to death for treason. At the beginning of the war, she was urged to leave France by American Embassy officials, friends and family, but refused, because astrological signs assured her the Germans would suffer a swift and certain defeat. Stein was so outspoken she's even on record saying that Hitler should receive the Nobel Peace Prize."

"Good grief."

"But ya know, it's amazing how many prominent people were attracted to fascist regimes -- Ezra Pound, Yeats, T. S. Eliot, Wyndham Lewis, Knut Hamsun, Céline, Heidegger, Robert Brasillach ..."

"William Randolph Hearst, Charles Lindbergh, John D. Rockefeller, and Allen Dulles," Joe added.

"Nancy Mitford," I said.

"Not to forget Joseph P. Kennedy. His support of Hitler essentially ended his diplomatic career."

"And who was this man Faÿ who protected Gertrude Stein and Alice B. Toklas?" I asked.

"Faÿ was a historian of American culture and Franco-American relations who studied at Harvard. He was director of the Bibliothèque Nationale and was chief henchman in charge of the repression of French Freemasons. He also stepped in at the request of Picasso when the Nazis were ready to seize Gertrude's art collection. The collection was spared.

"Stein wrote a letter on Faÿ's behalf when he was tried as a collaborator following the Liberation. A French court condemned him to *dégradation nationale* and forced labor for life, but he escaped to Switzerland a few years later. Funding to facilitate his prison break came from Alice B. Toklas. Later, Faÿ received a pardon from the French President – around the same time as Céline received his. Yes, Stein and Toklas did stay during the war, you're right about that. But the rest of us – we could not have, nor did we want to. And for many, escape was harrowing."

That led to the exploits of a courageous man named Varian Fry and of my equally brave, wonderful friend Charles Fernley Fawcett – movie actor, stuntman, filmmaker, songwriter, jazz musician, trumpet player, wrestler, adventurer, pilot, Foreign Legionnaire, Amazon explorer, horseman, freedom fighter, spy, swashbuckler, and courtly Southern gentleman, who had been my close friend in Rome.

CHAPTER SEVEN

Henry knew of American journalist Varian Fry and his amazing network in Vichy France that helped a few thousand anti-Nazi and Jewish refugees escape from Europe. He said, "While at Harvard, Varian Fry founded an influential literary magazine with Lincoln Kirstein. Following the occupation of France, he went to Marseille on a rescue mission. He and his volunteers, including your friend Charlie Fawcett, hid people and smuggled them out, putting them on ships at Marseille or taking them across the border to Spain and Portugal to catch passage to America. They saved over 2000 people, some of the most famous writers and artists of the century: Marc Chagall, Marcel Duchamp, André Breton, Lion Feuchtwänger, Hannah Arendt, Arthur Koestler, Jacques Lipchitz, Franz and Alma Mahler Werfel, André Masson, Kurt and Helen Wolff..."

Henry had heard stories about my friend Charlie's exploits and knew a number of people who knew him. He said, "There was a famous joke about Fawcett that made the rounds. A tourist in St. Peter's Square is looking up at the Pope on the balcony of the Vatican Palace. 'Who's that?' he asks a local. The local replies, 'I don't know who the fellow in the beanie is, but the guy next to him – that's Charlie Fawcett.'"

That joke always got a laugh, even if you didn't know Charlie. Henry said to me, "So you knew the infamous Charles Fernley Fawcett when you lived in Rome."

"I know him well," I answered. "Charlie is an utterly amazing man. Since the day we met, every morning I would wait for Charlie's phone call to tell me what was on the agenda for that day or night, who was in town, and where we would all go together. Sometimes we'd meet around noon on the Via Veneto, then have lunch with Charlie's visiting friends, or we'd go on excursions, or it would be something later in the day, a dinner, a party, dancing, whatever. We were all high on la dolce vita, mainly because of Charlie, always the organizer, always the energizer.

"There were days upon days and nights of outings, events, beach excursions, Via Veneto and Piazza Navona happenings, night clubs and after hours aperitivi and gelati at so many exciting places with Charlie, usually with an entourage in tow of Indian maharajahs, Greek shipping tycoons, international film stars, producers, directors, CIA/OSS spies, and assorted other interesting types who, immediately upon arrival in Rome, would always make sure their first phone call was to Charlie. Charlie knows everybody and everybody loves him.

"Charlie is known for never accepting a gift of any kind, not even a necktie, even though everybody wants to give him the world. He always declines. He is also, in addition to being called the 'honorary mayor of Rome,' the greatest facilitator known to man who delights in helping others and in arranging things to make lives better.

"Charlie pulled strings to obtain for me a vastly reduced ticket on Pakistan International Airlines from Rome to New York. Speaking of Pakistan reminds me of a plan Charlie had for me, never realized because of my own lack of foresight, for which I could certainly kick myself. Charlie knew I had started writing this book about the New York modeling business. 'You're a writer,' he told me, having read a couple of chapters. 'If you want to write something really important, I can arrange to have you be the guest of ...' and here, Charlie casually lists the names of top world leaders who are his bosom buddies in countries like Pakistan, Saudi Arabia, Ethiopia, and a host of others – President Goulart of Brazil, Saud bin Abdul Aziz, King of Saudi Arabia, King Mohammed and his son King Hassan of Morocco, and Heilie Selasie of Ethiopia were names Charlie mentioned, among many other exalted and extraordinary people, all of whom Charlie assured me would lay out the welcoming mat and be wonderful hosts! The idea was I should write about the role of women in these countries, a great deal of which, Charlie said, would not only be utterly fascinating, but little known to the world. This idea, Charlie said, would make a fabulous article or even a book.

"And you didn't take him up on the offer?"

"Regrettably, no."

"What an opportunity you missed."

"I know. I'm really sorry about it. I was still feeling so weak, even after being hospitalized for all those weeks. I was feeling rotten, besides which, someone I was close to was urging me to move to Hollywood. So I came back to the States. Why didn't I listen? Can you imagine such introductions?"

Henry said, "I know something of Charles Fawcett's story.

He and his siblings were orphans raised by relatives. At 15, Charlie had an affair with his best friend's mother. He and I share a similar experience in common. As a teenager, I too, had affair with an older woman. About his affair, Charlie said, 'If that's molestation, I would wish that on every young boy.' On that, I can heartily agree, doncha know. Charlie's affair didn't end that well," Henry continued, "nor did mine, ya know. After a few years, an unfortunate circumstance happened, and I bolted."

Joe said, "This important rite of passage should be available to young men everywhere."

Henry said, "It used to be perfectly acceptable, in fact, recommended, for an older woman to have an affair with a young man coming of age, to initiate him, in a manner of speaking. But today the woman is slandered for such behavior; this kind of relationship is condemned as immoral, and the woman can be prosecuted, even jailed. That's too bad; it's wrong. Young men can learn a great deal from an older woman. I know I did. As far as boys are concerned, if they're big enough, they're old enough, and the same should be true of girls as well, doncha know. "

I said, "Charlie's affair ended with a broken heart, and he headed to the Far East, working on steamships through the Panama Canal."

"I've heard so many Fawcett tales from friends," Henry said. "One story about him is that somewhere along the line, he persuaded Louis Armstrong to give him music lessons, and invited himself to lunch with Braque and Matisse."

I said, "An amusing incident Charlie told me about concerned his being at a train station, getting ready to board, when a little girl of maybe eight or nine years old spots him and says to her mother, 'Oh, look, Mamma, there's that man who's always *cornuto* – cuckolded – in all the movies.'"

That brought a good laugh. I continued, "Charlie's had so many incredible exploits. He was an artist's model, he wrestled in Poland for a living; joined the Polish army, worked with the ambulance corps in France, disguised himself as a Nazi officer to escape from Gestapo headquarters. He forged a British passport to fly RAF fighter planes, served in the French Foreign Legion and was part of French Resistance. He heard about Varian Fry's work in Marseille and headed there."

"Marseille was a very dangerous city," Henry pointed out.

"Yes, and Charlie's activities there were all the more so. He lived in the port, dealing with local gangsters, the *caïds* of the Marseille mafia were helping Charlie help Jews escape. He served with the OSS, and at the end of the war, he married (some say six, some say eleven, some say seventeen) Jewish women who'd been trapped in concentration camps, so they could leave Europe with an American visa. After the war, Charlie started an acting career, appearing in films shot in Italy, Spain, France, Yugoslavia, Portugal, Denmark – all over. He enjoys friendships with all the great international directors."

Henry said, "Ya know, his girlfriend for some time was Hedy Lamarr. Now there's one gorgeous dame."

"But being an actor didn't end Charlie's humanitarian efforts," I said. "He's continued responding to crises – smuggling refugees to safety from civil conflicts, organizing earthquake relief teams, fighting the communists in the Greek civil war. In the Hungarian uprising, he spent three months helping rescue refugees. During civil war riots in the Belgian Congo, once again, he was rescuing the disenfranchised. He lived among the headhunters of the Amazon. I could go on and on about Charlie. He's the product of an old Virginia family, a descendant of Thomas Jefferson and James Madison, a larger than life, swashbuckling figure off-screen as well as on. He was born with charisma, one of the most gracious and charming people ever."

"A remarkable man," Henry agreed. "I've heard much about his exploits; we have friends in common."

"Friends ... Charlie's like you in that respect, Henry. He has so many devoted friends, and a rare talent for cultivating them."

"We probably have a certain astrological aspect in common, if you will," Henry said. "With an incredible life like his, if anyone should write their memoirs, it's Charles Fawcett."

"Charlie never will. He's a keeper of secrets, the most trustworthy man you will ever meet, a man of enormous integrity. He's a genuine hero, but very modest about it – the last of the great Southern gentlemen."

Henry said that Charlie shared something in common with his friend and literary idol, Blaise Cendrars. "Cendrars wasn't quite the swashbuckler Fawcett is, but he had a varied and fascinating life nonetheless. In his own way, he too was a larger than life figure with an extraordinarily varied bio, too, ya know. He was a bee-keeper, a filmmaker, a chef, a movie house pianist, a watchmaker, and a traveler with the gypsies. He spent the First World War fighting with the French Foreign Legion, where he lost his arm in combat; he became an art critic, befriended Picasso, sailed the seven seas, shoveled coal in China, amassed and lost huge fortunes. He was as an assistant to Abel Gance in the filming of *La Roue* in the 20's. It was he who put together the montage of the running train, and suggested Hönegger to compose the music. He worked in Hollywood in the 30's, at the time of the filming of *Sutter's Gold*, and even had his own gossip column in a Hollywood newspaper. Modigliani painted his portrait, Braque designed the interior of his car. In the early months of the Occupation, Cendrars was a war correspondent attached to the British armies."

"So he stayed in France during the Occupation. Wasn't there an interesting life going on during that time, regardless?" I asked.

"I'm not sure what you mean by that. For some, if they collaborated with the Nazis, perhaps. For most people, it was a difficult time, doncha know, and it could be dangerous," Henry replied. "But yes, Cendrars stayed and it worked out fine in his case. Unlike me, Cendrars never had trouble earning a living, never experienced poverty. During the Occupation, he lived for the most part on the sale of green plants and medicinal herbs which he grew in his garden in Aix-en-Provence. He also had bees, which made him a lot of money. He made honey, doncha know, because it was easy work and well paid. All you needed were good customers. Now why didn't I think of that?

"Blaise Cendrars wasn't his real name, ya know. The name is a bastardization of *braise*, meaning embers, and *cendres*, the French word for ashes, adding ars at the end, meaning art. So Cendrars wrote on the ashes of outmoded literary styles to create his own pioneering art. He created this imaginative, magical and horrifying world, written in astoundingly beautiful prose. Reading Cendrars is like stepping into another universe. His fiction is unlike anything else you'll ever read."

Joe said, "His poetry influenced Apollinaire and helped shape modernism. By the way, Henry, we can add Apollinaire to our list of early deaths, along with John Reed. They died at 38 and 33 respectively. But to get back to Cendrars..."

Henry said, "Yas, yas ... Cendrars admired the divinatory quatrains of Nostradamus, which he described as a joy to him, written in a magnificent language, although they remained indecipherable. He read and reread them for forty years. Cendrars said, 'I gargle with them, I regale myself with them, I enjoy them, but I don't understand them.' He read nearly all the keys ever published, but found all of them meaningless, false, doncha know. Nevertheless, as a great French poet, Nostradamus is one of the greatest, he said, and I agree. Ya know, for years, we were all waiting for Cendrars's *Anthologie de la poésie française*, which never happened."

"That and his *La Carissima*, the mystical life of Mary Magdalene," Joe added.

"That's right," Henry said, "the only woman who ever made Christ weep. Cendrars said this was no less than the world's most beautiful love story. That book, which unfortunately never saw the light of day, was meant to tie in somehow with the tragic war years, I'm not sure how. Ya know, Cendrars said he was not an extraordinary worker, but an extraordinary daydreamer."

"Henry introduced me to Cendrars's work," Joe said. "I feel a real sense of loss that he's no longer with us. I wish more of his writing were available in English."

"True, true, because ideally, Cendrars should be read in French," Henry said. "Ya know, as a writer, Cendrars worked in an unusual way preparing some of his books. He would arrange the vocabulary he was going to employ. The first time he used this method was for *L'Homme Foudroyé*, for which he drew up a list of three thousand words in advance, and he used all of them. That saved him a lot of time, and, he said, gave a certain lightness to his work. I don't know how he happened on this system. He said language was a thing that seduced him, perverted him, formed, informed and deformed him, and that was why he was a poet."

"You'll have to try that method sometime, Henry," Joe said.

"I doubt it would work for me, Joe. I would miss the joy of spontaneity, in a manner of speaking, doncha know, even though I always shared such a common spirit with Cendrars," Henry said. "Cendrars said reading was a drug for him—he said, 'I drug myself on printer's ink.' I could say the same of myself. Hmmm ... hmmmm ...I share Cendrars' belief that writing is a noble privilege, compared with the lot of most people, who live like parts of a machine, existing only to keep the gears of society pointlessly turning. Like Cendrars, I pity them with all my heart. He spoke about the anonymous crowd he would watch from his apartment window, humanity pouring into or out of the métro at fixed hours. Truly, he said, that isn't a life. It isn't human. It's slavery ... and it reflects the absurdity of life itself.

"This was how I felt in New York," Henry said. "Paris for me was alive, it was electrifying, it was life enhancing. I was free, you see; I had freedom. I wasn't one of the working slaves pouring out of the metro at fixed hours. For that I will be eternally grateful."

"So Charlie Fawcett took off at 15, as did Cendrars, just like so many other young men did in those days," Henry said. "Frank Harris was even younger; he was only 13 when he set out to seek his fortune. He arrived in New York virtually penniless, took a series of odd jobs to support himself, including as a construction worker building the Brooklyn Bridge, doncha know."

"He'd never be hired today," Joe reflected. "Today, we have child labor laws."

"Those were the days," Henry began romanticizing. "A young man was free to explore life, prove his mettle. Frank Harris went to Chicago, after which he became a cowboy, then enrolled at the University of Kansas, where he earned a law degree and was admitted to the Kansas bar. Of course, he wasn't cut out for the law, either, but he got to see a great deal in his life. He even invented a card game called 'Dirty Banshee,' each card showing satyrs and goddesses coupling in a different way. His autobiography is notorious for the graphic descriptions of his sexual encounters, as Jeanne found out as a teenager at Jones Beach," Henry laughed. "Hmmm ... hmmm ..."

"It's really too bad there are so many restrictions on young men today," Joe lamented.

Henry agreed. "It's true, Joe. Young men are held back, supposedly for their own good. Back then, one could express far greater freedom, doncha know."

"You met Frank Harris, didn't you, Henry?" Joe said.

"In my early twenties, yes. He was the first great writer I met."

"Henry, when you left New York for Paris, even though you were a good deal older than those teenage adventurers we just mentioned, you showed a lot of guts, probably more guts than those younger men, because of your age," I said. "You were pushing 40, so you were risking a lot more than they did. What does a fifteen year old have to lose?"

Joe agreed. "No matter what happened along the way, these youngsters still had their whole lives ahead of them. As teenagers, they could afford to make mistakes. Youth is full of a sense of infallibility, an incredible belief in oneself and what wonderful things in life lie ahead. Later on, people become more cautious and jaded, only Henry never did."

"No, I've never been risk averse," Henry agreed. "I took risks, you're right about that, Joe. And somehow, not really by design at all, simply by chance, by pure accident, things worked out for me."

CHAPTER EIGHT

In our frequent talks about French literature, Henry remarked that more Nobel Prizes had been awarded to writers who wrote in French than in any other language., Romain Rolland; Anatole France; Maeterlinck, Bergson; André Gide; Mauriac; Camus; Saint-John Perse, and Jean-Paul Sartre (who declined the prize), to name a few.

Henry then asked me a few questions about my own writing, such as: "Have you always wanted to write?" and "How did you become interested in being a writer?"

I answered: "My great Aunt Marie, a retired school teacher, taught me the 3 R's, the basics of reading, writing and arithmetic well before I was old enough to attend school. Since I already knew everything the other kids were learning for the first time, the teachers used to leave me to my own devices. To amuse myself, starting in first grade, I began writing stories. The teachers always told my mother I was a born writer, that I would be a writer some day, and I believed it. I believed it up until I went to college. My freshman year at Vassar, I had an English teacher by the name of Anita Marburg Lerner, an ex-wife of Max Lerner, mother of his three daughters, who did not like my work, who said I had no ability at writing and could never be a writer, so I better focus on another goal."

"What a destructive thing to tell a young person," Henry said, amazed. "I've always believed in encouraging young writers, doncha know. Whatever the quality of their work, if they keep at it, they'll eventually hit their stride. The important thing is to believe in oneself and keep writing."

"Well, that put down was enough to stop me from writing for the next few years," I said. "Then, something happened that changed everything in my mind, and I was able to start again."

"What happened to change you?"

"One night in Rome, I was sitting on the Spanish Steps. It must have been around 10 pm. I turned around, and there was Anita Marburg Lerner's ex-husband, Max Lerner, sitting on the step directly behind me, a girl of about eighteen huddled by his side. I don't recall why we all happened to be sitting there, but someone introduced me to Max, and we ended up in conversation about his ex, my Vassar

English teacher. I told him the story about how Mrs. Lerner had disparaged my work and said I didn't have a prayer of becoming a writer so I better find something else to do with my life. Max said I shouldn't take her remarks to heart, because 'Anita always had to have one pretty girl in every class to pick on.'"

"So you snapped out of it and snapped to it," Henry said approvingly. Knowing of my courses at the UCLA Extension with Los Angeles Times book critic Robert Kirsch and the Leonardo Bercovici Workshop in the Novel, he asked, "What are you working on now?"

I said I was writing the novel begun in Italy (eventually published as *The Beauty Trap*, by Trident/ Simon & Schuster), getting up every day at 4 a.m., pounding the keys on a small Olivetti.

Someone asked, "Dare we inquire what your novel is about?"

"According to Mr. Bercovici, it's about the penalty of beauty. I didn't know that until I took the workshop. Lee Siegel, jr.. has read some of it and he likes it."

Henry said, "Your Bercovici was among those Hollywood writers who were blacklisted." I hadn't known that. Henry continued: "After his blacklisting, Bercovici went to Italy for awhile, married the beautiful Swedish film star Marta Toren, who died tragically young. Your teacher had an uncle, a very interesting man, Konrad Bercovici, who was extremely successful, very well known in his day, enormously popular as a writer, who wrote a great deal about gypsies. Are you familiar with him?"

"I am. Mr. Bercovici mentioned his uncle several times in class. So I looked for and found one of Konrad Bercovici's books at Larsen's. It was totally absorbing, and it had a great glossary of Romany words at the end."

"Konrad Bercovici is another writer who's been forgotten today, yet who was one of the most famous authors in the first half of the 20th century. He frequented the Hotel Algonquin group, that's how established he was. He was able to often travel back and forth to Europe, where he ran in circles with Fitzgerald and Hemingway. Modigliani painted his portrait."

"Like Cendrars and Rimbaud," Joe said.

"Yes, Joe," Henry said. "And Theodore Dreiser was a big fan of Konrad Bercovici, had copies of all his works in his library, and I must say, Bercovici was prolific. In Hollywood he was a sought after as a screenwriter for years, and was a good friend of Charlie Chaplin, Mary Pickford and Douglas Fairbanks."

"I know from Mr. Bercovici – we call him Nardo behind his back, by the way – his uncle was born in Romania and grew up speaking several languages. He was close to the local gypsies through the Roma with whom his father traded horses. Hence, so many of the books he wrote were about gypsies."

"*Gypsy Blood, Love and the Gypsy, Stories of Gypsy Life, The Story of the Gypsies - Gypsies, Their Life, Lore and Legends*," Henry recalled. "And in addition to his gypsy books, he wrote a host of others as well."

"Nardo told us when his grandfather – Konrad's father – died, the family moved to Paris around the time of the Dreyfus Affair. Konrad studied to be an organist. He married a sculptor and they emigrated first to Canada, where he worked as a journalist for a Yiddish newspaper, then to New York's Lower East Side, where he toiled in sweatshops, gave piano lessons, and played the organ for nickelodeons."

"Did you know his first book was an exposé of New York City private charities, with an introduction by John Reed?" Henry asked.

"No, I didn't. Amazing – all those accomplishments, and he's virtually unknown today."

"There was even a sensational international lawsuit that made huge headlines, between Charlie Chaplin and Bercovici, for which Bercovici's attorney was the famed Louis Nizer. The claim was that Chaplin had approached Bercovici regarding one of his stories as a motion picture, and in the course of friendly negotiations, Bercovici gave Chaplin his outline of *The Great Dictator*, the story of a barber who looks so much like Hitler he's confused with him.

"Chaplin denied everything in the claim, but Bercovici's lawyer, Nizer, was able to establish there had been a meeting in a Hollywood theater where Chaplin pointed out a Russian baritone in the audience whom he thought would be ideal to play an important role in the picture. The Russian was located as a witness, and in court saved the day when he recalled one of the great moments in his life being the possibility of appearing in a Charlie Chaplin movie. Chaplin had given the Russian his private telephone number. The Russian pulled out an address book in which the number was still written, in Chaplin's own handwriting, and that cinched things for Bercovici.

The case was settled with Chaplin paying $95,000 to Konrad Bercovici."

"Henry's met Charlie Chaplin," Joe said. "They met at Chaplin's home in Vevey, Switzerland. Georges Simenon took Henry there."

Henry said, "Chaplin is a fabulous storyteller, as you can imagine, and we three had a memorable, rollicking time of it. But the incident of Konrad Bercovici's lawsuit against Chaplin is one thing that never arose."

"Probably Chaplin would prefer to keep a lid on that event," Joe surmised.

I said, "Nardo told us his Uncle Konrad had an ignominious end."

"Yes, he was robbed and murdered by a gang of hoodlums – in Philadelphia, I think it was. He was still going strong well into his late 80's, and probably would have continued to live a good deal longer," Henry said.

Henry was interested in all things occult, mystical, metaphysical and spiritual. He said French author Romain Rolland, as well as the two Indian mystics Rolland wrote books about, Ramakrishna and Vivekananda, had influenced him significantly. "I really regret that Romain Rolland is so little read today; one seldom hears about him anymore," Henry said. "People no longer know who he is, he's practically unknown. He was such a giant in his day. Winner of the Nobel Prize in Literature."

Reading about Rolland's *La vie de Ramakrishna* in Henry's *Tropic* when I was living in Rome made me want to read the book, but I couldn't locate a copy. When Richard Burton and Elizabeth Taylor became a cause célèbre, Kurt Frings flew back to Rome to deal with the scandal that was breaking worldwide, and made a stop in Paris. I asked him to bring back the Rolland book. The staff at the Lancaster Hotel, where Kurt always stayed, dug up a copy of the classic work and Kurt gave it to me. I told Henry that I had devoured *La Vie de Ramakrishna* because of his recommendation.

Two of Henry's favorite quotes from Rolland were: "It is the artist's business to create sunshine when the sun fails;" and "There are some dead who are more alive than the living."

Henry said, "Romain Rolland described the mystical states

achieved by Ramakrishna as oceanic, states which Rolland had experienced himself. Rolland believed the universal human religious emotion resembles this oceanic sense. Ramakrishna taught that in spite of the differences, all religions are true, and all lead to the same ultimate goal—Brahman. Isn't that right? Ramakrishna's chief disciple, Swami Vivekananda, said his master never even learned to write his own name, but was an intellectual giant.

"Ramakrishna's first spiritual ecstasy happened when he was only six years old. He was so identified with his visions and spirituality that it was taking over his life, in a manner of speaking, so the family decided to get him married, thinking that would make him more down to earth. His wife was five years old when they were wed, Ramakrishna was 23. The marriage was never consummated. She became a follower of his teachings, and he called her the Divine Mother.

"His philosophy, Vedanta, isn't a system of preconceived ideas. There are no priests or authority figures. Vedanta is drawn from the Upanishads, the commentaries on the Vedas. It means the purpose or goal, the end of the Vedas. Its concern is self-realization by which we understand the ultimate nature of reality. Vedanta says each soul is potentially divine, and the goal is to manifest that divinity within by controlling both your internal and external nature. How you do it doesn't matter; the goal is what matters."

Joe said, "Henry has often quoted Ramakrishna's having said that religion is not for empty bellies."

"Although some religions do attract the poor," I said. "Catholicism, for one."

"Sure, sure," Henry said. "But Ramakrishna is talking about a different angle of religion – the search for meaning in life, the search for truth."

Henry went on to comment on Vedanta, the religion formulated by Ramakrishna, taught by his disciple Vivekananda. "Vedanta says Brahman is the only reality, that the world we experience is illusory. Maya, an illusory power of Brahman, causes the world to exist, and our ignorance of this reality is the cause of all suffering," Henry said. "Liberation can only be attained through true knowledge of Brahman. When you try to know Brahman through the mind, Brahman appears as God, separate from the individual. This happens because of Maya. In reality, there's no difference between the individual soul, Atman, and Brahman. Liberation lies in knowing the reality of this non-duality.

"Rolland said that skepticism, ridding ourselves of the faith of yesterday, prepares the way for the faith of tomorrow. It's something we're doing again right now," Henry said, "something that's done from time to time, over and over; it's necessary and it's a good thing. It happens in all ages, but people forget. How much will they remember? Why does each age have to start from scratch?

"There's a story in the Upanishads: There were two birds in a tree, one at the upper branch, serene, majestic and divine, and the other at a lower branch, pecking at fruit that's sometimes sweet and sometimes sour and bitter. Every time when the lower bird would eat a bitter fruit, it looked at the upper bird and climbed a branch up. This happened until eventually the bird reached the topmost branch. There it was not able to differentiate itself from the divine bird, and then it learned that there was only one bird in the tree, the upper bird, the real form of the other bird. This is the thought of Vedanta. The fruits in the story are Karma, the lower bird denotes a human soul, and the majestic bird denotes the Absolute.

"The only objection I have to that story," Henry said, "is how unlikely it is we will ever know the Absolute. Even HPB, Helena Petrovna Blavatsky, says we never will."

"That seals it, then," Joe decided.

"I would like to propose another author little read today who was huge in his own day. Lord Edward Bulwer-Lytton," I said. I had been introduced to this 19th century literary phenom by my friend Eve Bruce.

"Yes, yas, you are so right," Henry said. "Not many people have heard of Bulwer-Lytton in this day and age, but he was truly a giant in his time. Poet, playwright, novelist, politician, editor, occultist, and much more. Against his mother's wishes, he married a woman whom she disapproved of, and his mother cut him off financially. Needing to find a means of support, he began writing novels and became an enormous success at a very young age. He amassed a fortune from his works – *Zanoni, The Last Days of Pompeii, Vril: The Power of the Coming Race*. These phenomenally successful bestsellers initiated the birth of science fiction. In the 19th century, Bulwer-Lytton was regarded as the foremost writer of his day, at a time when Charles Dickens had already published several books, including *David Copperfield*.

"He coined many phrases that came into common usage: 'the pen is mightier than the sword,' 'the great unwashed,' 'the almighty dollar.' That famous line 'it was a dark and stormy night' was his. He popularized the fantasy genre. His plays were performed on the London stage for four decades. He developed the fictional detective and invented the occult subgenre. He created the haunted house genre, and pioneered the hollow earth novel. He created the catastrophe novel with *The Last Days of Pompeii*; he made the Newgate novels, fictional biographies of the criminal as antihero, into one of the most popular genres of the era, and the forerunner of the mystery novel.

"Dickens took the ending of *A Tale of Two Cities* from Bulwer-Lytton's *Zanoni,* Lovecraft was influenced by Bulwer-Lytton, George Bernard Shaw's ideas of the "Superman" came from Bulwer-Lytton's works. His *The Coming Race* is full of ideas and concepts that became standards in 20th century science fiction, including a version of atomic energy, android servants, anti-gravity flight, nuclear war, and the future evolution of the human body. He was only 25 when he wrote *Pelham*, which was the best-selling English novel of the entire 19th century. Does anyone read that book today?"

"*Pelham*? Never heard of it."

"*Pelham* had an enormous cultural impact. The book was so popular it changed men's fashion to this day in establishing black as the color for men's evening wear. Pelham made the Silver Fork genre of novel one of the dominant genres of the era. Bulwer-Lytton was also an editor of one of the most popular monthly fiction magazines of the century. He had a great influence on other writers, particularly Dickens; he offered support and encouragement to struggling writers and artists and worked toward creating effective copyright laws. That's not all. He even had a political career as a Member of Parliament, the House of Lords. And he was a prominent Rosecrucian occultist.

"Since youth, he had an interest in hermeticism, alchemy, astrology and Kabbalah. He was fascinated by the wisdom of Domenico Bocchini, who in the catacombs of Naples initiated him into the Egyptian Alchemy of Love. This alchemical school inspired several of his novels. He knew the French occultist Eliphas Levi, and the American Rosicrucian Paschal Beverly Randolph."

"Henry, why didn't you tell me about this guy before?" Joe asked. "I'll have to read him."

"*The Last Days of Pompeii* was one of the most important books in my life," Henry said, "and if we talk about Bulwer-Lytton, we need to also mention Paschal Beverly Randolph, another interesting 19th century figure. He was American – a free man of mixed-race ancestry – physician, abolitionist, occultist, spiritualist, trance medium, writer and publisher."

"I never heard of him either," Joe said.

I had heard of Paschal Beverly Randolph only *en passant*, having seen some of his out of print books at Larsen's, a second hand bookstore on Hollywood Boulevard, and didn't know his life story, as Henry was telling us. "He was the first person to introduce the principles of sex magic to North America, and to establish the earliest known Rosicrucian order in the United States. He founded the Fraternitas Rosae Crucis, the oldest American Rosicrucian organization, which dates back to the Civil War. He knew Abraham Lincoln and accompanied Lincoln's funeral procession train to Springfield.

"Here's another young man who struck out on his own to seek his fortune, so to speak. Orphaned when young, homeless and penniless, he ran away to sea to support himself, just like your friend Charles Fawcett, Michaux, my friend Cendrars, and Frank Harris," Henry said.

"By the time he was in his mid-twenties, doncha know, he was appearing on stage as a clairvoyant and advertising his services in magazines as a spiritual practitioner. He trained as a doctor of medicine, established a publishing company, wrote more than fifty books on magic and medicine, and was an avid promoter of birth control during a time when it was largely against the law to mention the topic.

"He traveled everywhere, all through Europe and as far east as Persia, where his interest in mysticism and the occult led him to study with local practitioners of folk magic and occultism. Randolph was a believer in pre-Adamism, the tenet that humans existed on earth before Adam and Eve. He wrote the book *Pre-Adamite Man*, about the existence of the human race on earth 100,000 years ago.

"He was initiated in Paris to the Egyptian Alchemy of Love,

and carried the sex mysteries back to North America."

"Just what is sex magic exactly, Henry?" Joe asked.

Henry took a drag on his ever present cigarette and said, "The Great Rite is a term for various types of sexual activity used in magical and spiritual rites. It holds that the energies of love and sexuality are the most potent forces the body contains, that sexual activity provides a conduit for human transcendence. The ritual act of sexual intercourse and orgasm taps into these hidden energies of the human body. In Gnostic Christian groups such as in the Magdalene mysteries, spiritual sexuality played an important role. Dante, Leonardo, Pico della Mirandola, Marsilio Ficino – all those Italians followed this belief. In the Renaissance, Ficino and Giordano Bruno wrote about the connection between eros and magick. This power may be harnessed in the creation of a solar body of light, in the direct experience of divine consciousness.."

"Maybe that was really the chief reason Giordano Bruno was burned at the stake," I suggested, "rather than for his cosmological and religious views."

"Possibly so," Henry allowed, and continued about sex magick. "The first system of spiritual sexuality in the United States came through Paschal Beverly Randolph, who expounded on the ritual sex practices of the Nusa'iri tribe of Syria," Henry said. "He described sexual intercourse as the highest, holiest, most important experience of man – but also the most abused."

"Wow, I never knew that," Joe said.

Henry continued, "The Great Rite is similar to the energy known as Kundalini in India. Vital energy is distributed through intersecting channels, the Ida and the Pingala, that are located around the median channel of the spine. Sushumna is the path along which the energy rises and falls. At orgasm, sexual activity produces an action of resonance within the blood.

"The Great Rite passed through Assyria, Chaldea and Egypt, where it became known as the Royal Art of Alchemy of Love. After Alexander the Great conquered Egypt, Alchemy of Love flourished among initiates of the Pythagorean School in Greece. Following the Roman occupation of Egypt, Alchemy of Love arrived in Pompeii and Naples, where it was preserved among initiates of the Hermetic tradition. Though the eruption of Vesuvius destroyed Pompeii, the Egyptian Alchemy of Love survived intact, but the true, sexual nature of the internal alchemical mysteries were forced underground.

"Preserved so that Lord Bulwer-Lytton and Paschal Beverly Randolph could carry it on as initiates," I said.

"Exactly. Two other remarkable 19th century figures," Henry said. "We mustn't forget these people. Without their legacy, where would we be today?"

CHAPTER NINE

Henry told us, "Joe and I were at a French restaurant the other night. When they brought the check, I made a joke about *le quart d'heure de Rabelais*. The waiter didn't understand so I had to explain. Does anyone know what I'm talking about when I mention the *quart d'heure de Rabelais*?"

No one did, so Henry clarified: "In France, the moment at a restaurant when the waiter presents the bill is still sometimes called *le quart d'heure de Rabelais*, in memory of a famous trick Rabelais used, to get out of paying a tavern bill when he had no money."

As has been said of Henry, he was a great talker with wonderful stories to tell, but at the same time, he was also a great listener who was curious about everything. He wanted to know more about my family and particularly about my early life. I answered his questions, telling him my paternal great grandparents, Peter and Rosalie Herche, had emigrated from Germany, settled in New York's Lower East Side, and had eight children, three boys who died in infancy and five girls who survived.

"See, I've always said girls are stronger than boys," Henry said. "This proves my theory, you might say."

"Peter Herche was a shoemaker," I said. "His fourth daughter, my grandmother, worked at the Waldorf Astoria Hotel as a telephone operator. She knew Oscar of the Waldorf and Nikola Tesla there."

Henry said, "You mentioned your other grandmother who was born and grew up in Brooklyn. Sadie Wright? Somehow, that name sounds familiar."

"If you ever listened to the radio program and later the TV show *It Pays to be Ignorant*, you may have heard my grandmother's name, because it was mentioned on a weekly basis. Sadie Wright was a running gag. Maybe that's why her name is familiar to you?"

"I recall that program, and I did listen to it," Henry said. "*It Pays to Be Ignorant* was a radio comedy show in the 40's that went on TV in the 50's. It was a spoof of programs like *The Quiz Kids*, *Information Please*, and *Doctor I.Q.* But why was your grandmother mentioned in it?" he asked.

"Gram was great friends with one of the performers, Lulu McConnell, who always talked about 'my friend Sadie Wright.' Audiences loved Lulu's Sadie Wright stories, and wrote in asking for more."

"Lulu McConnell," Henry reminisced, "I remember her. I actually saw her on Broadway. She was a hoot. Had a rasping voice, similar to a description I once heard of Ezra Pound's voice, 'like a thousand bees in a jar.' Great comedienne."

Joe said, "I listened to that radio show too. It was really funny."

"Yas, yaz," Henry said, "*It Pays to be Ignorant* was great satire. It featured a so called 'board of experts who are dumber than you are and can prove it.' A guy named Tom Howard was the quizmaster. I remember that name because I used to know a Tom Howard. Doesn't everybody know a Tom Howard? The cast was perfect. Some of these people had worked together in vaudeville and on Broadway.

"Questions were the likes of: 'What town in Massachusetts had the Boston Tea Party?' 'What is the name of the man who visits children on Christmas Eve?' 'How long does it take a ship to make a five-day journey?' The panelists would always get the answers wrong, but come up with outrageously funny lines instead that then launched them into wild comedy routines. The show had several running gags, too." Henry turned to me. "What can you tell us about your grandmother's friend, Lulu McConnell?"

"To me, she was Mrs. Simpson, and to my grandmother, she was Lula," I said. "Well, I know both from Mrs. Simpson herself and from my grandma that Lulu was originally from Kansas City, that her father was a dentist, and that she ran off to join a traveling theatre troupe when she was 16. See, Henry, young men weren't the only ones who used to run off in their teens," I said.

"More power to her," Henry said. "Women should be able to do whatever men do. If they have a dream, they should follow that dream. Women have been underestimated in our society, in a manner of speaking, doncha know?"

"Lulu ended up performing in vaudeville and Broadway shows with Nora Bayes, Clifton Webb, Eddie Cantor, Gertrude Niesen, Lillian Russell, Anna Held, and George Jessel. She discovered Jack Oakie. She was in the *Ziegfeld Follies*, she co-starred in a Rogers and Hart musical, *Peggy Ann*, that ran on Broadway and the West End, London. She made motion pictures in Hollywood.

"A lot of vaudeville and Broadway actors lived in my grandparents' town of Floral Park in those days, and were friends of my grandparents. After a New York performance was over, they would all pile onto the Long Island Rail Road and head back home, sometimes bringing fellow actor friends with them. They would walk the short distance from the Floral Park railroad station to my grandparents' home at 191 Tulip Avenue, where Gram would always have wonderful post theatre dinners ready for them. My grandma was a fabulous cook. The player piano was always on, unless my mother's sister, Aunt Helen, or somebody else wanted to play. Pre-Hollywood, Bob Hope, Jack Oakie, Wallace Beery, Alan Dinehart, and of course Lulu and her husband Grant Simpson, plus several other actors whose names escape my memory all came to my grandparents' every night. They were joined by the priests from Our Lady of Victory Catholic church across the street, who were always welcome even though my grandparents weren't Catholic."

"What wonderful memories," Henry said, "not your own memories, of course – but memories relayed to you by your family, which are often more cherished than the actual ones we ourselves experience."

"Lulu McConnell and Grant Simpson had a son, 'Bunk' Simpson, so named because he was born in a dressing room, and lived a gypsy life with his parents," I said. "Both Grant and Bunk Simpson died young. My mother grew up with the woman who married Bunk Simpson, Rose Brunella. Rose and Bunk had a daughter named Caroline. They also lived across the street from my grandparents. Rose and her sister Tess's parents ran a swank downtown Manhattan restaurant called Brunella's – I think it was in the financial district. My mother and grandmother twice visited the Brunellas at their villa in Lake Como, Italy."

Henry wanted to know more about my life in Italy. He asked, "Did you meet Italian film directors?"

"Yes, several. I lived catacorner from Visconti. Met Fellini. His office was not far from the restaurant Otello on the via del Babuino where a good friend of mine lived. I was supposed to have a role in Fellini's *8 ½* but got sick and went back to the States. Met Antonioni, de Sica, Rossellini, Lattuada, Mauro Bolognini, Dino de

Laurentiis, Alessandro Blasetti, was in one of his films and in a Rosselini film as well. Everyone was so accessible. Everyone hung out on the Via Veneto. Or you could just call up their office and say, '*Sono attrice americana,*' 'I'm an American actress,' and they immediately wanted to meet you."

"I can imagine," Henry said, a sudden smile brightening his face.

"I had an after dinner drink with the pope's dentist and his American mistress. This man had been dentist to three popes. His name was Dr. Hrushka. He asked me to dance and I said I was too tired, which was the absolute truth, as I was coming down with hepatitis (or whatever it was) and was totally devoid of energy. Dr. Hrushka became insulted and turned very arrogant, demanding, 'Who do you think you are, Joan of Arc?' I spent a lot of time with Elizabeth, Eddie, and the Burtons. Eddie's singing seemed to bother Elizabeth, who would always frown and exclaim, 'Oh Eddie!' You could see the foreshadowing of the breakup of their marriage."

"And Burton? Could you see that happening?"

"Funny thing about Richard Burton, and this has been mentioned by other women, too: he had the knack of making every woman in the room believe he was talking only to her. In my case, this was enhanced by the fact that Richard always sat directly opposite me at the dinner table, so I was a natural contact point for him."

"So you thought Burton had the hots for you!" Henry laughed. "Who was at the dinners they gave? Did you meet the *Cleopatra* producer?"

"Walter Wanger? Yes, I met him."

Henry said, "Walter Wanger has the same birthday as my sister, July 11."

"Walter Wanger – that's the fellow who shot his wife's agent in the balls and ruined his sex life," Joe pointed out.

"What was that guy's name again, Joe? The fellow Walter Wanger shot? Jennings Lang, was it?"

"Yeah, right, Jennings Lang. Wanger ended up serving four months at an honor farm a few miles outside of L.A. for that crime," Joe said.

Henry lit another cigarette. While I never kept track, I have the feeling Henry might have been a chain smoker. And yet, he did not seem to be constantly puffing. He would often allow the cigarette to burn in his fingers while he spoke, presumably ignoring it or forgetting about it for a while, then remembering and taking a another drag.

The conversation reverted to Rabelais, physician, monk, Greek scholar, writer of fantasy, satire, the grotesque and the bawdy. "He was first a novice of the Franciscan order, but got papal approval to switch to the Benedictines," Henry said. "His wonderful books *Gargantua* and *Pantagruel* were condemned by the church and the Sorbonne, but with support from the powerful du Bellay family, he was able to publish his controversial works, which were immensely popular. His books are filled with sexual double entendres, dirty jokes and ribald songs that can still shock modern readers.

"The early 16th century was a time of innovations in the French language, and Rabelais enriched it enormously in original, creative ways. He introduced dozens of Greek, Latin, and Italian words as well as many idioms. He invented new words and metaphors, some of which are still in use today.

"Rabelais taught medicine at Montpellier. Doctors graduating from the University's Faculty of Medicine today still take an oath under Rabelais's robe. Balzac considered Rabelais the greatest mind of modern humanity."

Joe said, "John Cowper Powys wrote books about Rabelais, and you met Powys, Henry."

"That's right, I did," Henry said. "Powys had a tremendous influence on me. He was a giant, I was a pygmy by comparison, so I was reticent about approaching him, I was so in awe of him."

"I will always remember Rabelais' last words," Joe said.

"Ah, yes, 'I go to seek a Great Perhaps' – *un grand peut-être*, Rabelais said. Very fitting, doncha know, something we have all wondered about – what happens after we die? Will we ever know? I doubt we will, surely not while we're alive, at any rate."

"Madame Blavatsky doesn't think we will either, Henry," I said.

"Well, she does allude to Devachan," Henry acknowledged, "but the nitty-gritty is always hazy."

A propos of origins, destinies, and wanting to explore the outer reaches of the human psyche, although I had initially considered having LSD with Timothy Leary in Mexico, I ended up going to the Hollywood Hospital in New Westminster, a suburb of Vancouver, B.C., where the drug was administered by J. Ross MacLean, M.D. Henry was curious about my experience there. He wanted to know, "What was it like? Was it everything you expected? How did it affect you?"

"I had a large dose; Dr. MacLean calls it a massive dose," I said. "500 micrograms of LSD, plus mescaline simultaneously. I had four experiences with the same dosage."

"And the results?"

"Overpowering. Destruction of the ego, a panorama of changing images with enormous meaning that came racing through my consciousness. I felt like I was both inside and outside creation, seeing creation's heart, its foundation and nucleus. I understood creation. I embraced the Platonic Eidos, not just as an intellectual concept, but viscerally. It was very emotional and very rhythmic."

Years ago, I was reluctant to ask Henry so many questions that today I wouldn't hesitate to ask. For instance, I never asked him if he had ever taken LSD. A parallel to my reluctance was expressed by the late Nora Ephron in a *Time* magazine interview: "There's some people I met that I not only wish I remembered more about, but I wish I had had the sense to ask them more questions .... I feel that I was way too respectful of some of the people I met, like Cary Grant, whom I should have just plopped myself next to and peppered with questions." Coincidentally, I had met Cary Grant in Rome, been in his company for several hours, and felt the same way as Nora Ephron. Now I sometimes felt that way with Henry.

Henry said. "Some say hallucinogens can be a viable tool toward greater spiritual awakening, but keep in mind, there is no ultimate key ... you're always at a point, albeit on a different level, opening a different door. It's like a Chinese puzzle box, so to speak."

In some ways echoing Anaïs, Henry offered a view that the experience described under LSD could happen to him in writing, at those times when a force would take over and everything would occur rapidly, almost like automatic writing. This speeded-up inspiration, almost like receiving dictation, to him was more important than images evoked under a drug could be, or even the immense psychological impetus that accompanied them.

As Norman Mailer said of Henry, "There is nothing like

Henry Miller when he gets rolling. One has to take the English language back to Marlowe or Shakespeare before encountering a wealth of imagery equal in intensity."

CHAPTER TEN

Marianne d'Anjou was a beautiful French-Canadian actress and registered nurse from Montreal who had mingled in the Hollywood world, which unfailingly complimented her on her beautiful face and body, and so decided why not? I can do this as well as any of these other girls out there trying for stardom. So she acquired an agent and began auditioning, succeeding in landing acting assignments in Hollywood, after which she also acted in France and Canada, supplementing her acting income with always available private duty nursing jobs.

Marianne was an incurable flirt, with the ability to throw her entire body into a conversation in a most beguiling fashion. She was adept at suggestive banter and the art of turning a male come-on into humor without offending. Marianne had perfected the art of the tease, and Henry was captivated by it. The fact that she was a francophone who spoke proper French, not "Canuck," was a further attraction. The fact that she had a charming French accent when she spoke English was yet another. Marianne's English was colorful, often hilarious, particularly when she would unintentionally use the wrong word. She had a peculiar habit of dropping the "h" from English words that began with that letter, so that a word like "hate" became "ate," and she would add an "h" where it didn't belong, such as "I heat," instead of "I eat." Marianne was one person with men, a distinct other with women. With women, she was composed, sweet, and sympathetic, whereas with men she was wisecracking, challenging, always throwing out one challenging joke after another.

In her vocation as a nurse, Marianne had worked for several well known Hollywood personalities – film stars, producers, businessmen, and other prominent individuals in the community. One of her clients was a Los Angeles bank president who a few decades ago had been Al Capone's driver, who had left Chicago to go legit in L.A. This very prominent financial figure and charity donor, well known to the Hollywood world, claimed he needed a nurse to take his blood pressure on a trip to Las Vegas, and Marianne was hired.

"Oh oh, I hear a punch line coming, and I think I can guess what it is," Henry said, enjoying the anticipation.

"You're probably right, Henry. This guy is actually a

notorious Casanova. He kept making passes the entire time in Vegas. Taking his blood pressure was just a big ruse."

"What's the name of the bank he's the head of?"

"You know the one, Henry," Joe Grey answered. "Everybody knows that bank. And we all know the notorious banker Marianne is talking about."

"I know them, Joe?"

"Sure, you do," Joe said, announcing the bank and banker's name for Henry and the rest of us, then adding, "The bank is hugely successful, it finances a whole slew of Hollywood films. Everybody knows its history."

Marianne said, "I later found out more about this bank and the banker. If you know the right people, you can deposit any amount there without the IRS ever knowing, if you're in with this guy we're talking about."

"Sure, it's a known front for the mob in L.A.," Joe explained for those out of the loop, who at that time included me. "This guy isn't the only Chicago organized crime hood who's come here to go straight. There's a whole contingent of them, and L.A. is the perfect place to do it."

Henry told Marianne, "You know, Marianne, you have a very meaningful name. Marianne is the national emblem of France, doncha know, an allegory of *liberté*. She's on coins and postage stamps; she's one of the most prominent symbols of the French Republic, she's displayed all over France, in all the town halls and courts of law. There's a famous bronze statue of her overlooking the Place de la Nation in Paris, she's sculpted as a warrior on the Arc de Triomphe, a bust of her stands in the Luxembourg Palace, the French Senate; the Hôtel de Ville, city hall, has a statue of her wearing a Phrygian cap, there's another statue of her in the post office of the Assemblée Nationale. Delacroix painted her, which is in the Louvre."

The discussion progressed to French literary figures, including François Villon, Montaigne, Rabelais, the Pléiade poets Ronsard and du Bellay; and others about whom Marianne was well informed.

Of Ronsard, Henry said, "He was the acknowledged chief of the Pléiade; his generation called him the Prince of Poets. He came from a well connected noble family, doncha know. His father was *maître d'hôtel du ro*i to François Premier, and as a child, Ronsard was attached as a page to the Scottish court. Mary Queen of Scots addressed him from her prison, and Torquato Tasso consulted him on his *Gerusalemme Liberata*. The Huguenots hated him and attempted to have him assassinated.

"Du Bellay was the son of Jean du Bellay, cousin of the powerful Cardinal Jean du Bellay and Guillaume du Bellay. Du Bellay and Ronsard met at an inn on the way to Poitiers. The historic Pléiade manifesto was written by Du Bellay. In it, Du Bellay details a literary program of renewal and revolution, in a manner of speaking. Du Bellay went to Rome as secretary to his cousin, the Cardinal. While he was there, he wrote sonnets, which were translated into English by none other than Edmund Spenser."

"Henry's nemesis," Joe said.

"That's right, I quit City College because of Spenser," Henry acknowledged, "because of my intense dislike for his exceedingly boring epic poem *The Faierie Queene*, celebrating the Tudor dynasty and Elizabeth I. I couldn't stomach it, ya know. In the eighteenth century, Alexander Pope compared Spenser to 'a mistress whose faults we see, but love her with them all.' Well, that's not how I saw it.

"At any rate, with reference to Ronsard: after his death, a reaction set in led by Malherbe, who harbored personal hatred of Ronsard, and for some time, Ronsard was forgotten until the early 19th century. It was Sainte-Beuve who helped reestablish Ronsard in his rightful place. An interesting thing is both these poets of the Pléiades went deaf as young men, ya know. Both Ronsard and Du Bellay. Quite a coincidence. And we can also add Du Bellay to the list of important figures who died young. He died in Paris at the age of only 38."

Henry asked if we knew Louise Labé, identified as *La Belle Cordière*, the Beautiful Ropemaker. "She was a female French Renaissance poet, daughter of a rich ropemaker, who married a ropemaker. She was active in a circle of Lyonnais poets. Calvin had a real thing against her; he referred to her as a cross-dresser and called her a common whore. There's been a four centuries debate on whether or not Labé was or was not a courtesan. Her sonnets are remarkable for their frank eroticism."

Pleased at their mutual interests, Henry inquired of Marianne,

"Don't tell me you're a veteran of the Napoleonic curriculum? You went to a French lycée in Canada, and that's how you happen to be so knowledgeable about 15th and 16th century French poets?"

"No, I was educated by the nuns," Marianne said. "And the nuns hated me."

"Of course they'd hate you," Henry said, turning on the charm. "You were beautiful and they were not."

Joe was a big fan of Montaigne and enjoyed quoting him. He offered to read us from one of his notebooks the Montaigne sayings he especially liked:

"'When I play with my cat, how do I know that she is not playing with me, rather than I with her?' 'Kings and philosophers defecate, and so do ladies;' 'The continuous work of our life is to build death;' 'Our religion is made to eradicate vices; instead, it encourages them, covers them, and nurtures them;' 'Nothing is so firmly believed as that which least is known;' 'Whether the events in our life are good or bad greatly depends on the way we perceive them;' 'I believe it to be true that dreams are the true interpreters of our inclinations; but there is art required to sort and understand them.'"

"Joe Grey and John Cowper Powys have both admired Montaigne's philosophy," Henry told the group. "I've been telling Joe he should join the Société des Amis de Montaigne "

"I might just take you up on that, Henry," Joe returned. "But I better not have to take a French test to be eligible."

Henry turned to Marianne again. He said, "Montaigne was one of the most influential writers of the French Renaissance, as you know. He was a Pisces. You're not by any chance a Pisces yourself, are you, Marianne?"

"No, I'm a Sagittarius."

"I should have known," Henry said, explaining how Sagittarius women were known for their charm, then continuing about Montaigne: "Montaigne influenced writers the world over, including Emerson and Nietzsche. His family was very rich; his father was the mayor of Bordeaux, as was Montaigne himself. Hmmm ... hmmm ...Ya know, Montaigne had one of the most interesting upbringings of any writer. Soon after birth, he was brought to a peasant cottage where he lived the first three years of his life, in order to draw him close to the common people, shall I say. After that, he was brought back to the family château with the intention that Latin should become his major language. The servants were given strict orders to speak only Latin to him. He was also given a German tutor who spoke no French. He became a brilliant man and died of quinsy, a condition we don't hear much about anymore in this day and age, basically abscessed tonsils, doncha know. He requested a mass, and died during its celebration."

"What a way to go!" Marianne exclaimed

On that note, Henry led us into a discussion about the famous Paris cemetery, Père Lachaise, and the celebrated individuals who were buried there: Abélard and Héloïse, Balzac, Modigliani, Sarah Bernhardt, Chopin, Isadora Duncan, Colette, Proust, Oscar Wilde, Gertrude Stein, Molière, and numerous others of renown.

"Père Lachaise is the most visited cemetery in the world, d'ya know," Henry said. "But when it first opened, it was considered too far from the city, so it attracted few customers. A public relations campaign changed that. What they did was to transfer the remains of cultural icons like La Fontaine, Molière, Abélard, Héloïse, and so forth. After that, everybody wanted to be buried there. Of course, the story of Abélard and Héloïse is one of the great medieval romances, isn't that right? Abélard, the noted philosopher, was hired to teach Héloïse, a rich young noblewoman. Their affair produced an illegitimate child. When he found out about it, Héloïse's uncle sent her to a nunnery and had Abélard castrated."

Searching for something in her satchel, Marianne pulled out a copy of a book borrowed from me, found on my shelves that I didn't even know I had. Seeing the book, Henry asked, "What are you reading there?"

"*Le Bal du Comte d'Orgel*, by Raymond Radiguet," Marianne answered. "I'm really enjoying this book. It's an incredible masterpiece, one of the most remarkable works I've ever read. And to think the author was only a teenager when he wrote it."

"Radiguet!" Henry exclaimed. "Sadly, there's another tragic early death – probably the earliest genius death in all literary France, only twenty years old when he died, Joe. He dropped out of school at fifteen to pursue writing, he befriended Picasso, Juan Gris and especially Cocteau, who became his mentor."

"Oh, he and Cocteau were lovers, then?" Joe asked.

"Gossip said yes, although Cocteau always denied it. And

Radiguet did have relationships with women, ya know. He died of typhoid fever contracted from eating oysters on a trip with Cocteau. Because of his early death, he had time to write only two novels."

"Yes," Marianne said, "His first and most famous was *Le Diable au Corps*."

"*The Devil in the Flesh*," Henry translated. "Did you see the wonderful film adaptation of that book? Directed by Autant-Lara, starring that beautiful actor, Gérard Philippe? The movie caused quite a stir. A young married woman has an affair with a sixteen-year-old boy while her husband is away fighting in World War I. The story was allegedly autobiographical, based on an affair that occurred when Radiguet was fourteen."

"His second novel, the one I'm reading now, also deals with adultery," Marianne said. "Cocteau had it published posthumously."

"Cocteau said something very memorable about Radiguet in his preface to the book you're reading, Marianne," Henry said. "He said, 'Yesterday's dead are eternal.'"

"Beautiful," Marianne said, "and so true."

"François Mauriac said of *Le Diable au Corps* that no adolescent before Radiguet delivered to us the secret of that age, that we have all falsified it," Henry added.

Marianne said, "Cocteau wrote about Radiguet's death. What he said was so moving."

"Yas, yaz," Henry agreed. "As Cocteau described it, Radiguet, feverish, said, 'Listen, listen to something terrible. In three days, I am going to be shot by God's soldiers.' When Cocteau tried to make other explanations for what was happening in Radiguet's mind, Radiguet said, 'Your explanations are not as good as mine. The order has been given. I have heard the order. There is a color that's moving around and people are hiding in the color.' Cocteau asked Radiguet if he wanted him to chase the people away, but Radiguet said, 'You can't chase them away because you don't see the color.' Then he sank. He moved his mouth, gazed in surprise at his mother and father, at his hands, and then he died."

"Raymond Radiguet," Joe repeated. "Wasn't he associated with the surrealists?"

"I wouldn't say so, particularly," Henry returned, "although he knew some of them. But the Raymond you may be thinking of, Joe, is probably Raymond Queneau. At one point, Queneau was associated with the surrealists, but he ended up separating from Breton and the others when they joined the Communist party. Queneau was interested in Eastern philosophy, as so many French writers and artists of that period were. For most of his life, Queneau worked at Gallimard, doncha know. His wife, Janine Kahn, was the sister of André Breton's first wife, Simone Kahn. Did you see the film adaptation of his novel *Zazie Dans le Métro*, directed by Louis Malle?"

"Yes, wonderful," Marianne said. "And do you know the Juliette Greco song *Si tu t'imagines?* Queneau wrote the lyrics."

Upon seeing Marianne consult her watch, a swift look of disappointment crossed Henry's face. "You have to go?" he asked.

Marianne said, "I don't want to, but I must –"

"You don't want to – so stay," Henry urged.

Marianne laughed. "I wish I could, Henry."

"Why can't you?"

Marianne glanced at me. She said, "Jeanne will explain."

"You can't tell us yourself?" Henry asked.

"Well, all right, I will," Marianne said. "I only meant Jeanne could verify the reason why I have to leave."

"Ok, let's hear it," Henry demanded, "and I'm going to bet the reason is a man."

"How did you guess, Henry?"

"In a manner of speaking, you might say I have a sixth sense about these things."

I said, "Marianne has a boyfriend –"

"So I gathered," Henry said.

"He's rather demanding."

"What are his demands?" Henry wanted to know.

"Dinner, for one thing," Marianne replied.. "He expects a good home cooked meal, especially on a Sunday night."

"What?" Henry said, "He doesn't take a beautiful woman like you out to dinner?"

"Sometimes, of course, yes. But he likes my cooking. He enjoys healthy meals."

"I would too, if you cooked them for me," Henry said. "But then this guy – what's his name, if I may ask?"

"Myron."

"I think Myron should take you out to dinner tonight so you

can stay longer this afternoon."

"Don't I wish," Marianne sighed. "But Myron has his mind set on something special tonight that I promised to cook for him. And after that, he has a television show he wants to watch, so I need to be on time with everything."

"You can't stay just a short while longer?"

Again, Marianne looked at her watch. "Well, maybe just a little while – but not too much longer."

Henry began talking about the different habits of writers and how they set about writing. He said, "Schiller kept a drawer full of rotten apples, which created a stench he required in order to work. Colette, after Willy locked her in a room, indulged in the ritual of plucking fleas from her dog to put her in the mood to write. Virginia Woolf and Ernest Hemingway both preferred to stand while they wrote. Agatha Christie's bathtub is her work space."

"And you, Henry?" Joe prompted. "How about you?"

"Writing with me comes about in a variety of ways, ya know. Sometimes it might even be routine, while other times, inspiration hits like lightning ... it becomes receiving from a higher source, like automatic writing; writing in white heat almost without rest, doncha know. But I have to say, most writing is done away from the typewriter, away from the desk. I'll say it occurs in quiet, silent moments, when you're walking or shaving or playing ping pong. That's when my best writing happens."

Henry was still going easy on the writing, he said, because of his eyes. "Ya know, James Joyce battled eye diseases throughout his life. He always had those thick glasses on you see him wearing in all his photos. When he wrote, Joyce always wore a white coat, which gave a kind of white light that reflected onto the page and helped him see better. Maybe I should try that, get a white coat ... look like a doctor ... hmmmm.... hmmmm," Henry mused.

"Now I really must be going," Marianne said apologetically, gathering her belongings again. "I hate to leave this fascinating company, but ..."

Henry gazed after her as she headed to the door, an expression of longing in his eyes, and sighed. "Beautiful, beautiful girl. Too bad about this guy Myron."

CHAPTER ELEVEN

In 1964-65, I was writing the book *Astrology and Your Sex Life* (published by Century Books) with Los Angeles based international psychic Contessa Maria Graciette. Hearing about our book, Henry was intrigued and wanted to know more about my co-writer.

At this point in time, Maria Graciette was the modern equivalent of my Virgil, having revealed to me previously undreamed of areas of occult knowledge. Maria was way ahead of the times, so far ahead that it took the Los Angeles metaphysical world, which was well ahead of the rest of the country, several years to catch up, and many people never did. Another way of describing Maria is that she was like a New Age Cassandra or a female John the Baptist. I told Henry she had opened my eyes to spiritual paths I never knew existed, all of which Maria was intimately acquainted with and had studied in depth for years.

Henry was a big astrology fan, astrology being just one of many subjects he and Maria shared in common. Maria had introduced me to the eccentric but excellent Los Angeles astrologer Roberta Wilson and to Hungarian emigré astrologer Zoltan Mason, who with his wife ran a wonderful occult bookshop on Lexington Avenue, New York, a block from Bloomingdale's, whose motto was "the only true sport is defying the stars." Maria took me to monthly parties given by noted astrologer Carroll Righter. Righter could immediately spot your sun sign, greeting you upon your entry to his Hollywood home, "Hello, Aries" (or whatever your sign). An autographed picture of his client Ronald Reagan occupied a prominent place on the living room piano. Maria had also taken me to meet the great Dane Rudhyar, whom Henry knew intimately.

It was thanks to Maria that. Maharishi Mahesh Yogi initiated me, pre-Beatles, when he was a complete unknown, and when Transcendental Meditation didn't even have a name yet. The day I received my mantra, I was sandwiched between Cobina Wright, Sr. and Efrem Zimbalist, Jr. Cobina wore a straw hat with a little black veil. As an aside, Efrem tested with me at Warners for a film role later played by Lee Remick. The test was arranged through Solly Baiano, who was one of the initial discoverers of Noreen Nash.

"Efrem Zimbalist and his half-sister, novelist Marcia

Davenport, are relatives of mine by marriage," I told Henry.

"Their mother was a wonderful opera singer whom I remember well, Alma Gluck," Henry said. "And of course, Efrem Zimbalist Sr. was one of the world's great violinists."

Maria had lived not only in her native Portugal, but in Spain, Morocco, Mexico, Brazil, Venezuela, France and Italy. Although still in her early to mid 30's, she had enjoyed a career in opera and film throughout South America. To Henry's questions about her psychic gifts, I answered, "Maria does psychometry, she reads coffee grounds, tea leaves, lips, skulls, palms, crystal balls, tarot cards, hair, nails, saliva, horoscopes, you name it. In Venezuela, she wrote a magazine column under the name 'Miss Star,' where she analyzed readers' lip prints."

"How did she do that?"

"Readers would make a lipstick impression of their lips, put in the mail for Maria to read, and Maria would reply in the magazine."

Henry asked, "But how would a man make a lip print? Men don't wear lipstick; at least, most men don't."

"The main readers of that magazine were women, but men could make lip prints without using lipstick. I'm not sure how they did it – I didn't ask. Maybe they used Vaseline. But Maria had male readers, too, and men did send in their lip prints." I continued, "Maria even reads feces."

"Reading feces! Now there's an unusual talent!" Henry exclaimed.

"Sounds fascinating," Joe agreed, making a face. "Ugh!"

"Feces, feces," Henry repeated. "Hmmm.... hmmmm....out of curiosity, how does she go about this type of analysis, so to speak?"

"I'm not really sure, I..."

"Does one create a sample on the spot, or bring it to the Countess ready made? I'm assuming specimens must come in different designs, shapes and shades, doncha know. Can the Countess tell if the specimen was a floater or a sinker once it's out of its natural environment?" Henry had the rest of the room in stitches with his conjectures. "Hmmm ... hmmm... no insult intended, but to tell the truth, the idea of that kind of a reading doesn't appeal to me!"

"Me neither," Joe agreed.

"Actually, Maria is so psychic she doesn't need any of these tools," I said. "She calls them points of contact, but they're not necessary."

Henry was curious. "How did you two meet?" he wanted to know.

"We met at the East West Cultural Center," I answered. "Have you been there, Henry?"

"I don't believe so, though it sounds like something I'd be interested in. Is it far from here?"

"Just past Hancock Park, east Hollywood, heading toward downtown. It's run by a red haired lady named Florence and a grey haired one called Judith, who teaches Sanskrit," I said. "Maria was in the audience at this lecture I attended, Florence introduced her; said Maria was going to be giving a talk there as well as at the Holland House Cafeteria and the Anderson Research Center. I went to all those lectures, spoke with Maria, had a great reading with her and we became friends. She was staying at the Knickerbocker Hotel when she gave me the reading."

"Ah," Henry said, "a famous, historic place, a big Hollywood landmark, doncha know. The Hotel Knickerbocker was a glamorous rendezvous site popular with celebrities, especially in the 20's and 30's, and on into the 40's and 50's." Henry reminisced, "Rudolph Valentino would often ride his horse there evenings to have a drink at the bar and dance with the ladies. D. W Griffith lived and died there. Marilyn Monroe and Joe DiMaggio conducted many an assignation there. In the hotel's heyday, Gloria Swanson, Bette Davis, and Errol Flynn all lived there; Sinatra and Elvis stayed there many times, doncha know. It was Houdini's home away from home, and after he died, his widow held a séance on the roof of that hotel."

Prior to her move to Hollywood, I had visited Maria at her home in Oakland, where I was impressed by her extensive collection of tarot cards from all over the world, awestruck by her library of metaphysical books in English, Spanish, French, Italian and Portuguese. Maria had a daughter Graciette and mother Romana, both of to whom she was fiercely devoted. Little Graciette was an exquisite child, around three or four years old at the time. Maria used to order Graciette, known as Gigi, "Meditate!" point her finger, and Gigi would immediately shut her eyes, place her hands in prayer position, bow her head, and obey. Maria had a way about her that people around her fell in line.

Maria and I took several trips together, including one to Hawaii with Gigi and Romana, the latter known as *"Vovo,"* a Portuguese diminutive for grandmother. Life was always an adventure with Maria. One of my early memories of her occurred at a gathering of spiritual enthusiasts at 100 South Rossmore in Los Angeles' Hancock Park neighborhood. Film icon Mae West, who lived just a few doors down and whose name and phone number were listed in the L.A. phone directory, was present that night to enthusiastically applaud Maria's dramatic rendition of *Granada*, performed with Maria leaning on a concert grand piano, tossing both arms and a gossamer scarf in the air. Maria craved the limelight, came alive under its spell. Larger than life, she loved dancing, particularly Latin rhythms, speaking before crowds, and giving advice.

She was a Doctor of Divinity and read for many Hollywood figures, including three men I dated, actor Glenn Ford, game show producer Mark Goodson, and television mogul Jim Aubrey, who served as President of both CBS-TV and ABC-TV. Strong willed, opinionated and outspoken, Maria was never one to mince words; consequently, some people objected to the honest insights she gave in readings because they didn't want to hear the truth. Noreen told me a friend of hers to whom she recommended Maria had been shocked and upset by Maria's predictions of health problems.

Hearing about her, Henry's curiosity was piqued. He wanted to meet Maria, so I introduced them. Maria arrived at the Siegels' in customary colorful attire. She was partial to styles of various ethnic origins – Indian saris, Hawaiian mumus, Mexican and gypsy clothes in bold colors – turquoise, royal purple, royal blue, red, orange, magenta, bright green. These she would often pair with white Courrèges boots, which were all the rage then. She loved gold – gold jewelry, gold trim on clothing. She also loved diamonds.

"Countess? Doctor?" Henry asked, "Which do you prefer?"

"Call me Maria."

Maria, a January 24 Aquarius, was a born extrovert. It is impossible to recreate here Maria's unique manner of speaking English, which she called "Ingels." Some Maria-isms were: "would, could, should" came out as "woo, coo, shoo;" "he doesn't want" was "he no want"; "he has" was "he have;" she frequently dropped certain pronouns, as in Spanish and Italian usage: "it's true" became "is true;" "your" became "you," as in "you dress is beautiful." Often past tense sentences were stated using present tense. The word "point" was pronounced "poont."

Most conversations between Henry and Maria centered on the metaphysical, both traditional and the offbeat – Buddhism, Vedanta, Theosophy, UFO's, life on other planets (which Henry decidedly believed in), hollow earth, astrology, reincarnation, Atlantis and Lemuria. For all these topics and more, Maria was a natural match with Henry.

"There's so much going on in L.A. It's a virtual schmorgasbord – like a contemporary metaphysical version of Hemingway's Paris, *A Movable Feast*," Henry said. "Southern California, particularly Los Angeles., has a long metaphysical tradition, doncha know. Spiritual groups have been located here for decades – the Vedanta Society, the Theosophists, Yogananda's Self-Realization Fellowship, Manley P. Hall's organization – L.A. has always been a magnet."

"They call this the New Age, but spiritual activity has definitely been going on for a very long time," Maria said.

"Sure, sure," Henry agreed. "A few decades ago here in L.A., Aimee Semple McPherson was the phenomenon *du jour*. By the way, did you know the actor Anthony Quinn played in the McPherson Four Square Church band, and that he was an apprentice preacher?" As an aside to Joe, Henry said, "Quinn's parents fought with Pancho Villa. His father was an Irish mercenary and his mother was Mexican."

Henry continued, "Actually, the Civil War and World War I were fertile spiritual periods in the United States, though many people don't realize it. As they say, there's nothing new under the sun – *plus ça change, plus c'est la même chose*."

Maria told Henry I had been contracted to write an erotic book called *The Video Jungle*, published by Century Books, under the pseudonym of Albert E.R. Sibyl. I don't remember how I came up with that nom de plume. Henry thought it was pretty funny. Maria joked that he should read the book, and maybe he could even learn something about sex.

"It sounds interesting," Henry allowed.

"Like something Henry should read when his eyes improve," Joe said.

"No!" I protested.

"Why not?"

"I just did it for the money," I explained.

"There's nothing wrong with that. Don't apologize," Henry said. After all, Henry had done the same thing, together with Anaïs Nin and Caresse Crosby, so he understood.

The following week, when I went alone to the Siegels, Henry asked, "Tell me more about your Portuguese friend. She's quite unusual – flamboyant, if you will. You think she's a good psychic?"

"Definitely," I responded. "She has uncanny insights into human nature, she's amazingly intuitive and a great judge of character."

"In the long run, that's more important than giving predictions," Henry observed. "People desperately want to know the future, want to believe what's coming is going to be better than the present or the past. But actually appraising a person's strengths and weaknesses, looking at their nature and at one's own, is more important, isn't that right? Nevertheless, out of curiosity, has she ever predicted anything for you that came true?"

"Yes, several times. I also had a past life reading with her, and that was really an incredible experience."

"What did she tell you?"

"She said in a past life in Egypt, I was named Ayesha."

"Ayesha? That's a famous character in Rider Haggard's novels." British novelist H. Rider Haggard was one of Henry's favorite authors.

At Henry's request, I elaborated on the past life reading as told by Maria. Movie star Glenn Ford had been my secret lover in Egypt, which explained our attraction in this life, Maria said. Disapproving upon discovering our affair, my father took a bow and arrow and mortally wounded Glenn. Maria said my father in Egypt had reincarnated as my father in this present life, and that Glenn and I had a child together in that life who had returned as my brother in this life.

"Good story," Henry said. "True or not, it pulls at the heartstrings, and it has the ring of truth, so to speak, so that it could be true, who knows? And who cares? Some things don't need to be literally true. They're true on a certain level, a very important inner level. Obviously you identified with it."

Maria was back the following Sunday, when the subject of

Rider Haggard arose again, and Henry quoted a question Haggard posed: "What is imagination? Perhaps it is the shadow of intangible truth; perhaps it is the soul's thoughts." Henry wanted to know if Maria and I had read Haggard's books. Maria had several years ago; I had read him only recently.

"I found *Ayesha* and *She* in the library of a friend, Norman Hickman," I said. "The books originally belonged to Norman's parents." Maria and I spent time together in New York on various occasions, where our home base was always Norman's spacious co-op at the elegant River House on 52nd Street overlooking the East River. Norman, a gracious host who referred to Maria as "the Portuguese Princess," always treated us royally, tossing parties in our honor and taking us to the best restaurants and night spots in town.

An investment banker with the firm of Wood, Struthers & Winthrop, Norman was the author of *The Quintessential Quiz Book* and *Quizzes for Whizzes*, and was associate producer of two documentary films, *The Finest Hour* about Winston Churchill, and *A King's Story* about the Duke of Windsor, both which were nominated for Academy Awards. I was Norman's date at the Oscars those two years. (He didn't win either year). Norman was close to the Churchill family – Sarah and Randolph Churchill always stayed with him when they were in town, either at the River House or at Norman's country home in Southampton. As for Sir Winston, I believe the Hickmans and the Churchills were related as cousins. Norman had a lot of Churchill memorabilia, such as handwritten letters and autographed photos from the former Prime Minister. Rider Haggard, incidentally, was one of the Churchill family's favorite writers.

Henry said, "In addition to the two Haggard books about Ayesha, Haggard is also the author another very popular book you may have read, the swashbuckling adventure *King Solomon's Mines*, which is considered the first novel in the Lost World genre. I devoured his books, doncha know. They rank as my all-time favorites, and Haggard's books are among the best-selling books of all time, if you will. Did you see the movie version of *King Solomon's Mines*?"

"No, but I heard it was a great picture."

"They should do a remake," Joe said.

"Rider Haggard was in love with a woman, Lilly Jackson Archer, whom he wanted to marry, only he wasn't established yet financially and Lilly married someone else," Henry told us. "Several years later, when Haggard was a successful author, Lilly contacted him. Her husband had embezzled funds and disappeared, abandoning the family. Haggard assumed financial responsibility for Lilly and her children. Lilly eventually reconciled with her husband, who gave her syphilis before dying of it himself. Haggard continued to support Lilly until her death."

"Rider Haggard loved psychic things," Maria enthused. "Psychic phenomena, metaphysics, the spiritual, paranormal phenomena."

"Ayesha is a wonderful character," Henry said. "She's the near-immortal, beautiful and ruthless ruler of a lost civilization, a femme fatale ageless beauty, lost soul who refuses to die till her beloved returns to earth. Haggard wrote *She* in 6 weeks, d'ya know. It was never rewritten. Genius! Back in the thirties, Helen Gahagan starred as Ayesha in the movie. Gahagan married the actor Melvyn Douglas. She was elected to the U. S. House of Representatives and had a celebrated affair with Lyndon Johnson. She ran for the Senate but lost to Richard Nixon. It was she who invented the name 'Tricky Dicky,' by the way. Ironically, John F. Kennedy contributed to the Nixon campaign against her."

"That's a switch," Joe said. "Then there's the recent film version of *She*, starring the gorgeous, incredible, fabulously beautiful Ursula Andress."

When Maria mentioned that Soraya, former wife of the Shah of Iran, had a part in that film, Henry, always the romantic, lamented, "Such a sad story about Soraya. Her infertility caused the unfortunate rupture of the marriage. Medical treatments failed. The Shah needed an heir, so he had no choice but to divorce her, doncha know. And the marriage started off so auspiciously, with omens heralding a wonderful, long and successful life together. Theirs was a fairy tale wedding, you might say, with incredible gifts sent by the world's top leaders – Truman, Stalin, the King and Queen of England, the Aga Khan. A couple of thousand guests attended, tons of flowers were shipped from abroad, the bride wore Dior, the Shah gave her expensive jewels and furs as wedding gifts, lay the world at her feet. It was all over the headlines when Soraya said she was sacrificing her own happiness for the greater good, and the Shah said nobody could carry a torch longer than he. He remarried and an heir was born. And

Soraya has been offered several movie roles in addition to the role in *She*."

Henry noted that Soraya was born in Ispahan, a place he said he would like to visit. I asked him, "Do you know the poem by Leconte de Lisle, *Les Roses d'Ispahan?*"

"Sure, sure," Henry enthused. "Beautiful poem. Part of the prevalent orientalism of 19th century French literature, art and music. The Parnassian movement crystallized in de Lisle; his verse is full of exotic local color. He sees the world as what Joe's favorite writer, Lord Byron called, 'a glorious blunder.' To the Gnostics as well, Earth is a mistake, a cosmic blunder. Incidentally, Leconte de Lisle was elected to the Académie Française in succession to Victor Hugo."

"Gabriel Fauré composed a song from the poem *Les Roses d'Ispahan*," I said. "It's one of my favorite chansons."

"You sing it?"

"I do." And I quoted the beginning lines: "*Les Roses d'Ispahan dans leur gaine de mousse / les jasmins de Mossoul, les fleurs de l'oranger / ont un parfum moins frais, ont une odeur moins douce / o blanche Leila, que ton souffle légère.*"

Henry had had his horoscope done by several prominent astrologers, including, among others, Conrad Moricand, by his good friend Sidney Omarr, and by another good friend, the man known as the dean of modern astrology, Dane Rudhyar. Soon, Maria gave Henry an informal astrological reading. I made notes of what she told him:

"The Sun in your chart gives you great charisma. Mercury in your chart makes you cerebral, curious, a deep philosophical thinker, a true intellectual and very quick-witted. Mars gives you energy, enthusiasm, courage and the willingness to risk.

"Your life path is influenced by the number 3, which highlights communication, creativity, and originality. Both your Sun and Venus are in Capricorn. You have a great need for freedom and a rare gift for sharing knowledge and information. For you, love is a quest for the Absolute.

"Your chart has a predominance of planets in the Southern hemisphere. You were destined to become known to the public as an important cultural figure.

"The Eastern section of your chart, your Ascendant side, shows ego and magnetism. The Western part, the Descendant side, represents other people, relationships, communication, and your adaptability toward them. The planets in the Western hemisphere of your chart indicate you are flexible, friendly, and excel at communication.

"Your 7th, 8th and 9th houses influence communication. A predominance of water signs gives you unusual sensitivity, making feelings and emotions important to you. Love leads you to greater understanding.

"The 1st, 4th, 7th, 9th and 10th houses are your strongest, most dynamic houses, the 7th house being particularly strong, representing other people, marriage, contracts, and partnerships. Friendships and acquaintances are extremely important to you. You have an enormous ability to nurture relationships. You're extroverted and love an audience.

"The 10th house, representing your career, public life and ambitions, is prominent in your chart. You've had your ups and downs, but you always come through much the wiser. Your 9th house emphasizes travel, which plays a major role in your life, including actual travel, philosophical and metaphysical travel, and spirituality.

"Your three most important signs are Capricorn, Scorpio and Aries, so you display some of the characteristics of each of these signs. Capricorn gives you a serious side, makes you steady and tough. You are very sensitive, particularly in love. The Scorpio in your chart makes you passionate, charming and a keeper of secrets, Aries gives you enthusiasm, fire, honesty, and the ability to always be able to reinvent yourself, to live in different places and adjust to new environments. You have a great weakness for Aries women, due to the aspects in your astrological chart. Scorpio women also appeal to you.

"Eager to explore the unknown, you're always looking for exciting discoveries and new horizons. You are sensible and down to earth, charming, attractive, intuitive, with a great deal of integrity, honesty and enthusiasm. You are loyal and adventurous, and you can also be gullible. Your emotions are secretive, intense, and sensual; you are often consumed with erotic thoughts and your magnetic nature gives you the power to seduce women. You are aware of the fascination you exert on others. Friendships play a key role in your life."

"True, true," Henry agreed, "I've had great friendships all through my life. That's always been the key thing in my horoscope: I'm a person who is destined to make wonderful friends. That's probably the biggest factor in my life. I've been helped all my life by friends; I've had many great friends, lifelong friends."

"And you are very psychic, Henry. You have the definite gift of clairvoyance."

"Yas, yaz, that's absolutely true," Henry agreed. "I am that, I have that."

Maria had introduced me to Henry's friend Dane Rudhyar, renaissance man, pianist, avant-garde composer, philosopher, writer, occultist, astrologer. Oddly, the occasion had taken place in a dark, out of the way room in a derelict section of Hollywood. A tall, imposing figure cloaked in black, Rudhyar sat at an upright piano facing a wall, raised his arms to hold his hands aloft for several seconds until beginning the music, as his long thin fingers evoked strange melodies on the instrument. To me, he looked like a benevolent warlock.

"Amazing that Dane Rudhyar moved here too," I said. "Henry, Anaïs, and Dane Rudhyar, all three of you moved to California, all of you so attached to Paris in the 30's."

"No, that's wrong," Henry corrected. "Anaïs and I, yes, but not Dane Rudhyar. Rudhyar was long gone from Paris by the 30's. Anaïs and I both left at the start of World War II, but Rudyhar preceded us by more than a couple of decades."

"Oh, I thought you three were contemporaries whose lives intersected at specific points and places in time," I said.

"Anaïs and I, yes. But Dane Rudhyar, which wasn't his real name, incidentally, doncha know ... his given name was Daniel, and I don't recall the surname, if I ever knew it – Rudyhar was a pseudonym, too. As I recall, it was a Japanese Zen teacher he met in America who inspired him to take the name Rudhyar, a combination of several Sanskrit words, including the name of the god Rudra. But Rudhyar left France long before Anaïs and I did, around the time of the First World War. It had to do with his music, which was performed in New York when he was a young man, only around 20 or 21."

"I didn't know that."

"In fact, his composition was among the first polyphonic music performed at the Metropolitan Opera, during the Great War, ya know. Rudhyar's most distinctive music is for piano. His works are almost all composed of brief movements, and they employ dissonant harmony. His musical approach was influenced by Henri Bergson and theosophy. He viewed composers as mediums, in a manner of speaking. He wrote that 'the new composer' was no longer a 'composer,' but an evoker, a magician."

"Didn't Eric Satie believe something similar?"

"Satie referred to himself as a 'phonometrician,' meaning someone who measures sounds. Rudhyar envisions himself as a seed man of the New Age cultural evolution. He was instrumental in bringing astrology and Jungian psychology together."

"Humanistic astrology," Maria said, "is the subject of Rudhyar's great book *The Astrology of Personality*. Alice Bailey, who coined the term New Age, encouraged him; she published his first book."

"Rudhyar also wrote several novels, ya know. He wrote extensively on music too, he wrote books about Debussy, dissonant harmony, Hindu music. And he was into transcendental art. The idea behind transcendental painting was to paint images of Jungian archetypes."

I said, "Many people say he's the most important astrologer of the 20th century."

"Rudhyar's initial writings were articles in *American Astrology* and *Horoscope* magazines," Henry said. "He wrote about a thousand articles on astrology in those magazines."

"I read those magazines. I discovered them in Penn Station when I was eight years old," I said, "and I remember the name Dane Rudhyar on so many of the articles. I thought his name sounded so interesting – foreign and exotic. Every month, I would ride my bike two miles away to this little stationery store on Old Country Road in Mineola where they carried the astrology magazines. I think they cost a quarter then, maybe even less. I paid for them with the allowance my grandmother gave me, which was 25 cents a week."

"Rudhyar wrote that the stars don't cause events in life; they are psychological forces at work, but we have free will to respond or not respond to those forces," Henry said.

"Similar to what Carroll Righter says: 'the stars impel but do not compel,'" Maria said.

Henry had written: "Astrology does not offer an explanation of the laws of the universe, nor why the universe exists. What it does ... is to show us that there is a rhythm to the universe, and that man's own life partakes of this rhythm."

In addition to interpreting his astrological chart, Maria gave Henry a reading about his past lives, some of which pertained to incarnations in Atlantis and Lemuria. Atlantis, Lemuria, life on other planets, flying saucers, hollow earth, the origins of life – Henry loved these subjects and was in his element when we spoke about them.

A topic of interest to Henry we explored concerned a peculiar race that lives alongside us humans. Henry expounded: "It's said there's a parallel race among us, a race that is without souls. They are merely human replicas, clones or jinns, if you will. It's said that three billion of these entities, or whatever you want to call them, exist right here, right now. They look and act like the rest of us humans, but they don't belong to the same spirit group as true humans. Their purpose is to propagate negativity. They have no conscience, no empathy or remorse; they are totally pathological, sociopathic beings. They often hold important positions as world leaders."

"Yes," Maria agreed. "What you say is very true, Henry. It is our exact circumstance, what we humans are up against."

"Even though I'm not a fan of Rudolf Steiner's writing style – heavy handed, pedantic, tedious, dull, soporific – nevertheless, I find what he wrote in his book *Lucifer, Christ and Ahriman* quite interesting," Henry said. "He called this soulless race living amongst us the Ahrimanic Powers, if you will. That concept unlocks a mystery. It explains why this world we live in is so rotten. This is really an outstanding piece of information, doncha know. I think some of it Steiner got from Zoroastrianism. Ya know, he originally was with the Theosophists, but split off to form his own group, which he called Anthroposophy.

"This idea of Steiner's – you might really call it a revelation– helps us see what's wrong with the world. From one point of view, you might say we're doomed if we allow these soulless ones among us to override our consciousness, if we give them power, so to speak."

"Do we have a choice?" Joe asked. "When the soulless people are in power positions, they make the rules, they hold the reins."

"Our choice is not to surrender to them, but to maintain our integrity," Henry affirmed. "As I said, I was never a great admirer of Steiner and his ponderous prose, but I think he hit the nail on the head with his Ahrimanic Powers explanation."

"That's the point," Maria said. "We have to watch, just like the shortest word in the Bible advises, be alert so not to be defeated. You're right, Henry, it's our choice. We have free will to make that choice."

"Sure, sure," Henry said, "but unfortunately, we're not doing a very good job of it. Look at us. Look at the direction the world is going – look at what has always been, is now and, we can assume, always will be."

Maria said, "What you just said, Henry, this is our great challenge as humans. We confront the opposing force so we learn. We meet the challenger, we fight, and through that, we gain higher consciousness."

"That's the best light of seeing it," Henry said, "I agree with you on that point, Maria. I do find the soulless semi-humans an enticing theory. It certainly answers many questions. But as to ever really unlocking the key to the universe, I don't believe that's possible."

Maria said, "Madame Blavatsky said Satan is the true and only god of our planet."

"That's right," Henry agreed, "and interestingly, she didn't include any description of wickedness or depravity. She explains that he whom the Christian dogma calls Lucifer was never the representative of evil, but on the contrary, is the light-bringer, which is the literal meaning of the name Lucifer. According to Blavatsky, the church turned him into Satan, meaning 'the opponent,' to fit him into Christian dogma. A similar view is shared by the Gnostics."

Joe asked, "If there's a subhuman, negative, pathological species as you and Maria describe, Henry, couldn't there also be a superhuman, positive species that's superior to us humans, who look like us, and who are here among us?"

"Sure, sure, there likely could be. That's another popular theory, Joe," Henry said. "Hmmm ... hmmm ... I can see it being a reality in principle, but I'm not convinced there are too many instances of these superior beings among us intervening in our affairs by performing noble works in this day and age, at least that we know or hear about, isn't that right? Naturally, we have reports of the great avatars, Buddha, Jesus, the saints and masters, but who is there on such an exalted level today? These superior beings are a rarity who only appear on a seldom, almost never basis."

"If they exist today, why are they presumably hiding from sight?" Joe asked. "They should come out and enlighten us. The world could use their wisdom and guidance."

"Amen," Henry said. "Until we recognize the next avatar, we'll just have to struggle on our own ... hmmm ... hmmmm."

CHAPTER TWELVE

Maria had given Henry a copy of the astrology book we wrote, *Astrology and Your Sex Life*. Joe was reading aloud from it: "'Maria is gifted with the powers of psychometry and precognition to an unusual degree. In 1962 Maria accurately predicted the death of Pope John XXIII and five top secular leaders, as well as the assassination of President John F. Kennedy ... A particular goal of Maria's is to make people aware, understand and feel the reality of love in both the spiritual and sexual sense. 'We are here,' Maria says, 'to ... give love as a consuming fire.'

"'Countess Maria Graciette has established the Maria Creative Womanhood Foundation for the purposes of esoteric study, higher meditation and divine healing, as well as to teach people, especially women, how to achieve harmony in life and how to have richer sex lives. ...In this book, Dr. Graciette reveals some hitherto unpublished secrets of inspired love and sex, all with a sound astrological basis.

"'Sex is creative energy... that begins as an impulse at the root of the spinal column, or kundalini as it is called in Indian philosophy. If more women would develop their kundalini power, men would never stray. If more men would develop their kundalini power, women would be their willing slaves.'"

"I'm all for that, "Henry said. "Who wouldn't be?"

"'In Tibet today the Masters still choose disciples to initiate into Tantra Yoga, the Yoga of sex,'" Joe continued reading. "I was one of the fortunate ones to receive these sacred teachings, which enables gaining insight and understanding into the creative power that is in the nucleus of ourselves.'"

Maria explained to Henry, the master sexologist, that "...Sex acts like a generator, and a generator in good working order can electrify all parts of the organism.... Without this generator in good working condition, the body declines."

Henry agreed, "I concur. Sure, sure ... sex certainly keeps the body toned and vibrant."

Maria said, "Physical decline results from practicing lower sex, you know."

"Lower sex?" Henry was stumped. "What's that? I've never heard that term. Lower as opposed to higher? What's the criteria for figuring which is which?"

After offering a definition I don't recall, Maria said, "Sex is meant to be a beautiful, elevating experience, a union and a communion that builds to ecstasy."

"With great passion, of course."

"Yes, passion and more, much more – beyond passion. Ecstasy is beyond passion. Passion can be deceptive," Maria said. "Passion can happen from lust, and the mind can trick us, but ecstasy is pure, it is a union of mind, spirit, body, being, soul, everything, it is an overflowing and exchange of pure energies."

"Sex is one of the highest forms of spirituality ... a great art, I have always believed," Henry declared.

Joe took up reading again: "'Energies from the kundalini flow ... throughout the entire body, electrical charges circulating, invigorating, giving renewed current of life and spirit. Ecstasy is produced as an extension of sex ...Thus does nature afford man the opportunity of transcendence ... the chance to expand his consciousness in sex...'"

"Now you're talking about love, love with a capital L," Henry said, "a rarity, to be sure, something we all seek but seldom find, doncha know. Hmmm ... hmmm... ya know, people think of me as a human sex machine, but the truth is, I was always looking for love."

The figure of Count Saint Germain intrigued both Henry and Maria. Henry said, "St. Germain is the greatest mystery man of the past several hundred years and maybe more, if you will." He went on to elaborate, "Here's this guy, this fabulous figure, showing up mysteriously in the high courts of Europe, then disappearing as mysteriously as he appeared. He was a scientist, alchemist, linguist, poet, philosopher and more. He had an enormous presence and great influence. The story claims he rarely if ever ate, and that he knew how to turn ordinary stones into valuable jewels which paid his expenses. Many believed he was immortal, and in a way he was, or at least the stories of his existence present him that way, if you will. When he would arrive at the age of fifty, they say, he would perform a secret rite, a forty day fast in which he used an elixir called the 'Master's White Drops.'

"After he was about a month into the fast, he'd start shedding and replacing his skin, hair, eyes, and teeth, resulting in complete rejuvenation by the 40th day. It was said he was behind the writings of Francis Bacon and Shakespeare; he's alleged to have founded Rosicrucianism and Freemasonry, and was even instrumental in the creation of the United States of America. He was in Tibet for most of the 19th century. He was supposedly last seen about forty years ago in Rome by Charles Leadbeater, the theosophist.

"Supposedly he now resides in the Himalayas, and only comes out in the world on rare occasions, because of the increasing pollution and negativity on the planet."

Joe asked, "If he's such a master with so many great powers, why should pollution and negativity affect him? Shouldn't he be able to overcome things like that?"

"Good question, Joe," Henry agreed. "I'm only telling you what I've heard and read about the man."

Joe said, "I like to think more advanced beings than humans can and do exist. I don't like to think the extent of life possibilities ends with us."

"Well, theosophy and other systems say that Venus is the most spiritually advanced planet in our solar system, and those beings living on the etheric plane of Venus are said to be hundreds of millions of years ahead of us in their spiritual evolution," Henry said, and asked Maria if she agreed with that.

Maria did agree, adding, "The governing council from Venus is called the Seven Holy Kumars. They sent Sanat Kumara to Earth to guide us. Sanat Kumara built his headquarters as the city of Shamballa, on the etheric plane over the Gobi Desert."

"Shamballa," Henry echoed. "Theosophy believes the streets in Shamballa are laid out just like the Champs-Elysées."

"That's very true," Maria affirmed. "And Washington, D.C. is modeled on Shamballa."

"Sure, sure, supposedly George Washington was divinely inspired when he chose Pierre L'Enfant to create Washington," Henry said.

"Shamballa is so beautiful," Maria said. "The big temple there has a beautiful golden dome. It's surrounded by seven small temples, one for each of the seven rays. The temples are situated on a grand boulevard, just like Paris."

"You sound like you've actually been there," Henry said.

"I have," Maria said, "many times."

"How did you get there?" a puzzled Joe wanted to know.

"Through the etheric, in astral projection," Maria replied nonchalantly. "By out of the body travel."

Henry, a staunch believer in flying saucers and life on other planets, said he'd welcome the chance to go on a space ship. In the infinite corners of his imagination, anything could be reality. "The possible, the probable, the certain, the uncertain, the impossible possible truth – where does it all lead? Even the most preposterous things have a grain of possibility in them, a grain of truth, and we should never lose sight of that, ya know," Henry said.

Maria gave him a copy of her book *My Adventure in Tallulah Falls*, Georgia, the story of her being taken on a UFO. "There've been several UFO sightings in Tallulah Falls this year," Henry said. "People spotted a saucer hovering across a highway there. When it vanished, it left a distinctive smell behind, something like embalming fluid or brake fluid. A dozen witnesses who saw the craft complained of a stinging, burning pain on their arms and face. They said the saucer made a hissing sound like a million snakes."

Henry said, "Life on other planets is totally plausible, if you will. People can debunk the possibility of life being capable of being supported under conditions of planets without oxygen or with an atmosphere of poisonous gas, but it always amuses me, because they're judging by earth standards, using the conditions we live in on this planet, our physical attributes, whereas other forms of life or modes of consciousness wouldn't have to share our characteristics. They wouldn't have to physically resemble us or have our faculties, if you will. They could exist in intense heat or cold, not needing to eat the same kind of food we eat, or eat at all. They may not have mouths, ears, eyes, but other sensory organs, or no sensory organs as we know them, and so on. This is the fallacy people never address when they declare there can't be such a thing as life on other planets. Of course there is life on other planets – absolutely!"

"Of course there is!" Maria agreed.

"Going to Venus would be well worth it, especially since they obviously must know something about love, doncha know – something we could all learn from them, in a manner of speaking," Henry said. "That's really the essence of why we're here, to experience love, to expand our capacity for love. Love is the biggest lesson we're learning in our incarnations. It's really the answer to everything."

"Life didn't start on Earth or even in our solar system," Maria said. "It was seeded here at intervals."

Henry said, "Some say human life originated in Lyra, spread to the Pleaides, then went – some say to Uranus, some say to Venus – just how long ago is debatable ... some say 150,000 years ago, 50,000 years ago, millions of years ago. We don't know for sure. No matter. Extraterrestials, I believe, are very real and I also believe they're much more civilized and humane than we are."

Joe said, "So Henry, don't you place any stock in the stories about negative aliens, evil entities?"

"I believe that could be possible as well. And I definitely believe there's a negative part of the ego in all of us that must be cleansed and changed. We all have our dark side. Are you familiar with Robert Ernst Dickhoff?" Henry asked, and told the rest of us, "Dickhoff is a writer on the paranormal, founder of the American Buddhist Society and Fellowship, who writes books relating to UFOs and the hollow earth theory. He believes UFOs might be Garudas that capture humans and kill them for food. He was one of the first UFOologists to consider UFOs possibly being unfriendly, whereas most UFOlogists prefer to think of aliens as benevolent, so to speak."

Maria had known several UFOlogists that Henry was aware of, including George Adamski and George Van Tassel. Henry said, "George Adamski fought in the cavalry regiment at the Mexican border during the Pancho Villa Expedition. He's known for his communication with Venusians."

Maria said, "Yes, a spaceship from Venus landed close to him. The visitors took Adamski on a trip of the solar system. They told Adamski they lived in underground cities, so they're not exposed to hostile conditions on the planet's surface. There are some wonderful photographs of Adamski's UFO adventures."

"Those pictures are famous," Henry said. "Ya know, Cecil B. de Mille's top cinematographer, Pev Marley, who was married to the movie star Linda Darnell, declared that if Adamski's pictures were fakes, they were the best he'd ever seen. And more than a dozen experts from the J. Arthur Rank Organization concluded the object photographed had to either be definitely real, or else photographed from a full-scale model."

Maria said, "Queen Juliana of the Netherlands was interested in Adamski's experiences, and invited him to the royal court. He also met with Pope John XXIII."

"Maria met with the pope too," I said. "He told her a lot of interesting things, hidden secrets, esoteric knowledge that the multitudes don't know about."

"You'll have to tell us about that, Maria," Henry said, but Maria said she'd been sworn to secrecy and couldn't.

As for the other George, George Van Tassel, he was a retired test pilot for Howard Hughes who lived at Giant Rock and operated the Giant Rock airport. Maria attended his annual spacecraft conventions along with thousands of others. Giant Rock itself was a seven story high boulder in the Mojave Desert covering 5,800 square feet of ground, the world's largest freestanding boulder. Native Americans considered it sacred. Around Giant Rock, the skies were full of UFOs.

Maria said, "Among other things, George Van Tassel runs the Giant Rock café. His former employer Howard Hughes flies into the airport on weekends to get a slice of the famous pie Van Tassel's wife makes." Maria said that Van Tassel led weekly meditations in an excavated room under the Giant Rock, where he received instructions from aliens and from Nikola Tesla for a rejuvenation and time machine to revitalize human cells using the natural energy of the atmosphere. Van Tassel called his device the Integratron. It was 38 feet high and 50 feet in diameter. With his Integraton, people believed Van Tassel had tapped into the universal knowledge of the century.

"He says the body is an electrical device, that aging is a matter of our cells just running out of power. The Integraton recharges cells and brings about renewed youth and longer life," Maria explained

"I think we should all go there and get recharged," Henry said.

"Good idea, Henry," Joe seconded.

Maria spoke of another interesting device: "There's a transportational device that lies buried under the sands of southern Iraq. It first came here when aliens began interacting with humanity thousands of years ago. It was shut down around 1600 BC. If reactivated, the device would allow transportation between Earth and our home planet."

Henry said many people had made a case for the earth being hollow. "They say in the Himalayas there's an entrance to the subterranean kingdom of Agartha, where life exists in the inner earth."

Joe asked, "But how would they live without the sun?"

Maria said, "The earth's interior has its own sun. One can catch glimpses of it – it's behind the aurora borealis. Earth's inner sun remains hidden within the Earth for cycles of 3600 years. When it shows itself, it marks a new epoch in our planetary history. The last such time was around 1500 to 1600 BC during the great Exodus of the Bible."

Henry elaborated. "They say the true nature of our planet has been hidden for centuries. Ancient wisdom tells us not only is the earth hollow, but all the other planets in our solar system are hollow, too. Access to the interior of the earth is through openings at the north and south poles."

"We heard a lot about the hollow earth from Jules Verne, didn't we, Henry?" Joe said.

"Yes, and it's a thoroughly fascinating subject, isn't that right? One wants to believe these stories are possible, and who knows, they well could be. However, some scientists say hollow earth habitation is impossible," Henry said. "While scientists recognize that the Earth's core is responsible for creating our planet's magnetic field, physically traveling to the core is problematic, because of rapidly increasing pressures and temperatures. Still, it's plausible that advanced beings could overcome this, or maybe already have, ya know."

Maria said, "Admiral Byrd made two trips where he viewed the entrance to the hollow earth. He flew over the north polar opening; he saw it with his own eyes."

Henry added, "There was a Norwegian sailor named Olaf Jansen. He and his father claimed to have sailed all the way in and mingled with the inhabitants for a full two years in the 19th century."

"Science has to catch up with reality," Maria declared. "The fact is, there are literally hundreds of large cities beneath the earth interconnected by tunnels. The inhabitants use magnetic propulsion with high speed shuttles to travel around. Some of the cities are located in or under mountains."

Maria said that a mile under Mount Shasta in northern California was the domed city of Telos, where over a million and a half descendants of Atlantis and Lemuria lived. "The city was built over 14,000 years ago as a haven from war and destruction," Maria said. "Telos is connected to hundreds of other cities and to the main Agarthean hub beneath the Gobi desert. The citizens of Telos are scientifically advanced. The city's main power source is a huge central crystal the size of a skyscraper."

Henry supplied further information. He said, "Edmund Halley, discoverer of Halley's Comet, was one of the earliest proponents of hollow earth. Halley concluded that there are other bodies within the Earth to account for the varying directions of the Earth's magnetic field. He proposed four concentric spheres, all inhabited and nestled inside each other, each with its own magnetic field. The outermost is of course the Earth. Halley said all of the earth's inner shells are bathed in perpetual luminous light. He postulated that the aurora borealis was the result of escaped gases coming from the Earth's interior."

"It's said that Earth contains a repository or library of universal knowledge collected from all parts of the universe," Maria said. "In secret vaults, coded within the very core or fabric of the planet itself is information so powerful it could render its possessor practically invincible."

"A very enticing thought," Henry said. "How can we access this incredible wisdom? I feel we will never know either the origins or the end of earth existence. Have you read *The Urantia Book*?"

"Oh, yes. It's fascinating."

"It's over 2000 pages long and covers the whole spectrum of earth's history, beginning 900 billion years ago," Henry said, "And according to Hindu scripture, man has been on Earth for over 120 million years, d'ya know? We're supposedly in the 28th cycle – there are 30 in all – of 4,320,000 years, which are divided into four stages.

"The Golden Age of Man lasted over 2 million years. In those days, humans were 31.5 feet tall, physically immortal, and lived 100,000 years before going voluntarily into a deep sleep and leaving the body to return to their spiritual home. Then came the Silver Age, which lasted around a million years, in which man was 21 feet tall and lived 10,000 years. Next came the Copper Age, lasting 720,000 years. Humans were 10 feet tall and lived 1000 years. And now we're living in the Iron Age, our present age, which is 360,000 years long, during which man's average height is less than 6 feet. Mankind's decreasing physical stature over millennia reflects his continual moral or spiritual degeneration, so to speak."

"But a new Golden Age will occur," Maria said. "Man will return to his original physical and spiritual stature during the next 144,000 years."

"This must already be happening, because people have been getting taller," Joe said.

"Sure, sure," Henry said. "They claim that in middle earth, giantism is common due to the lower gravity and better climate, if you will, that most inner earth inhabitants are between 9 and 12 feet tall, and have lifespans of between 600 to 1000 years."

"It certainly makes you think," Joe ventured.

Henry said, "It does, doesn't it? And all this doesn't even have to actually be true, because there's truth involved, no matter what. If for no other purpose, these stories affect our subconscious. They're true on one level, and maybe they're factually true as well, but they don't have to be factually true to affect us deeply."

Maria said, "There's a degree of truth in everything, if you can understand and extract it."

Henry said, "What we're tasked with here is to go the distance, to dig deeper, as deep as we can get. Krishna, Buddha, Jesus and many others less well known all conquered their human nature to become immortal masters, and we must do the same."

Another point of common interest between Maria and Henry was Ashley Montagu, who had written a book called *The Biological Superiority of Woman*. Henry said, "You know, he has this compelling theory that women are more developed than men, that the male is a degenerate female. The male is uglier, less sensitive, and less smart than the female. Women are more in tune with nature, they're less destructive, doncha know. Supposedly, the reason the male voice is deeper is because he operates at a lower vibration, and because man's reproductive organs hang out, which has an effect on why he has a shorter life span than his female counterpart... hmmm ... hmmmm...."

Maria said, "I watch Ashley Montague all the time on Johnny Carson, on *The Tonight Show*."

Henry said, "Montagu studied at the London School of Economics, where he was one of the first students of Bronislaw Malinowski. Malinowski, you may know, wrote about the coital practices of the Trobriand Islanders, whose sexual approach is similar to Tantra Yoga and Karezza. They prolong intercourse until the souls of their dead ancestors emerge. Among these Trobriand Islanders, there's no incidence of divorce or infidelity and the people achieve a degree of happiness unheard of in the West."

"Wilhelm Reich also wrote about the Trobriand Islanders," I said.

"That's so, and what happened to Reich is a travesty," Henry said. "That said, nevertheless, Reich was at fault for thinking he could ignore the law. Everything could have been resolved differently. He should not have ignored the subpoena. He could have fought the charges, but he failed to appear in court, the kiss of death. Whoever gave him legal advice put the nail in his coffin. Reich could have saved himself. As it was, he died too young."

Another mystic who came up in discussion was Allan Kardac, whose books, Maria said, were wildly popular all over South America.

"Allan Kardac is a pseudonym," Henry said, "chosen from a previous incarnation when Kardec was a Druid. He was a science and math teacher in Paris who became interested in spirit-tapping. Franz Mesmer's animal magnetism was popular at the time, and Kardec wanted to understand what was causing the physical effects attributed to spirits, if you will. His books explore relations between the spirit and material worlds. Camille Flammarion, the famous French astronomer, said 'Spiritism is not a religion but a science.' Flammarion gave Kardac's eulogy. Kardec is buried in Père Lachaise, along with so many other greats. The inscription on his tomb says *Naître, mourir, renaître encore et progresser sans cesse, telle est la loi'* – 'To be born, to die, to be reborn again, and so to progress unceasingly, such is the law."

"Beautiful," Joe said.

Henry and Maria agreed that Manley P. Hall, who presided over the Philosophical Society on Los Feliz, was an incredible genius, "a brilliant man. He speaks extemporaneously, ya know, no notes at all. This guy sits down and stays put for the next hour, during which the most fascinating information just pours out of him. Remarkable storehouse of knowledge," Henry said.

"Very impressive," Maria agreed. "Manley Hall is a fantastic speaker."

"His organization has a wonderful library. It's known as the finest metaphysical library in the world," Henry said.

Maria said, "There's nothing Manley Hall doesn't know about in the occult, spiritual and metaphysical field. I love to go Sundays to hear him speak. And his books are wonderful. He's written so many of them."

Maria mentioned that a story about Padre Pio, the Capuchin priest who was famous for the stigmata, appeared in the Italian magazine *Tempo*, in an issue in which I was on the cover and the subject of a four page story. Henry asked to see the magazine, so I brought it to show him. Maria had visited with Padre Pio. "Whatever you say about him, he is a powerful presence," she said. "By the time he was five years old, he had already made the decision to dedicate his life to God."

"Padre Pio has something in common with Vivekananda," Henry said, "who was having spiritual visions at that age."

"Padre Pio believes the love of God is inseparable from suffering, that suffering is the way the soul reaches God," Maria said. "His followers believe Padre Pio was attacked by the devil, physically and spiritually. Padre Pio had a vision in which Christ appeared and pierced his side, leaving Padre Pio with a physical wound. This occurrence is considered as a transverberation or piercing of the heart, indicating the union of love with God."

"Transverberation?" Joe questioned. "I never heard of it. Is it something that just happens to Catholics?"

Henry explained, "St. John of the Cross described transverberation as the soul being inflamed with the love of God, attacked by a seraph who pierces it with a dart, which leaves the soul wounded, which causes it to overflow with divine love. I guess it could happen to anybody, regardless of creed, except the Catholic saints seem to be the major ones we hear about, doncha know."

Maria said, "Padre Pio said he felt a perpetual wound in the depths of his soul that caused him agony. He experienced religious ecstasy, after which he received the stigmata, the five wounds of Christ. He wears fingerless gloves to conceal his hand wounds."

"That's controversial," Henry pointed out. "Padre Pio has been accused of being a self-mutilating psychopath, you know. He's been accused of faking his stigmata, using carbolic acid to self-inflict the wounds."

"The Vatican was initially skeptical," Maria agreed. "He's been subjected to many investigations of the supernatural phenomena around him, his ability to bilocate, to smell perfumes that aren't present. Investigations are proving positive."

Henry said, "Some believe the stigmata, religious ecstasy and extremism are a hysterical reaction to sexual repression. My feeling is, they may have a valid point." Henry never put anybody or any idea down; he was always open minded, respectful and polite. He never panned anything outright, but you knew the difference when he was a full supporter and when he was leaving a verdict open.

Maria said, "Padre Pio is famous for a quote, 'Pray, hope and don't worry.'"

"Hmmm.... hmmmm...." Henry mused. "Is that really the best we can do?"

An Italian film version of Machiavelli's play *La Mandragola*, starring Rosanna Schiafino, Totò, and Jean-Claude Brialy, directed by Alberto Lattuada, had recently been released. I was eager to see it, having met both Totò and Lattuada and having studied the Machiavelli play at Vassar with my brilliant drama professor, Leon Katz.

"Wonderful actor, incredible face," Henry said. "Totò is one of the greatest artists of the 20th century, he's Italy's answer to Buster Keaton and Charlie Chaplin, an heir of the commedia dell'arte tradition."

I said, "In Italy, he's nicknamed *il principe della risata*, 'the prince of laughter.'"

"Ya know, Totò was the illegitimate son of a Sicilian woman and a Neapolitan prince who didn't legally recognize him until he was in his 30's, when he got his biological father to adopt him in exchange for a life annuity. From this, Totò became an heir of two noble families and can legitimately call himself a prince."

Maria said, "I hear he's wonderful in *La Mandragola*."

Henry said, "The *mandragola*, which we call the mandrake root in English, is said to grow from the sperm of a hanged man, and is alleged to be an aphrodisiac, doncha know."

Maria said, "It works. I can tell you that it definitely works. It's very similar to Pega Palo."

"Pega Palo? What's that?" Joe asked.

Maria said, "It's a root that resembles a man, just like the mandrake root does. Pega Palo is indigenous to the Dominican

Republic. You soak the root in alcohol, drink the concoction, and wow! Does it work!"

"So it's an aphrodisiac, then," Joe concluded.

"And how!" Maria exclaimed.

Henry perked up. "How does one find this Pega Palo? Is it available in this country?"

Maria leaned over confidentially and murmured something about talking to Henry privately about the subject later. I'm not sure what happened after that, whether there was a follow up, but I knew a little about Pega Palo myself. Back in New York, I had a Cuban dentist (who turned out not to be a real dentist, which is a separate story), Dr. Armando Crucet, who gave me a bottle of Pega Palo. Just as Maria said, Pega Palo was a root with a marked human resemblance. Dr. Crucet said he and his wife Rita had used some Pega Palo over one weekend and had lost twelve pounds, that its sensual effects were not to be believed. It was incredible stuff, Dr. Crucet swore, and I should definitely try it. I never did get to do so. I was on my way to Florida to shoot the movie *A Touch of Flesh*, in which my role was that of a disturbed, armed and dangerous narcissistic teenage nymphomaniac. My fencing teacher Phil Gerard and his girlfriend would be staying in my apartment while I was gone. Before leaving, I told Phil that I had left a bottle of Pega Palo in the refrigerator, explaining what it was. Upon my return, the Pega Palo bottle was empty; Phil and his girlfriend had used it all up.

To Maria, motherhood was sacred; she cherished relationships with her mother and daughter as the crowning jewels of her life. She hit a sore spot with Henry with a remark she made on motherhood: "We have many people in our lives, people who come and go. We can have many friends, spouses and lovers, but we have only one mother." This statement did not sit well with Henry, considering his difficult relationship with his mother. The observation made him uncomfortable, caused him to bristle, one of the few times I saw his naturally sunny, cheerful disposition noticeably shift, as a look of sadness crossed his face and he extinguished his cigarette.

Maria had a special affinity with people born the same day as she. One of these was Sharon Tate. When Sharon became the second actress signed by Marty Ransohoff and was sent to Jacobina Caro and

Jeff Corey for training, she didn't have a car and didn't drive, so I would pick her up and take her back and forth to our mutual acting and body movement classes. Sharon was living at the Hollywood Studio Club on Lodi Place, where Marilyn Monroe and Kim Novak as young starlets had also stayed. Upon our return from classes, Sharon would often invite me upstairs to her small quarters to pore over her scrapbooks and photo albums. She would talk about her family, her two sisters, her parents, being an Army brat, and time spent in Italy, where her father was posted with the armed services. Sharon was one of the sweetest and loveliest persons you would ever want to know, fresh, naive, thoroughly unspoiled, and as yet unwise to the ways of the world. When Maria and Sharon met, they established an immediate rapport, in part due to the shared January 24 birthday. But I noticed Maria shudder. I could perceive she was picking something up, something that wasn't good. When I asked her about it, Maria could only say, "I don't want to talk about what I see. I don't want to give it power. I just hope I'm wrong, that's all." Unfortunately, Maria wasn't wrong, but was clairvoyantly glimpsing Sharon's horrible, tragic fate.

On another note, Maria had critical words for me. She felt I should be encouraging Henry romantically. "You throw away opportunities," she admonished. "The Universe opens a door for you and you shut it. Charlie Fawcett offered to send you to Morocco, Ethiopia, Saudi Arabia, Brazil, Pakistan and all over the world. You could have been a guest of top world leaders everywhere, but you didn't go. Who do you think you are, that you can afford to refuse possibilities like that?"

I started to reply, but Maria kept on. "The Miss Rheingold contest was down to just a few remaining girls, and you didn't show up for the finals. They chose you for the lead in a movie, *The Blob*, opposite Steve McQueen, and you turned it down – to appear in summer stock in Maine! That was Steve McQueen's first movie and it made him a star. It would have helped you, too. You were chosen for the ingenue lead in the road company of Tennessee Williams' play *Sweet Bird of Youth*, and you said no, you gave a phony excuse. Fellini wanted you in *8 ½*, and you left the country. Why do you deny everything the Universe offers that could help your life?" Maria demanded.

Declining to listen to any explanations, she continued, "You think you can keep saying no to everything that's offered you? How many chances do you think the Universe will give? You have not arrived yet; you need to take every opportunity to build your life so you can one day be in the driver's seat. You made mistakes in the past. You don't understand how accepting smaller things can lead to bigger things. Stepping stones is what the Universe keeps offering you, but you don't acknowledge them. You need a foundation. Now you have this opportunity with Henry Miller."

"What opportunity?"

"Henry likes you. He gives you openings, but you shut him out."

"I don't want to be romantically involved with Henry," I protested.

"Oh, please. You make so many conditions, so many decisions against your best interest."

"I told you before, Maria, Henry's way too old for me."

This was not the first time Maria had mentioned the idea that I should cultivate Henry romantically, "stimulate his erotic nature." She already knew I was not in favor of it.

Maria asked, "What's the big deal to have a romance with Henry Miller? You could make him very happy, and he would take you to Europe, besides. You would love that. It would be so interesting to be in Europe with Henry Miller. Listen, you could do a lot worse. In fact, you have done a lot worse – don't pretend you haven't." Maria kept on, "Henry tries to flirt with you. You don't flirt back. Why not?"

"I told you, I don't want to lead him on."

"Henry is a charming man. He is delightful. He has a beautiful temperament. Few men have that kind of wonderful nature. You and Henry have a lot in common. Henry likes Aries women. He likes you."

"Henry likes women, period. He's a romantic. He's always in love. He starts fantasizing. He can't help it; he loves the impossible dream –"

"Sure, fantasy keeps Henry going. He doesn't care if it's real or not. Fantasy is his medicine, he thrives on it. He doesn't ask that much, he just wants a woman to participate in the fantasy. It's almost like phone sex. Completely harmless."

"Not to me."

Shaking her head, Maria said, "You turn your nose up at all the opportunities the Universe places in your path. You don't acknowledge them, you don't accept them. Henry is one big opportunity you're missing, that some day, you will regret."

"Maria, Henry's totally wonderful, agreed, but romantically is a different story."

"All right," Maria said, symbolically washing her hands of the matter. "Just don't ever say I didn't advise you."

If only Henry and I were of the same generation, I thought, everything might be different.

CHAPTER THIRTEEN

Anyway, I had a current romantic interest in my life, a man who was only ten years older than I, a much more suitable age. My *affair de coeur* with Hollywood hyphenate Andrew McCullough began auspiciously on an intense note. From its inception, Maria did not approve and predicted it would never work out. And she was right; it didn't.

Andy was a tall, good looking Harvard graduate writer/director, self-styled black Irish poet who had made his reputation as an award winning director in New York live television. In Hollywood, much of Andy's directing was for *The Donna Reid Show*. He was immensely charming and articulate, strong, masculine, sensitive and perceptive. He wrote wonderful plays. He was serious about his own work and spoke eloquently about the work of other writers. One of the things that appealed most to me about Andy was his erudition, his immense knowledge of literature – fiction, plays, poetry.

Andy spotted me one night as I was dining at the Aware Inn, a casual natural foods restaurant with a pleasant ambiance in West Hollywood that was popular with the Hollywood set, frequented by stars from Bill Cosby to Hedy Lamarr and Jane Fonda. Wishing to meet me, Andy asked Elaine Baker, wife of the owner, if she could arrange it. Elaine's husband Jim Baker, who had served time for killing two men, would start two more famous L.A. restaurants, The Old World and The Source. Later, Baker would redesign himself as "Father Yod," grow his copious, curly salt and pepper hair long, don white robes, and live a life of mythic proportions as a Hawaii spiritual guru, where he had a following of young acolytes, including fourteen wives with whom he fathered many offspring. He was killed, still in his 50's, in a hang gliding accident.

But back to Andy. In the throes of romance, we drove up the scenic California coast past the Hearst Castle on the winding, two lane coastal highway. The fog along the Monterey Coast drifted in spurts, relieved by spasms of sunbursts. Overcome by Big Sur's magical, wild beauty, my thoughts drifted to Henry, imagining him living here among the redwoods, the tamarack and pine, the white ash, the fields of yellow poppies sprinkled with magenta wildflowers growing on hillsides among the rocks. Henry was here! The area seemed imbued with his presence, even though it had been a couple of years since he'd lived here.

We got out of the car to behold cypress trees shaped by the winds. Out in the ocean near a sea lion's fief, wild gander swooped in squadrons, swiveling through the air in long undulations. Goslings assembled on the beach to practice wing drills. I couldn't get Henry out of my mind, he was so associated with this ambiance. He stayed in my consciousness as the sun sank into the sea; he lingered during walks in the forest and up the golden hills, with the redtail hawks soaring above. Evenings at open air sulphur baths, the Pacific roaring below, the sweet, pungent smell of smoke and burning wood – all of it evoked Henry. Even eating ambrosia burgers at the cliff hanging Nepenthe Restaurant made me think of Henry. His spirit seemed to linger over the area, as if the place were infused with him. Despite knowing he wasn't here anymore, I still sought him and felt an emptiness, a strange dislocation of the ethers, not finding him.

"I was in Big Sur for a few days last week," I told Henry. "I was looking for you there."

"Looking for me in Big Sur?" Henry laughed. "I don't live there anymore. I'm here! As you know!"

"Yes, but you left your indelible imprint there."

Andy was interested in meeting Henry, so he came with me to the Siegels. Henry and Andy, familiar with many of he same writers, provided us with a discussion on some of them that afternoon. Andy usually dominated a conversation, often on a topic dear to his heart, politics, but that subject didn't arise this time; Henry was notoriously anti-politics. "Politics is a thoroughly foul, rotten world," he commented. "Politics debases everything. We get nowhere through politics. The politicians are all corrupt and eating at the taxpayers' trough. It's disgusting."

With most groups, Andy was the impressive star, the well informed talker. If he wasn't expounding on politics, he was, as the black Irish poet, expounding on Joyce, Yeats and others. On this occasion, he shared the stage with Henry, not dominating it. In Henry's company, Andy proved a good listener, good questioner, and offered his own ideas less than listening to Henry's. Andy was extremely well read, with a firm foundation in American, British, and

Irish literature. Henry and Andy talked about George Bernard Shaw, Singhe, Yeats, Joyce, O'Casey, Oscar Wilde. They enumerated other famous Irish writers:

"... Congreve, Sheridan, Oliver Goldsmith, Edmund Burke, Bram Stoker, Jonothan Swift, Brendan Behan -- "

"Might we also even mention Beckett, even though he writes in French? Brian Moore?"

Lest Irish women writers be overlooked, I put in, "How about Lady Gregory, Elizabeth Bowen, Edna O'Brien..."

"Especially Edna O'Brien," Henry echoed enthusiastically, "a wonderful writer ... a pioneer, a great favorite of mine."

They continued with other Irish writers. Henry said, "At the turn of the century, the Irish playwright Justin Huntly McCarthy wrote a play, *If I Were King*, imagining the French poet François Villon matching wits with Louis XI, climaxing with Villon finding love in the king's court and saving Paris from the Duke of Burgundy when Louis makes him Constable of France for a week. This was a stage and screen favorite for the next several decades."

Andy picked up the ball: "*If I Were King* was filmed several times. John Barrymore starred as Villon in *The Beloved Rogue*."

"Yes," Henry added, "and Rudolph Friml's operetta *The Vagabond King*, also based on the McCarthy play, was filmed twice – in the thirties with Jeanette MacDonald and in the fifties with Kathryn Grayson. A propos of Villon, there's Bertolt Brecht's *Baal*. The main character of *Baal* is based on Villon. Some of the lyrics Brecht wrote for *The Threepenny Opera* are translations or paraphrases of poems by Villon."

Joe was saying that some questioned whether a man by the name of François Villon actually existed.

"Whether he existed or not," Henry said, "Villon, as whomever, was a great innovator. While he understood the medieval courtly ideal, he chose to write otherwise, celebrating lowlifes, thieves, and other criminals. He was an innovator in language."

This brought Henry to Ezra Pound's opera *Le Testament*, which, he said, "takes passages from Villon's *Le Testament* for its libretto and demonstrates radical changes in language under Villon, changes that Pound believes profoundly influenced English poetry."

"Isn't Ezra Pound one of your admirers, Henry?" Joe asked.

"Well, I suppose you could call him that, in a manner of

speaking," Henry said. "Sure, sure, he's known to have thrown a few compliments my way. Originally, he wanted my opinion on money, doncha know. The topic of money was of enormous interest to him. It was almost as if he'd discovered the key to the universe with his theories of usury. As for Pound's work, the *Cantos* is considered his masterpiece – but not to me. I prefer his earlier works for sheer beauty of language; I feel they surpass the later ones.

"Aside from his own writing, Ezra was a major discoverer, editor and promoter of other writers. He helped an amazing number of fledgling giants of the age, if you will: T. S. Eliot, James Joyce, for instance. We can thank him for the publication of *The Love Song of J. Alfred Prufrock*, James Joyce's *A Portrait of the Artist as a Young Man*, *Ulysses* and *Finnegan's Wake*. The Imagist movement in poetry owes him, H.D – Hilda Doolittle, in particular.

"Yas, yaz, so many authors are indebted to him – Robert Frost, Hemingway, Marianne Moore, e.e. Cummings, Lawrence, Wyndham Lewis, Archibald MacLeish, William Carlos Williams, Yeats. He helped Margaret Anderson with her *Little Review*. He blue-penciled *The Wasteland* and Hemingway's short stories, he secured funding for Ford Madox Ford's literary review, which published works by Hemingway and Joyce, Gertrude Stein, and of course Pound himself."

"Not to forget how he helped popularize poets of past ages besides Villon," Andy said.

"That's right, such as Guido Cavalcanti," Henry agreed. "He brought Provençal and Chinese poetry to English-speaking audiences. He introduced the west to classical Japanese poetry and drama. He translated Greek, Latin and Anglo-Saxon classics."

"Pound has been called a crackpot, and he probably is, but nevertheless, clearly the man is a genius," Andy affirmed. "He entered college at 15; he learned nine languages."

"Surely one of the most versatile talents of his time. He worked with A. R. Orage, wrote for Orage's magazine *New Age*; he was a force behind Margaret Anderson and her *Little Review*; he was friends with Marcel Duchamp, Tristan Tzara, Léger and others of the Dada and Surrealist movements," Henry said. "Besides all that, most people don't know anything about Pound's music, ya know. He worked with George Antheil and wrote two operas, *Le Testament de Villon* and his opera about Guido Cavalcanti. He also wrote pieces for solo violin which he composed for his mistress of fifty years, the American expatriate violinist Olga Rudge. She, by the way, was one of the movers, along with Pound, of the Vivaldi revival."

Andy said, "Pound believed the cause of the First World War was capitalism, specifically usary, as you mentioned, Henry, to which he believed the solution was fascism. He thought he could stop us from involvement in the Second World War. He went to Washington, where he met with politicians to no result. His fatal flaw, of course, was being a fascist anti-semite and embracing Mussolini and Hitler. He wrote antisemitic tracts for Italian newspapers. He wrote that Roosevelt was a closet Jew and signed the letter 'Heil Hitler.' He was on record for saying Hitler was a Joan of Arc, a saint."

"When they arrested him for treason, he was placed in a six-by-six-foot outdoor steel cage lit up all night by floodlights and left for weeks in isolation in the heat, denied exercise and bed. After two and a half weeks he started collapsing under the strain."

"Who wouldn't?"

"Since he was judged unfit to stand trial, he was incarcerated in a psychiatric hospital for over twelve years. It was only thanks to a campaign by fellow writers he was finally released."

Andy said, "When asked by the press when he had been released from the mental hospital, he replied: 'I never was. When I left the hospital I was still in America, and all America is an insane asylum.'"

"He may have had a point there," Henry observed. "I can't say I totally disagree."

"He went back to Italy," I said. "That's when my Vassar Italian teacher and her daughter traveled all over Italy with him."

Andy said, "Pound boasted that there was a link between his creativity and his ability to seduce women, and he had a very interesting romantic life."

"Yaz, yaz," Henry agreed, "Apart from all the side action he enjoyed, he had a steady mistress for over half a century, along with a wife, both of whom gave birth to his children. The children were raised separately by surrogates. None of the three parents had anything to do with their upbringing. Clearly, none of them really wanted children."

"There was so much outrage after the treason charge. Arthur

Miller considered him worse than Hitler," Andy said.

Joe said, "Pound wasn't the only writer who got in trouble for being on the wrong side politically. There was Céline."

"One of Joe's favorite authors," Henry said. "And mine, naturally."

Joe said. "Henry did me the great service of introducing me to Céline."

"We all love Céline," Henry said. "He influenced so many of us. Certainly one of the most provocative and influential writers in recent times. He developed a new style of writing that thoroughly modernized literature, doncha know. *Journey to the End of the Night* is among the greatest and most brilliant novels of the 20th century."

"You know, Henry," I said, "I first read Céline because of your writing about him. Then when I was in New York for a few months during the summer, I took a course at the New School with Alfred Kazin, and reread *Journey to the End of the Night* there. I read it in English this time."

"Céline was a pen name," Joe said.

"That's right; he took his grandmother's name," Henry said. "Céline married, had a child, and promptly deserted the family. He was a physician, doncha know, with a private practice in Montmartre specializing in obstetrics. Céline writes – wrote, I should say, since he's passed on – wrote such great black comedy. He violated literary conventions, used slang, vulgar speech in the tradition of Villon, only more so, if you will. Those wonderfully chaotic visions of human suffering, laughter in the face of tragedy, his use of ellipses to enhance rhythm... he was a great innovator and masterful storyteller. So many of us owe Céline a debt – Beckett, Sartre, Queneau, Genet, Vonnegut, Günter Grass..."

Joe said, "Now if it weren't for his politics ..."

Henry said, "Unfortunately. Leading up to the war, Céline was campaigning for an alliance between France and Nazi Germany, for the protection of the white Aryan race."

"Similar to Knut Hamsen," Joe said.

"Quite similar, yes. During the Occupation, Céline continued publishing antisemitic writing, critical of Jews and their influence in France. After Germany lost the war, Céline fled to Sigmaringen along with the rest of the collaborators, then made it to Denmark. He was convicted in absentia in France, but after a while, was granted amnesty and returned to regain his literary fame. He wrote *D'un Château l'Autre*, describing his exile in Schloss Sigmaringen. He lamented his ruined reputation but never apologized for his antisemitism, even made additional statements of holocaust denial and how early in his life he had recognized the Jews as exploiters."

Joe, who was Jewish, declared, "Well, if you want the truth, I don't give a shit if Céline and Hamsun were antisemitic. What counts is they could write, and that goes for Ezra Pound, too."

Henry said, "Isaac Bashevis Singer calls Hamsun the father of the modern school of literature in every aspect— subjectiveness, fragmentariness, use of flashbacks, lyricism. Hamsun was a Nobel Prize winner, doncha know. Ernest Hemingway said Hamsun taught him to write; Hemingway recommended Hamsun to Fitzgerald. André Breton quoted Hamsun's novel *Hunger* at length in his Surrealist Manifesto. Hamsun is the Dickens of my generation."

"*Hunger* led Henry to start *Tropic of Cancer*," Joe said.

"True, true," Henry said. "In Hamsun, we assuredly have one of the most innovative literary stylists of the century. He wrote beautifully, poetically, savagely. He believed literature should explore the human mind; he pioneered stream of consciousness and interior monologue. His women are wonderful, unobtainable Hamsun showed us the way. His philosophy of what's necessary to be a writer is similar to Rimbaud's."

Opening his notebook, Joe quoted, "The writer ...'must immerse himself in the unpredictable chaos of perception, the delicate life of the imagination held under the microscope; the meanderings of these thoughts and feelings in the blue, trackless, traceless journeys of the heart and mind, curious workings of the psyche, the whisperings of the blood, prayers of the bone, the entire unconscious life of the mind.'"

Next up for discussion were the Transcendentalists, who had influenced Henry enormously. "Thoreau worked in his family's pencil factory for most of his life," Henry told us, then directed his remarks to Andy: "Speaking of your alma mater, Thoreau's maternal grandfather led Harvard's student Butter Rebellion, the first recorded student protest in the Colonies. And another Harvard tidbit: Thoreau refused to accept his Harvard diploma because it was on sheepskin."

Andy laughed. "Thoreau had his ideals, that's for sure."

"He did," Henry agreed, "and here's more in that vein: he

was teaching school, but resigned rather than administer corporal punishment. He was jailed for his refusal to pay taxes because of his opposition to the Mexican-American War and slavery. Definitely a man of principle, isn't that right? He was also one of the first American supporters of Darwin's theory of evolution, doncha know, and of course, his writing influenced not only me, but many others ... Gandhi, Tolstoy, Proust, Yeats, Hemingway, George Bernard Shaw ... Emma Goldman even referred to him as the greatest American anarchist."

Joe said, "I love his remark to his aunt in his final days, when she asks him if he's made his peace with God. Thoreau answers, 'I did not know we had ever quarreled.'"

"His last words were "Now comes good sailing," Henry said.

"Chalk up another early death, Henry," Joe said.

"Right, Joe. Thoreau died at only 44."

Joe said, "In *Walden*, Thoreau spoke of the 'the stupendous and cosmogonal philosophy of the *Bhagavad Gita*.'"

"Yes, the Transcendentalists were heavily influenced by the Vedas," Henry said, and turned to Walt Whitman. "Whitman is my spiritual ancestor. He had a tremendous influence on me. He was born in Long Island, by the way, in the Town of Huntington – that's around your neck of the woods, isn't it?" Henry asked me.

"Not far. It's in Suffolk County, and I'm from Nassau, but Huntington is only about 15 or 20 miles from my parents' home in Mill Neck. Andy's from around that region, too."

"Great Neck," Andy said. "Closer to the city."

Henry said, "Whitman moved to Brooklyn, where as a boy he was lifted in the air and kissed on the cheek by the Marquis de Lafayette. He left school at eleven years old and went to work, which was not uncommon in that day. He worked for several newspapers, including *The Long Island Star*. He taught school for a while. Imagine, a man with a 5th or 6th grade education, teaching, writing, editing. He became editor of *The Brooklyn Eagle*."

"Henry and Whitman share a lot in common," Joe said. "Henry's a Whitman man – 'a man without responsibility, a liberated man, a character cynical about the pretenses engulfing him,' as he says in *Tropic*."

"Sure, sure, Whitman and I see things alike, from a mystical standpoint, as it were. He suffered the slings and arrows because of his writing, as did I, doncha know," Henry said. "Whitman became the brunt of criticism due to the sexual themes in *Leaves of Grass*, for writing about death, prostitution, and homosexuality, taboo subjects. He tried to obtain a government post but was turned down on account of the sensationalism of his writing, but he redeemed himself after Lincoln died with his poem '*O Captain! My Captain!*' and got a job working in the attorney general's office."

"Henry has been compared to Whitman many times," Joe said. "John Dos Passos compared him to Whitman."

"He affected me deeply," Henry acknowledged.

Andy said, "If we're talking about Thoreau and Whitman, there's another Transcendental writer we should mention, who, like Thoreau, was a Harvard man."

"Ralph Waldo Emerson," Henry said, "who also had a great influence on me. A propos of Harvard, Emerson was Class Poet. He graduated at 18 and went on to Harvard Divinity School. But he abandoned the ministry. He said the profession was antiquated, that we were worshiping the dead forms of our forefathers, as it were."

"Same thoughts as Romain Rolland," Joe commented.

"Yas, yas, And Emerson created quite a scandal at Harvard when he gave a graduation address at the Divinity School, in which he discounted the Biblical miracles. Christianity, he said, had turned Jesus into a god like Osiris and Apollo. His comments outraged the establishment, he was denounced as an atheist and wasn't invited back for another thirty years."

Andy said, "His writing was rooted in the transcendental philosophy of Kant, Schopenhauer, Vedic thought, Swedenborg."

Henry said, "Later in life, Emerson started having memory problems; he would forget his own name. When asked how he felt, he would say, "Quite well; I have lost my mental faculties, but I am perfectly well.""

"An important distinction, to be sure," Andy said.

"Emerson has been called the American Montaigne," Joe said.

Henry was always very gallant and admiring of the dazzling Noreen Siegel. On this particular occasion, he complimented her several times on how beautiful she looked, on her special glow. Both Henry and Andy were fascinated with the way Noreen pursed her lips, and made much of it, Henry implying that Noreen was keeping a secret from the rest of us.

I brought up the subject of the controversial French Luchaire family, something I wanted to hear what Henry had to say about, but Henry and Joe were preparing to leave. Henry said, "I want to talk about that. Let's do it next week, shall we?" So Luchaire would have to wait. Nor did we discuss him the following week. Krishnamurti took precedence.

Andy had invited me to hear Krishnamurti speak in Ojai, the town in Ventura County where Krishnamurti had resided for many years, on property purchased by the woman who adopted him and raised him as a son, Annie Besant. Krishnamurti was a great favorite of Henry's, and Andy was impressed with him as well. The two spoke glowingly in praise of the world renowned guru. Was I missing something? Contrary to popular opinion, I was not enthralled with Krishnamurti. Despite his being revered by a lot of important world figures, he didn't register with me.

After a short discussion between the two, Henry directed a question at me: "Well, you've been quiet. You were there. What do you have to say on the subject?"

Tentatively, I began, "I don't like to be a dissenting voice, but..."

"Go ahead," Henry invited "You've every right to your opinion."

"Well, I'm sorry, I don't share your and Andy's enthusiasm. I don't think Krishnamurti is saying anything profound or original, and his personality is unappealing to me. I don't see the attraction."

"Continue. We want to hear your thoughts."

"The things he says are such platitudes. He seems full of himself, arrogant, smug. He strikes me as a rather unpleasant man. He's not particularly likable, not to me, at least."

Andy intervened, paraphrasing a quote from Nietzsche about how you don't have to like a person for him to be your best friend; the tailor who makes you a great suit is your best friend because he performs a service that enhances you, concluding, "You don't have to like Krishnamurti to be affected by him, Kirishnamurti is a master of reality."

Henry said, "You mention his platitudes, while Krishnamurti says men are reluctant to accept what is easy to grasp. Do you think this might be the problem for you?"

"Possibly," I conceded, "but still, I could never be his follower ..."

"Krishnamurti doesn't want you to be his follower," Henry returned. "He says man is always seeking salvation not through his own efforts but through an outside source, an outside system, a group or person, while what man needs is to become his own liberator. It's you who must emancipate yourself. You can never be free if you're someone else's disciple, if you place a guru over you."

"Man is his own liberator!" Andy echoed. "That's Krishnamurti's message."

"Okay," I said, "but Krishnamurti believes in the masters, doesn't he?"

"He does affirm the existence of masters, sure, sure," Henry agreed. "He says everyone believes masters exist, but believing is not enough. The important thing is to change ourselves, for us to become masters ourselves. For that, man must be stripped of his illusions, false ideals and beliefs, all his crutches."

"Just like Vedanta, and many other approaches," I pointed out.

Henry said a book about Krishnamurti by Carlos Suares, which he had initially read in Paris and since reread many times, had been a source of inspiration. "In Paris when I first heard of Krishnamurti, friends would read passages aloud from Madame Blavatsky, whom they called HPB, from Annie Bessant, Leadbeater, Rudolf Steiner. When he was only thirteen or fourteen, Krishnamurti was chosen by those Theosophist leaders who followed HPB – Bessant and Leadbeater – as the coming Savior. He was told he was the Messiah, the incarnation of Lord Bodhisattva Maitreya, the fifth Buddha. Krishnamurti believed what they told him, that he was the true successor of Jesus. He believed it for some time. Eventually he renounced that role, freed himself of vanity and every form of self-importance."

"Did he really? He seems full of self-importance to me," I argued. "It's not that I disagree with his philosophy, it's that I find him boring, pedantic, snobbish, and disdainful, like he places himself above the common herd. It's not what he says but how he says it that annoys me."

Andy stepped in, to say, "George Bernard Shaw once called

Krishnamurti the most beautiful human being he had ever seen. From having seen pictures of him when he was young, I can understand how Shaw would say that."

"That was back when Krishnamurti was a Theosophist," I said. "Yet Shaw ridiculed Theosopy, as in his play *Getting Married*, with the character of the Theosophist, Mrs. George." I knew this, having appeared in that same play at Vassar, directed by Leon Katz.

Henry continued talking about the positive aspects of Krishnamurti that so moved him: "He understands that meditation is an art. You learn it by practicing without technique, by watching the self in daily activities like walking and eating, speech, gossip, your reactive emotions, your hate and jealousy – becoming aware of these things."

"That's similar to Gurdjieff," I said, "and others."

Henry compared Krishnamurti to Vivekananda's ideas on limitation (*Moha*) and freedom (*Mukti*). He said, "It may seem that the purpose of spiritual practice is to make you into something other than what you are now, but in fact, the purpose is to reveal the full glory of who you really are. Spiritual practice removes limitations, frees you, and opens the conduit of Divine Power that lies behind what you believe yourself to be. 'Thou Art That' is not an intellectual formulation, Vivekananda says; it's the truth that's hidden behind our current limited view of ourselves. This ties in with Krishnamurti, that true meditation is the ending of thought, leading to a different dimension, beyond time."

Andy said, "Krishnamurti says world problems have their roots in our thinking, that our thoughts lead us to create a divided world. He says man wants the world to be changed, without acknowledging that the world problem is a reflection of the individual's problem."

"Exactly," Henry said. "Man is stultified by hope and fear. The myth he lives is that he may one day escape from the prison which he's created for himself, which he attributes to others. To this end, to overcome limitations, Krishnamurti founded several schools around the world."

"If he doesn't believe in systems, groups, and so forth, why found schools around the world?"

Bypassing my question, Andy said, "He says every moment should be lived as the now. That may sound banal, but it's very profound."

Again, I protested: "Being continually in the now is pretty nigh onto impossible. And why is it so desirable? A lot can be said for introspection, know thyself, for going back over your life, reappraising your past experiences. Also, we need to look ahead and plan the future. You can't do either of those if you're always in the now."

"Krishnamurti's tenets of evolution, reincarnation and karma I heartily subscribe to," Henry said, to which everyone agreed. "His message is living in the moment without fear, accepting, surrendering to everything that happens. He influenced Joseph Campbell, Aldous Huxley, Alan Watts ... and so many others."

While I didn't relish the role of devil's advocate, once again, I put in my two cents. "The spiritual teacher Meher Baba was critical of Krishnamurti. He said, 'Krishnamurti a new world teacher? God forbid ....You cannot compare Ramakrishna with Krishnamurti.. He does not have the slightest idea, not even a wisp, of the real Truth.'"

Andy said, "Sounds like professional jealousy to me."

Henry said, "As I've said many times, after years of struggle and search, I found gold with Krishnamurti."

Case closed.

CHAPTER FOURTEEN

The following Sunday, Henry, ever curious, asked about Andy. "Tell me more about that good looking man you were with last week. Is he your boyfriend?"

"Well, we've been seeing one another for the past several months. We have dinner together nearly every night, so I guess you would call him that."

"Oh, so this is serious, then?" Henry prompted. "I liked him. He's certainly well read. He's a Harvard graduate, he said?"

"Yes. He roomed with Jack Lemmon at Harvard. Jack was head of Hasty Pudding. Andy's taken me over to the Lemmons' home in Beverly Hills on a few occasions, and by the way, Henry, like you, Jack plays the piano."

"You appeared quite entranced with this man, if you don't mind my saying."

"I didn't realize it showed."

"Oh, it shows all right. One sees that immediately," Henry said, then asked, "So is there a future in the cards?" When I told Henry the problem was that Andy was anti-marriage, Henry said, "Hmmm ... hmmm ...I suppose he must have been previously married, then, which is what makes him marriage shy. Maybe he's being cautious based on past experience. But in a manner of speaking, I'm the last person who should be venturing an opinion."

"Why?"

"To me, it's only natural to marry a woman you fall in love with, isn't that right? I've certainly done it over and again, doncha know. But then, I'm an incurable romantic. I have no inhibitions as regards marriage. I'm all for it."

"Andy says he's a romantic, too."

Again, I brought up the topic of the Luchaire family, which Henry promised we were going to talk about but hadn't yet. Henry asked, "How is it you know about this family? Everyone in France knows who they are, they're a distinguished family of artists and intellectuals – but not well known in the U.S."

"When I was growing up in Long Island, Channel 5, then called the Dumont network, sometimes broadcast in Italian. The musical introduction was a Rossini overture. The channel signed off at midnight with the *Star Spangled Banner*. It was a great channel. They showed this 30's movie called *Prison Without Bars*, starring Corinne Luchaire. That was the first I ever heard of Corinne. Then I read about her life in an article in *Life* magazine, and came to know about her father as well. I thought she was so interesting, such a compelling, gifted actress."

"She was hauntingly beautiful in that picture," Henry agreed. "*Prison Without Bars* was her film debut. Mary Pickford called her the new Garbo. She had a certain air of mystery, a quality of *je ne sais quoi*."

I said, "That movie was directed by Leonid Moguy. I met Moguy on the beach at the Lido during the Venice Film Festival. The incident was written up in a 2 page spread in an Italian magazine, together with a photo of me in a bikini, which, believe it or not, the magazine retouched so it would look like the bikini wasn't as brief as it was. We spoke French, Moguy and I, after which he heard me speaking English to someone and said I should never speak English, because I had so much more charm in French."

"I know what he means ... hmmm...hmmm," Henry said, apparently sharing Moguy's opinion. "Another film Corinne Luchaire was famous for was *Le Dernier Tournant*, which was the first motion picture made from James M. Cain's novel *The Postman Always Rings Twice*. She was a brunette in that film. Much better as a blonde, doncha know – my opinion, at least. Another of her films was directed by Marc Allegret, who was once married to Simone Signoret, who had worked as Corinne's father Jean Luchaire's secretary."

"Hard to believe! Direct opposite poles, politically."

Henry said, "The film industry was active during the German occupation. In Paris, entertainment was going full blast, with an especially glittering social life for those who favored the Nazis. Those who cast their lot with the Gestapo felt they had good reason to, and some of them paid dearly for it after the war, including Corinne's father, Jean Luchaire. Luchaire may have seen the Nazis as a way to power and money, in addition to his political leanings."

Since the Luchaire family was unknown to most of those present, Henry spoke more about them. "Corinne Luchaire's father, Jean Luchaire, was a collaborationist, a leftist idealist who believed in a closer alliance of France and Germany, having actively promoted rapprochement as far back as the 1920's, ya know. He opposed the Versailles Treaty for being unfair to Germany. He was friends with Otto Abetz, together with whom he organized groups for Franco-German friendship. He founded newspapers, for which the likes of De Jouvenel and Pierre Mendes-France wrote articles. Despite the rise of Hitler, he still thought lasting peace was possible through political compromise between the two nations. He was a pragmatist, declaring that France should deal with Germany regardless of who was the country's leader. He said, 'Stresemann was nicer than Hitler, but Hitler is Germany.' Luchaire just went too far, he stepped over the line, and paid for it with his life.

"Luchaire's wife was the daughter of Albert Besnard, one of the leading French painters of his day. The Luchaires had several children, some of whom became involved in the arts, the most famous, of course, being their daughter Corinne. Corinne actually grew up around Nazis; her mother was Gustav Stresemann's mistress and moved to Germany with the children. Stresemann, for those who may not know him, was a prominent leader in the Weimar Republic. He is the man who could have saved us from Hitler, had he not died prematurely (and some say mysteriously). Hmmm ... hmmm... After the fall of France, when Abetz was the Third Reich ambassador in Paris, Luchaire held an important position as president of the Press Association, loyal to the Vichy government. Corinne became the brightest star in Vichy society. By then she was Otto Abetz's mistress, and the toast of Paris.

"The Luchaires escaped from France before the liberation, taking refuge in Sigmaringen, the Vichy government in exile. After VE Day, American liberators delivered them to the French. Corinne spent several months behind bars, was tried and sentenced to ten years' national indignity. Her father was found guilty, condemned to death for treason, and was shot. Abetz was sentenced to twenty years' hard labor.

"In my opinion," Henry said, "the swift execution of Jean Luchaire was probably a rush to judgment. After the war, guilt made the French eager to quickly punish traitors of all stripes, isn't that right? Unlike some of his contemporaries, Luchaire was not a Jew hater; on the contrary, he had many Jewish friends and Jewish relatives. Some believe his real sin was ambition and desire for money, which led him to cast his lot with the Germans."

"And what happened to Corinne?" Joe wanted to know.

"Another young death," Henry said. "Corinne died at only 28 years old. Just before that, she published an autobiography about her life under the German occupation. A sad story, a tragic death. She suffered from tuberculosis and never got treatment. She died bleeding to death at a bus stop."

Urged to tell more about the Luchaires, Henry crushed out his cigarette and continued, "The family had so many distinguished members. On his father's side, Jean Luchaire was the grandson of respected historians, the medievalist Protestant Achilles Luchaire and Jewish historian Jules Zellner. Then there was Luchaire's father, Julien Luchaire, a handsome man of great culture. Unlike his son, Julien chose resistance. He wrote a book about the difference between his and his son's beliefs. During the Occupation, along with numerous other artists and intellectuals, Julien and his third wife, who was Jewish, took up residence in the southern zone in Clermont-Ferrand, to protect his wife's family.

"Julien created the French Institute in Florence, the first of all French Institutes in the world. He also created the forerunner of UNESCO. He wrote histories of the popes, the church, the Borgias, political revolutions, Siena. He was a member of the French Academy. He wrote plays, including one directed by Raymond Rouleau that starred Corinne, which was made into a film.

"His first marriage was to the daughter of the philosopher and historian Lionel Dauriac. She was an economist and book editor at one of the big French publishing firms, Stock. Their two children were Jean and Marguerite, known as Ghita. Julien's third wife, Polish-German intellectual Antonina Silberstein, was a writer known as Antonina Valentin, who wrote biographies of Leonardo da Vinci, Mirabeau, Goya, Einstein, Picasso, El Greco, H. G. Wells, Streseman, and others. And lest this sound too incestuous, Antonina had also been the mistress of Streseman.

"As for Julien, after the war, he was ostracized because of his name and never really came back in style. He was a brilliant scholar whose day had passed, who paid the price for his son's sins."

"And Ghita Luchaire, Jean's sister? What happened to her?"

"Ghita married the psychoanalyst, dadaist/surrealist Dr. Theodore Fraenkel. Their friend Man Ray did an exquisite and very famous photo of Ghita, photographing her upside down. Ghita had beautiful long, thick, wavy blond hair, which, captured by Man, cascades to the ground. That photo is very well known," Henry said. "You must have seen it."

Henry lit another cigarette and took a deep drag. "Fraenkel was a friend of André Breton, too," he said. The two met in medical school, shared much in common, d'ya know, formed groups and wrote manifestos and tracts together, acted together, exhibited artistic works in the same dadaist venues. Both were strongly influenced by Jacques Vaché, who was one of the chief inspirations behind the Surrealist movement. As Breton declared, they were very taken with Rimbaud, Jarry, and Apollinaire, but it was Jacques Vaché to whom they owed the most. Vaché is yet another young death – he died at only 24 from an overdose of opium; some say it was suicide. He was known for wearing a monocle."

Continuing, Henry said, "Dr. Theodor Fraenkel was an interesting fellow, ya know. You've all seen him in that famous Max Ernst painting of the major surrealists, 'The Reunion,' sitting dead center, wearing spectacles. He participated in the demonstrations organized by Breton, Louis Aragon, Paul Éluard, Francis Picabia, and Tristan Tzara; he contributed to their magazines, appeared in their plays. At the Salon Dada he exhibited a sculpture; he wrote poetry. But years later, he refused to sign the leaflet written by the surrealists against Louis Aragon, and broke off relations with his friend of many years, Breton, because of it. Most all of his many letters to Breton disappeared, perhaps destroyed by Breton in a fit of anger. Fraenkel was also a close friend of Robert Desnos and Antonin Artaud. During the Spanish Civil War, Fraenkel joined the Republicans – along with George Orwell and a host of other idealists, and during World War II, he was with the Free French in England. I told George Orwell he was nuts, an idiot to go fighting in Spain, and I would have told Fraenkel the same thing, had I known him."

Henry flicked an ash into a nearby ashtray, took another puff, exhaled, and said, "Fraenkel's first wife was the beautiful and gifted Bianca Maklès, who acted under the stage name Lucienne Morand. Bianca was tragically killed when she fell off a cliff. She was one of the four celebrated Maklès sisters, each who married well known French intellectuals. Sylvia Maklès married the writer Georges Bataille and the psychoanalyst Jacques Lacan. Like her sister Bianca, Sylvia was an actress, best remembered for her part in Jean Renoir's *A Day in the Country*. She acted in several other Renoir films and worked with a number of other important directors – Prévert, Marcel Carne, Marcel Pagnol, Autant-Lara.

"Rose Maklès was the wife of painter André Masson, who was associated with surrealism, whose work Gertrude Stein was mad for; Stein was a prominent collector of his paintings. In World War II, the Nazis condemned his work as degenerate. With Varian Fry's help, Masson escaped France and ended up in Connecticut. Upon arrival in New York, U.S. customs officials inspecting his luggage found his erotic drawings. Denouncing them as pornographic, they ripped them up in front of him. His work became an important influence on American abstract expressionists, in particular, on Jackson Pollock. Simone Maklès, the fourth Maklès sister, married the writer, editor, critic, publisher, philosopher and politician Jean-Baptiste Piel."

Henry crushed his cigarette into the nearby ashtray. "Blaise Cendrars had a good friend, one of the surrealists, Robert Desnos, who was also close to Fraenkel. Cendrars used to drink with Desnos in a bar on the rue de Rivoli under the arcades, a couple of steps from the Place de la Concorde, from where you could see all Paris pass by without moving from your table. Desnos played a key role in the surrealist movement; he had a particular talent for automatic writing. He was also friends with André Breton, with whom he later had a falling out."

"Seems like a lot of people had their differences with Breton," Joe said. "But that surrealist novel Breton wrote, *Nadja*, is really interesting, Henry."

Henry agreed. "*Nadja* cast an unforgettable spell over me, ya know. Still does, after all these years. Breton included two unique photos in that book of Desnos sleeping. Desnos was also good friends with Picasso, Hemingway, Artaud, and Dos Passos. As a journalist, he published many critical reviews on jazz and cinema. He published poetry, novels and wrote a film script that was directed by Man Ray. Miro, another friend of Desnos, made plans to collaborate on a *livre d'artiste*, plans that were put on hold first because of the Spanish civil war and then World War II.

"During war, Desnos was with the Resistance. He was arrested by the Gestapo, deported to Auschwitz, then sent to Buchenwald, and finally to Theresienstadt. One day Desnos and others were taken from their barracks. They knew right away they were on the way to the gas chamber. Suddenly, Desnos jumped out of line, grabbed the hand of a woman in front of him and began to read her palm. He predicted a long, happy and successful life for her. One by one, everyone wanted their palm read. Desnos predicted the same destiny for all – long lives filled with happiness and abundance. The guards became so disoriented they were unable to go through with the planned executions.

"Desnos never was executed, but died of typhoid just weeks after the camp's liberation, another relatively young death – he was 44. The poems he wrote during his imprisonment were supposedly accidentally destroyed following his death. Some of his poetry has been set to music by a number of composers, including Poulenc."

Joe said, "So many sad stories and early deaths – Corinne and her father, Rimbaud, Desnos, Radiguet, and so many others. Henry, you mentioned Jarry, one of the inspirations of the surrealist movement. Didn't he die young too?"

"He did," Henry said, adding, "Alfred Jarry was a symbolist writer. His play *Ubu Roi* is considered a forerunner to the surrealist theatre of the 1920s and '30s. He contributed to absurdist literature and invented a fictional philosophy called pataphysics. He also wrote what is cited as the first cyborg sex novel, *Le Surmâle, (The Supermale)*.

"I suppose Jarry would rightfully be considered a midget, doncha know, as he was less than 5 feet tall. He lived in an apartment of unusually truncated dimensions. He could barely manage to stand up in the place, and his guests all had to bend over or crouch. Picasso was fascinated with Jarry. After his death, Picasso acquired Jarry's revolver and many of his manuscripts. He also made a famous drawing of him.

"Like Corinne Luchaire, Jarry died of tuberculosis, in his case, aggravated by drug and alcohol use. He was 34 years old. His last request was for a toothpick."

CHAPTER FIFTEEN

Henry asked several times, "How is your friend Marianne? When are we going to see her again?" He wanted to know her status, what was going on with her boyfriend, how serious was it, and so on. I repeated that Marianne was living with a very jealous psychologist, Dr. Myron Brodsky, to whom she felt she always had to not only please but cater to well beyond what most women would accept. Henry seemed disappointed at not seeing enough of Marianne. I continued, "Marriage is important to Marianne. She wants so much to marry Myron, but Myron doesn't want marriage. He's happy being divorced and wants to stay that way."

"Like that Harvard man friend of yours, the one who roomed with Jack Lemmon," Henry noted. "Marianne shouldn't have a problem if she wants to be married, though. She's a fantastic woman. Any man would be lucky to have her for a wife."

"True, but she's stuck on this guy Myron. What can you do?"

Henry said, "You know, sometimes the most incredible women will put up with men they shouldn't give the time of day to. It never ceases to amaze me, how women so often fall for the wrong men, that they seek approval and love from someone who can't give it, who's all wrong for them ... isn't that so? No doubt this Myron doesn't deserve her."

"You hit the nail on the head, Henry. Myron doesn't have a clue what a beautiful person Marianne is. He doesn't appreciate her fine qualities. He's very self-involved."

"What a louse. Who needs a guy like that?"

"Marianne does everything for Myron. She cooks and cleans, does his laundry, irons his shirts, picks up after him, straightens the apartment, keeps the place spotless – it would be a mess, were it not for her."

"This fellow doesn't know how good he has it, ya know? All that devotion, a beautiful woman catering to his every need in a way bordering on slavery, a woman who loves him beyond measure, who'll do anything to please him. Nothing's too good for this man. His shit don't stink, doncha know."

"Yes, he's really arrogant and egotistical."

"How unfortunate for Marianne. Why any woman would want to be with a man like that has always puzzled me. Why do women do this? Ya know, women are so much more evolved than men."

"Myron is selfish. He expects her to devote weekends to him – when it suits him."

"How did Marianne meet this character?"

"They had a car accident on Sunset Boulevard."

"If that's not fate, I don't know what is. Obviously, you're not crazy about Myron."

"I have a problem with him. The thing is, Myron made an unsolicited and unappreciated pass at me. They were dropping me off after dinner one night, and Myron left Marianne in the car to walk me to my apartment. At the door, he suddenly grabs me and bellows in my ear, 'I have to have you!' I was really annoyed. And at the same time, I was embarrassed for him."

"Embarrassed? Why should you be embarrassed for him?"

"That he was so obtuse, that he just presumed ..."

"Conceited of him, to be sure, especially to phrase it in that manner. No compliments. Hmmm ... hmmm ...nothing about your beauty, your intelligence, your spirit, your soul, why he was attracted to you, that he appreciates your mind. Just that he has to have you. All about him, yas, yaz...."

"And it was even worse, because Marianne is my friend, she's like a sister to me, so for him to do this to such a good friend ..."

"Not to defend him, but I understand his actions, the mentality behind it, ya know? I'm not saying I approve of his approach, or that I haven't indulged in some of that myself – hmmm ... hmmm – it's that I've seen men going after a woman with this tactic, and if I may say, some women do respond to the aggressive male's technique. Some men overpower a woman, and the woman is flattered to be desired so ardently. How did you leave it with him?"

"I told him no way. I said, Look, Myron, Marianne is my fiend, and I would never do anything to hurt or betray her."

"That was considerate of you. Quite a few women I've known were of the exact opposite bent, doncha know. It can be a free for all out there; rules don't apply. As they say, all's fair in love and war," Henry said.

"Unfortunately, yes."

"Hmmm ... hmmm... the problem for many men is they don't know how to love a woman, how to give of themselves," Henry said. "Your friend Marianne is not only a great beauty, but a truly lovely person – caring, sweet, gentle, romantic – *elle est très sympat, c'est une fille formidable* — and if I may say, *elle a du chien.*"

"You're so right, Henry. *Elle a du chien, bien sûr, et elle est très sensible davantage.*"

"*Oui, tu as raison.*"

CHAPTER SIXTEEN

The strange and tragic story of Mercedes Ospina haunts me still today, many years after I met Mercedes and introduced her to her idol and man of her dreams, Henry Miller. I still puzzle over what was going on in Mercedes' life at that time, what may have or may not have been going on between Henry and Mercedes, and what really happened at the end. In my mind's eye, images of her persist, always clad in a kelly green pant suit. In my mind's ear, I hear her unusually compelling and lovely voice. I see her quiet, dark haired teenage sister and her petite mother, visiting from South America. We are, the four of us, walking on the beach at Malibu, then suddenly, Mercedes leaps ahead of us and jumps in the air, exclaiming, "Henry! Henry! Henry! I love Henry Miller! Henry! Henry Miller is a god! Henry Miller is God! I love you, Henry Miller!" She then executes a pirouette followed by a cartwheel, stands up, and runs toward the ocean. Mrs. Ospina and her youngest daughter smile indulgently. Who could know that Mercedes Ospina, a young woman in her early to mid-twenties, would not live till autumn of that year, 1965?

I met Mercedes through Norman Hickman, who phoned from New York about her, saying she was from Colombia, South America, was reputed to be a talented actress, that she had just left New York for Hollywood to pursue her acting career. Not long after I hung up, Mercedes phoned.

"Norman Hickman gave me your number," she began, in perfect English. "He speaks highly of you. I'd love to meet you. Can we get together?"

We chatted briefly, and the next day, I picked Mercedes up at the small Beverly Hills hotel where she was staying,. We lunched together at a Hollywood natural foods restaurant. Mercedes was a very attractive, fashionable brunette young woman, cultured, well read, well informed, a graduate of Le Lycée Français in Bogotá, Colombia, who spoke fluent French and English as well as her native Spanish.

It was the first of many times I would see Mercedes, always wearing the same kelly green pantsuit. Pantsuits were just coming in style, and Mercedes was ahead of the curve, expressing surprise that I was wearing a dress, not a pantsuit myself.

She had come to Hollywood in hopes of making her mark on the silver screen, Mercedes said, and had three interesting avant garde film roles to her credit: Andy Warhol's *The Life of Juanita Castro*, shot in New York at Warhol's Factory; *Un Alma Pura (A Pure Soul)*, written by Mexican novelist Carlos Fuentes, filmed in Mexico, directed by Juan Ibáñez, which was one half of a three hour film called *Los Bienamados (The Well Loved Ones)*; and a Colombian feature, *El Detective Genial (The Genial Detective)*, in which she played the female lead and received star billing.

"*El Detective Genial* is a comedy," Mercedes said. "It was directed by René Cardona Jr., a Mexican director, writer, screenwriter, actor, and producer. He's a Taurus, and we got along famously. He wants me to do another picture with him soon."

All three of these films were to be released that year. In fact, *Juanita Castro* had already been released in March, while the other two were scheduled for August. Significantly, Mercedes had no agent, a decided drawback in Hollywood, but was hoping that networking would lead her to the right someone who would get behind her and push her career to stardom. Knowing the Hollywood system as I did, I feared Mercedes was naive, unprepared, overconfident and taking a risk arriving with such high hopes and so few professional resources.

I learned Mercedes was one of four girls, that her youngest sister, 16 year old Sandra, together with their mother, would soon be arriving from Colombia for a visit. Having been schooled at a French lycée, Mercedes was knowledgeable in French literature. We conversed both in English and French, and spoke about some of our favorite authors, Baudelaire, Villon, Zola, Sartre, Camus, Andre Gide, Mauriac, and others. We had similar tastes and quickly established an excellent rapport.

Henry's name came up. When she heard I actually knew Henry, Mercedes became excited, saying she worshiped the ground Henry Miller walked on, that he was the greatest writer of the 20th century, that she was dying to meet him, and could I, oh, would I introduce them? So I invited her to the Siegels. When I picked her up the following Sunday, Mercedes was once again clad in the same kelly green pantsuit. Over a period of a few weeks, I never saw her wear anything else.

Needless to say, Mercedes immediately went totally gaga over Henry. She was enthralled, thrilled in his presence. Henry was very attentive to her, recognizing her as the beautiful, chic, sophisticated and worldly young woman she was. Henry asked Mercedes about her experiences in the acting world, the people she'd worked with, particularly in the Warhol and Fuentes films.

Mercedes' voice had a unique timbre and transparent quality. Addressing Henry's questions in her unusually beautiful voice that was characterized by mellowness with a variety of modulation, Mercedes said, "*The Life of Juanita Castro* is high-camp farce. We had a lot of fun doing it. It's a subversive satire on Latin American politics, Fidel Castro's in particular, on the Cuban Revolution as seen through the eyes of Castro's sister Juanita. It pokes fun at machismo and totalitarianism. The movie is partly based on a *Life* magazine article in which Juanita denounced her brother Fidel, revealed her brother Raul was a transvestite, that Fidel had once appeared as an extra in an Esther Williams movie and wanted Marlon Brando to play him in a film version of his life, with Raoul to be acted by Frank Sinatra. My sister Marina plays Che Guevara in the film."

"Who else is in it? Anyone we would know?" Joe asked.

"Marie Menken, Ultra Violet and Elektrah have roles in it," Mercedes replied.

"Has the film been released?" Henry asked.

"Oh, yes, it premiered early this spring at the Cinémathèque in New York City."

"How did this Warhol film come about?" Henry wanted to know.

"Waldo Diaz-Balart was the catalyst. His sister Mirta was married to Fidel Castro, as you may know," Mecedes said. "They were divorced right before Fidel came to power. Diaz-Balart is now living in exile in a beautiful 19th century townhouse on West 10th Street on the north side of Tompkins Square Park. He's reputed to have left Cuba with one million dollars in cash."

"Which would explain the 19th century townhouse in the Village," Henry remarked.

Mercedes said, "Waldo invited Andy, Ronnie Tavel, the screenwriter, my sister Marina and me to dinner. The conversation turned to the political intrigues of the Cuban revolution, particularly the in-fighting on the part of the Castro family, and most particularly

Juanita Castro. Andy became fascinated and said we should do the life of story of Juanita Castro. Waldo has a role in the film too. We shot *Juanita Castro* at the Factory."

"And you played Fidel Castro?!"

"That's right. The male roles are played by women. Fidel, Raoul, and Che Guevara are all played by women."

"Interesting," Henry said. "What was the rationale behind the idea of having women play men?"

"I think that question invites endless speculation, which could go in several directions. Ronnie Tavel has never definitively stated why he wanted it that way."

"What are the speculations you refer to?"

"Well, a few years before this film was made, the CIA had plotted, if not to castrate Castro outright, at least to try to make him less virile by putting female sex hormones in his food. They figured his beard would fall off and his voice would become high-pitched like a woman's. Once his macho image was ruined, they thought he could easily be overthrown."

"An obsession with Fidel's sexuality seems to a factor in several CIA projects," Henry said. "And who plays Juanita Castro?"

"Marie Menken. She's an abstract painter and filmmaker who's been called the queen of American avant garde cinema."

"I know of her reputation," Henry said. "She's was mentor and muse to several underground filmmakers – Kenneth Anger, Stan Brackhage, Jonas Mekas, Maya Deren, and of course Andy Warhol."

"Didn't Anaïs appear in films by some of the ones you mentioned, Henry?" Joe asked.

"Kenneth Anger and Maya Deren's films, I believe," Henry said. "I'm familiar with Marie Menken's work as a filmmaker. She's created stunningly beautiful films with handheld cinematography. She's allegedly the inspiration for the character of Martha in Edward Albee's *Who's Afraid of Virginia Woolf*, and her volatile relationship with her husband – he's a filmmaker, too, Willard Maas – reportedly is the basis of that play."

Answering further questions about *The Life of Juanita Castro*, Mercedes said, "The format is reminiscent of Pirandello's *Six Characters in Search of an Author*, in which the playwright or stage manager, played by Ronnie Tavel, the screenwriter, goads a group of actors into doing an improvisation on Fidel and family."

Henry wanted to know about *Un Alma Pura* as well. Mercedes replied, "It was photographed by Gabriel Figueroa. He is wonderful. He was the cinematographer on John Huston's *Night of the Iguana*, and some of Bunuel's films as well. Manuel Barbachano Ponce is the producer. The director is Juan Ibáñez, a young man of only 26 or 27, who is just brilliant. This film is considered experimental, a part of the new Mexican cinema, *el Nuevo Cine*, which has been compared to the French *Nouvelle Vague*, to Goddard and Resnais, and to Italian directors Fellini and Antonioni. This is truly avant garde cinema, and very exciting. Gabriel García Márquez, Gabo, as he's called, is a good friend of Carlos'. They asked each other, what will we do? Shall we save the Mexican cinema or write our novels? Gabo and Carlos are now collaborating on films together."

"And still writing their novels as well, hopefully," Henry said.

To Henry's questions, Mercedes said that others who appeared on screen in *Un Alma Pura* included author-screenwriter Carlos Fuentes himself; British/Mexican surrealist painter Leonora Carrington, and a whole group of both Latin American and US intellectuals, most of them literary associates of Carlos. "There's Carlos Monsiváis, the Mexican journalist, Mexican novelist Juan García Ponce and Chilean writer José Donoso," Mercedes began, and reeled off more names:

"From the US, there was a group of Carlos' American friends and colleagues: Nelson Aldrich, United States Senator from Rhode Island, grandfather of director Robert Aldrich and related to the Rockefellers; author William Styron, a very close friend of Fuentes; Jason Epstein, co-founder of *The New York Review of Books*, editor and publisher at Random House for Norman Mailer, Vladimir Nabokov, Gore Vidal and countless others; *Village Voice* cartoonist Jules Feiffer (who shares a January 26 birthday with Epstein); novelist Bruce Jay Friedman (*A Mother's Kisses*); conservative pundit Norman Podhoretz of *Commentary* magazine; Carol Southern, wife of author and screenwriter Terry Southern (*Candy, The Magic Christian, Dr. Strangelove*)."

"Quite a cast," Henry said.

"Oh, that's not all," Mercedes said. "There's also the fabulous Sergio Aragonés, *Mad* magazine cartoonist who came to the United States with just twenty dollars in his pocket; British journalist Sally Belfrage, Hans Koning – Koningsberger; American writer Frank

Conroy, who's an accomplished jazz pianist, by the way; playwright Jack Richardson, whose first play won an Obie and a Drama Desk Award – he's married to Anne Roiphe; actors Erika Carlsson and Bernard Faber – he was born in Paris and has appeared in a lot of Italian movies.

"Not to forget John Philips Marquand, who under the name John Phillips published the novel *The Second Happiest Day*, his father being the immensely popular Pulitzer Prize winning author of such enormous bestsellers of the 1930s and 40s as *H. M. Pulham, Esq., The Late George Apley, Point of No Return* and the *Mr. Moto* spy stories."

"Mr. Moto!" Henry exclaimed. "Joe, didn't you appear in one of those Mr. Moto movies?"

"Sure did – *Mr. Moto's Gamble*. It was one of my first Hollywood jobs, back in the late 30's."

"Before Dean Martin and Frank Sinatra became famous," Henry said, citing two of Joe's buddies who always saw to it that Joe worked in all their films.

Mercedes said, "I really enjoyed being in the company of all of those noteworthy individuals. Marquand was interesting."

Henry said, "The Marquands are descendants of the Transcendentalist writer Margaret Fuller, and Marquand *père* is a cousin of Buckminster Fuller. Through marriage, he became a part of the Rockefeller family."

I added, "His sister-in-law, Blanchette Hooker, is married to John D. Rockefeller III. Mrs. Rockefeller is a noted art collector, a great benefactor of Vassar, a major donor to the Vassar Art Center."

"Marquand served at the Mexican border at the time of the Revolution, doncha know," Henry added. "So many interesting people were there at that time ....Ambrose Bierce disappeared there, never to be heard of again, and nobody knows to this day what happened to him. Well, at least Marquand survived, to give us some very fine books. Marquand, ya know, became one of the most popular novelists in the country," Henry continued: "His satires of the upper class are hilarious and very accurate. But the academic literati turned up their noses at him because of his so-called hack work, writing for slick magazines like *The Saturday Evening Post* when he needed to make money."

"Purists don't think a writer should have to make money," Mercedes said. "Marquand's son says his father's financial success is definitely the reason academia ignores him."

"Maybe somebody can tell me why a two hundred and some odd year-old *Saturday Evening Post,* inaugurated by Benjamin Franklin, doesn't qualify as literature, but being published in *Playboy* does," Henry said. "Marquand's social portrait of twentieth-century America should be likened to Balzac's *Comédie Humaine,* but unfortunately for Marquand, the critics just refused to take him seriously."

"Henry," Joe said, "Those same critics might have been talking about you."

"So you know Carlos Fuentes," Henry said, "you worked on this interesting film with him."

Mercedes said, "Carlos not only wrote the story and screenplay, but also has a role in the picture. It's made in Spanish, of course, but Carlos speaks flawless English."

"I've heard he's an intriguing and cultured gentleman, and quite a man with the ladies, doncha know ... hmmm... hmmm," Henry said. "Didn't he spend a good part of his early years in the United States?"

"That's right. His father was a Washington diplomat. Later, Carlos lived in Havana during the Cuban revolution."

"That must have been interesting to hear about, considering your playing Fidel Castro in the Warhol film," Henry said, then asked, "What is Fuentes' *Alma Pura* about?"

"Claudia, an aristocratic young woman, travels to Switzerland to retrieve the body of her brother, Juan Luis," Mercedes replied. "In flashback we see that Claudia and her brother had an incestuous relationship, and that she managed to drive her brother's fiancée, Claire, to her death... with tragic consequences for all three."

"It sounds like a picture I'd like to see," Henry said, then told us, "Ya know, I've heard that when he starts the writing process, Fuentes poses himself a very valid question. He begins by asking, 'For whom am I writing?' This is important, knowing your audience, even if that audience is yourself – or shall I say, perhaps especially if your audience is yourself."

"Carlos is a fascinating man," Mercedes said, "a man of enormous wit, charm and talent, and certainly one of the most admired writers in the Spanish speaking world. His first novel, *La Región Más Transparente – Where the Air Is Clear –* put him on the map.

It's the story of a man who abandons his revolutionary ideals to become a powerful financier."

"I haven't read that one yet, but it's on my list," Henry said.

"You'll love it, Henry," Mercedes promised. "Carlos is a truly great writer. The book paints wonderful vignettes of Mexico City, inequality and corruption, using the techniques of interior monologue and subconscious exploration you admire so much in writers like Knut Hamsun. Another one of Fuentes' novels, *The Death of Artemio Cruz – La Muerte de Artemio Cruz*, is considered a seminal work in South American literature. That novel explores the corrupting effects of power and how the revolutionaries' original ideals became distorted."

Henry asked if there was any significance in the title, *Un Alma Pura, A Pure Soul*. Mercedes said, "In the introduction to the story on which the film is based, Fuentes references French writer Raymond Radiguet's novel, *Count Orgel's Ball, El Baile del Conde de Orgel*, a quote from which he takes the title of the story: 'The unconscious maneuvers of a pure soul are even more singular than the wiles of vice.'"

"Interestingly, we were just talking about that book recently," Henry said. "Another friend of Jeanne's was reading it."

"Since then, I've read it too, Henry," I said. "A wonderful book."

Mercedes said, "The Radiguet book is also referenced a couple more times in the story, not just in the introduction. It apparently made a big impression on Carlos."

"It's a book one wants to read and reread for sheer admiration of how well that genius young man could write," Henry declared. Then, to Mercedes, he said, "You say Leonora Carrington plays a role in the film. I'm familiar with Carrington's work as a surrealist painter. She's originally British – and is also a writer – who's lived most of her life in Mexico."

"Salvador Dali calls her the world's most important female artist," Mercedes said.

"I know something about her," Henry said. "She comes from an unlikely background, considering the events in her life. Like Caresse Crosby, who was presented to the King of England, Leonora was presented as a debutante at the court of George V."

Mercedes picked up the story: "When she was twenty,

Leonora ran off to Paris with Max Ernst, who was 25 years older than she. Ernst left his second wife for her, and introduced her to his friends – Picasso, André Breton, Man Ray, Dalí, Miró, Arp and all the rest. They would meet regularly at the Café des Deux Magots in St. Germain des Prés.

"When the war was starting, Ernst was arrested by the French for being a hostile alien, and thanks to friends, was discharged, but right after that, was arrested by the Gestapo. He escaped and fled to America with Peggy Guggenheim, which caused Leonora to have a nervous breakdown. She ended up in Spain and Portugal, where a Mexican diplomat friend of Picasso's married her to get her out of Europe.

"In New York she had solo shows at the Museum of Modern Art. Her marriage of convenience was dissolved in good faith, and she moved to Mexico, where she met up with Breton, Dali, Frida Kahlo, Diego Rivera and all the others in that group at that point in time. Her art is full of animal imagery and occult symbolism, alchemy, the Kabbalah."

"Yas, yaz, her paintings are mysterious, magical," Henry said.

Mercedes nodded. "Dark canvases dominated by large, sinister-looking houses, strange, menacing tall women in black cloaks; ethereal figures; horses, dogs, birds."

"Ernst loved birds, too. He painted them all the time."

"One of her books, *La Maison de la Peur*, is illustrated by Ernst. Ernst taught her everything, she said."

"Before Leonora," Henry said, "Ernst had left his first wife and family, entered France illegally, and lived for some time in a *ménage à trois* with Paul Éluard and his then wife Gala. Ernst and Éluard collaborated on *Les Malheurs des Immortels* and other projects. Later, as everyone knows, Gala left Éluard and married Dali.

"Ernst had quite a varied career," Henry continued. "He collaborated with Joan Miró on designs for Diaghilev. He appeared in Buñuel's film *L'Âge d'Or*. He sculpted and spent time with Giacometti. Arp and he were friends for fifty years. Prior to marrying his third wife, Peggy Guggenheim, Guggenheim acquired many of Ernst's works, which she displayed in her museums. The marriage didn't last, doncha know. Ernst married for the fourth time in a double ceremony with Man Ray here in California. They lived in Sedona for a while. In the U.S., Ernst was instrumental in the development of abstract expressionism."

"We mentioned André Breton," Mercedes said. "He was a good friend of Leonora's, both in Paris, New York and Mexico. As founder of Surrealism, Breton said Mexico is the most surrealist country in the world."

"And he defined surrealism as 'pure psychic automatism,'" Henry said. "Breton met Trotsky in Mexico; they wrote a manifesto together. As for Trotsky, I used to see him in a tearoom on Second Avenue in New York, doncha know. And a propos of Breton, he joined the French Communist Party, but they expelled him. The Vichy government banned his writings, too. He escaped to the US with the help of Varian Fry." Henry's perpetual cigarette was now approaching butt status, as he exhaled a cloud of smoke. "Breton is an avid collector – paintings, photography, trinkets, kachina dolls. There's more than five thousand items in his Paris apartment.

"But tell us more about your Carlos Fuentes film, Mercedes," Henry asked, returning the focus to Mercedes. "Did you have a good part in the picture? Were you the female lead?"

"No, I have just a small role," Mercedes answered. "Carlos actually wrote the story and the screenplay especially for Arabella Árbenz. She is the star."

"Arabella Árbenz – is she a new actress?" Henry asked. "I've not heard of her."

"Arabella was well known in Paris as a runway and photographic model, where she used the name Bella Nova. Arabella is an extraordinarily beautiful woman, and you could say she's notorious," Mercedes said. "Her father was President of Guatemala, Colonel Jacobo Árbenz Guzmán. His picture was on the cover of *Time* magazine."

"Ah, so she's well connected in important circles, you might say."

"Well, she's been the mistress of millionaire lovers like Baron Philippe de Rothschild and Mexican television magnate Emilio Azcárraga Milmo, known as El Tigre. El Tigre installed her in an elegant penthouse in Mexico City. He gave her a Mercedes-Benz convertible that she smashed up the first time she ever drove it. He showered her with gifts and paid for her every whim. Not that she needs the money – her mother's family is from El Salvador and they're filthy rich."

"Did you two become friends during the filming?" Henry asked.

"Yes, indeed. I like her very much. She can be a bit stubborn, but then, everybody has their faults."

"Hmmm ... hmmm," Henry said, obviously intrigued with the description of Arabella. "How old is this woman? Early 30's, perhaps?"

"No, she's 24," Mercedes said.

"That young – hmmm ... hmmm," Henry remarked, his thoughts trailing off.

"Young, yes, but Arabella has had a remarkable life. She's lived all over the world -- New York, Paris, Switzerland, Mexico, Czechoslovakia. Moscow, Uruguay, Guatemala, El Salvador, Cuba. Arabella has always been a rebel. And she is an extremely intelligent, learned woman. You would be amazed how well read, how educated she is. Besides Spanish, she speaks English, Italian, French and Russian.

"In her Paris modeling days, she was known to be wildly extravagant. She would take over night clubs to toss terrific parties, and would never be seen using the same limousine twice in the same week. She posed for artistic nudes in Paris and also in Mexico. She has a very beautiful body. One of the nudes of her is by the famous photographer and cinematographer Gabriel Figueroa, our cameraman. And in *Un Alma Pura*, she appears in full frontal nudity, the first time a Guatemalan woman has appeared naked in motion picture history."

"Hmmm ...hmmm," Henry mused, a smile spreading across his face, as he was no doubt conjuring fantasies of the beauteous Arabella.

"Does Henry have a girlfriend?"

The key in the ignition had barely been turned when I was startled by Mercedes' question. My answer was I knew next to nothing about the present status of Henry's private life; all I knew was he was divorced from his fourth wife, or at least I thought he was.

"Oh, I hope he doesn't have a woman in his life," Mercedes said, "because I am so, so, so absolutely, insanely and desperately in love with this man!"

I was surprised by her ardor and by hearing her repeat, "I love him, I love him, I love him! Henry, Henry! I want you, Henry, I want Henry! Oh, Henry!"

When we pulled up in front of her hotel, as if transported to another dimension, Mercedes looked at me with imploring eyes and said, "I must know everything about Henry, past and present. I must find out if he has a girlfriend. Please, can you find this out for me? I really need to know."

From that day forward, Henry Miller was the central focus of Mercedes' life. Henry had become her world. Every time we spoke, he was the nearly exclusive topic. Mercedes meant what she said; she adored Henry, she worshiped him, she was mesmerized by him, she wanted him. I wondered how a young woman of her age could be so obsessively attracted to a man in his mid-seventies, a man half a century her senior, to the extent of seeing him in a romantic light. If Henry was far too old for me, it was hard to understand one of my contemporaries falling in love with him. I touched on the subject of Henry's age with Mercedes, making every effort to be diplomatic.

"You don't think he's too old for you?" I suggested in one of our conversations.

"Age is meaningless," Mercedes asserted. "It's just a number. What counts is the inner man, the soul, the essence of a man. Henry is absolutely the most phenomenal, the most incredible human being I have ever met I've dreamed all my life of knowing and loving someone like him."

I tried to point out as gently as possible that age comes with irreversible disadvantages, that a man in his 70's can't embody what would be expected of one who was 30 or 40; it was just not humanly possible.

Mercedes disagreed. Knowing the May-December love story of Leonora Carrington and Max Ernst, perhaps Mercedes envisioned herself in a similar role with Henry, even though the spread in their ages was greater than that between Leonora and Max. Perhaps reading my mind, Mercedes brought up the Carrington/Ernst affair, comparing her feelings for Henry potentially leading to something as exalted and unique as the relationship between Ernst and Carrington, yet even more so.

"Their love affair ended at the outbreak of WW II, perhaps because Ernst was an opportunist and saw a better life for himself with Peggy Guggenheim, who had a lot to offer him in terms of advancing his career and reputation. In that sense, Ernst really used Peggy Guggenheim. But nothing like that can interfere with Henry and me. We are meant to be together. I know it."

I listened without comment, not wanting to criticize or offer advice, as Mercedes went on, "I just want the chance to be special to him, to be the only woman in his life, to show him I am the one woman with the key to his soul," she persisted. "I understand Henry the inner man, his pain, his need for love. I know he was in love with June and with Anaïs, but neither of these relationships could give him what he needed. June was cruel, a tormentor by nature, Anaïs had two or three other men at the same time as Henry, so each in her own way, despite any positives, each of them was playing Henry. I would be totally devoted to Henry, I would give my all to him, that's the big difference."

A few days later, she called to ask if I had found out if he had a girlfriend yet. I said I still didn't know. In fact, I didn't want to ask anybody, because asking would have made me uncomfortable.

"Henry is so sensitive," Mercedes gushed. "People don't appreciate Henry's enormous sensitivity. And Henry is so kind, such a loving man. All his life, Henry has sought but never found love. You know, it's horrible the way he was crucified by people who don't have a right to lick his boots. All that hypocrisy about his writing about sex ... to identify him chiefly as a writer of salacious books is a sacrilege. No one understands the real Henry. I do! I understand."

I didn't know what to say, so I mostly kept quiet as Mercedes continued, "Henry had no anchor, he was poor and essentially homeless. Henry was a man suffering for lack of a loved partner. He had to transfer all his thwarted love instincts into pornography as a protective shield to cover his pain. He wrote about these sexual experiences that had a tawdry, lurid feel to them, because he was frustrated and because that was the only kind of sex he could get, given his poverty. Henry was always seeking true love, which he never found. I understand that. I want Henry to know I understand. I want to show Henry what love is. It's not too late for him.

"Henry is a living god," Mercedes went on. "Henry Miller is absolutely the most fabulous man I've ever met. I feel his presence deeply, deeply, at the bottom of my soul. I feel there is a great oneness between us. It's a very rare thing, the feelings I have for

Henry, the incredible way in which he and I are linked."

When Mercedes' mother and youngest sister arrived in town, the four of us lunched together at the Sea Lion, a restaurant in Malibu with a view of the ocean below. Both Mrs. Ospina and her youngest daughter, Sandra, were impressively fluent in English. Mrs. Ospina, a sweet and very polite woman, expressed interest in me and wanted to know more about me. Somehow, probably because of the movie in which Mercedes played Fidel Castro, we got on the subject of the Cuban faux dentist I'd had in New York, the colorful Dr. Crucet.

I was saying, "Dr. Crucet made me two crowns, and all went well up until the time he had to fit them. He kept filing them down, until I was left with a far different bite than I originally had. My bite has never been the same since."

"Oh, that's really too bad," Mrs. Ospina sympathized. I noticed Mercedes wasn't listening, that her gaze was far off, her head turned to one side.

"Then I found out he wasn't a really a dentist."

"Not a dentist? He was an impostor?"

"Yes. He was a pretty crazy guy. His fingernails were weird too. The Batista government had pulled all his nails out."

"Oh, terrible. They tortured him," Mrs. Ospina shook her head disapprovingly.

"What did the nails look like?" sixteen year old Sandra, mouth agape, asked.

"Yellow and brown, stubby, with ridges. They were so ugly I didn't want to get a really close look. They were disgusting."

Mother and younger daughter were aghast, but Mercedes's mind was elsewhere as I continued, "He told me he had done work on Marlene Dietrich, and that from her dental bones he could tell she was older than she was admitting."

"Interesting," said Mrs. Ospina. "I wouldn't be at all surprised."

"I wonder how a big star like Marlene Dietrich ended up going to this man for her dentist," dark haired Sandra mused.

"I also wonder how such a person could even practice dentistry in New York City," Mrs. Ospina said. "Wouldn't he have needed a license?"

"I'm sure he would have. I can only guess he either forged

one or got it through some kind of bribe or payoff," I said.

"And how did you meet this so-called dentist?" Mrs. Ospina wanted to know. "How did he happen to become your dentist?"

"He was recommended to me, strangely enough, by the husband of my dad's secretary, who was a New York State patrolman."

"Yes, that is very unusual," Mrs. Ospina agreed.

Mercedes had started to get fidgety. She looked preoccupied, bothered by the conversation. Clearly, she had no interest in what we had been talking about. Suddenly, she broke in and started talking about Henry.

"Henry suffered," she told us, "but that suffering was necessary to realize the incredible person Henry became, the Henry of today. Henry has done a great work apart from his books; the greatest work of art he has achieved is Henry himself." Once the spigot was turned on, Mercedes went full throttle on her favorite subject of Henry: "Henry is so far above and beyond the way he has been portrayed by the media. Henry is a great intellectual, a philosopher, a deep thinker, a seeker, sage, and mystic. He hasn't been given the credit he deserves. He's a man of tremendous wisdom, an artist and a musician of enormous talent. He's light years from the merciless way the media described him, putting him down as a filthy book writer."

Sandra looked puzzled by her sister's intensity, even embarrassed. Mrs. Ospina, glancing at me with a benevolent smile, seemed overwhelmed by Mercedes but made no comment. I surmised the three of them must have had endless conversations in the same vein, all about how wonderful Henry was and how much Mercedes loved him. Being family, mother and sister must have been accustomed to Mercedes' gushing excesses.

Following lunch, the four of us went for a stroll on the beach. All of a sudden, throwing up her rams, waving them in the air, Mercedes leapt ahead of us, twirling around and crying out, "Henry! Henry! I love you, Henry Miller! Henry Miller is a god! Henry Miller is God! I love you, Henry Miller!"

As Mercedes ran toward the ocean. Mrs. Ospina and Sandra both smiled tolerantly, as if they had witnessed this type of behavior many times before.

CHAPTER SEVENTEEN

I had no idea whether Mercedes was making progress in reaching Henry's heart, mind, soul and beyond. While I could certainly understand her admiring Henry and basking in his charisma, on a male-female romantic basis, my understanding stopped. Was it emotional attachment to a father figure? Mercedes seemed to want more, something indefinable. But who was I to criticize? Henry had had young wives before, wives decades younger than he, and age surely hadn't mattered to him, so given his record, Mercedes could conceivably have a chance. And if the age difference didn't bother her, it was not my place to interject my own prejudice.

A followup Sunday at the Siegels, Henry told us that a friend had given him some background information on Arabella Árbenz's father: "The Colonel was President of Guatemala from 1951 to 1954. He was ousted in a coup d'état engineered by the United States government, by our CIA under Allen Dulles, and replaced by a military junta. United Fruit Company that owns Chiquita Banana is Guatemala's largest landowner. They were threatened by Árbenz's Marxist land reform initiatives and lobbied the CIA to get rid of him."

The topic switched to French poetry. Mercedes' love for the poetry of Rimbaud pleased Henry, who wrote a book on Rimbaud and regarded the French poet as one of his greatest literary influences. Henry said, "Rimbaud died young. He was only 37 when he died. His best known works were produced while in his teens. In fact, sadly, he gave up writing before he was 20."

Mercedes, her eyes glued lovingly to Henry's, nodded. "I know. Victor Hugo called him an infant Shakespeare."

"Modigliani did a wonderful portrait of him," Joe interjected. "Henry owes a great debt to Rimbaud."

"Sure, sure, Rimbaud is very close to me in spirit," Henry affirmed. "He and I share a common mother problem, in a manner of speaking. Rimbaud helped me recognize my mother fixation. I'm not done with it yet, ya know. It's been a good decade since my mother's gone, and there are still those unresolved issues." Henry told us more about Rimbaud's life. "Rimbaud's father deserted the family and his mother raised the children very strictly, so much that Rimbaud ran away more than once to escape her. She would punish her kids by making them recite a hundred lines of Latin verse by heart, and if they made even one mistake, she'd deprive them of meals."

"The mother thing," Joe said, shaking his head. "The bad mother is such a big part of Henry's life."

"Joe was lucky to have a mother he loved. I was not," Henry said. "Mine was a mother from hell, and I do feel a tremendous bond with Rimbaud in that respect, ya know." Henry continued on Rimbaud: "In his teens, Rimbaud sent some of his poems to Paul Verlaine, who sent him a ticket to Paris. Rimbaud lived with Verlaine and his wife; the two men were having an affair. Rimbaud described *this ménage à trois* as a *drôle de ménage* with his pitiable brother and a crazy virgin – Verlaine's wife, that is, who wasn't really a virgin, since she was pregnant. Rimbaud portrayed himself as the infernal groom.

"The two poets scandalized the Paris literary world, leading a wild, drunken life with absinthe and hashish, doncha know. They took off for London, lived in Bloomsbury and in Brussels. When their relationship deteriorated, Verlaine, in a drunken rage, picked up a revolver, fired it at Rimbaud and wounded him. Verlaine was arrested for attempted murder and sentenced to prison.

"After Rimbaud gave up writing, he enlisted in the Dutch Army, went to the Dutch East Indies, deserted, and eventually sneaked back into France. He went to Ethiopia, where he became friendly with the father of the future Emperor Hailie Selassie. He developed what he initially thought was arthritis, was misdiagnosed and had his right leg amputated. The post-operative diagnosis was cancer."

"He died in 1891 – the year Henry was born," Joe said. "One genius leaves the world, another enters it."

"Such a sad story," Mercedes said, with tears in her eyes, her entire being focused on Henry.

"Rimbaud was truly a *poète maudit*," Henry said.

"Yes, yes!" Mercedes exclaimed, "a tortured soul. His belief of what's necessary to become an artist is a form of self-flagellation. The poet makes himself a seer by disordering of the senses, he said."

Henry expanded on the thought. "His poetic method entailed reaching the unknown through derangement of the senses, consuming all poisons but keeping their essence, if you will. You're right, Mercedes, he believed the artistic process involved great suffering, torture and superhuman strength to arrive at the unknown."

Mercedes said, "My favorite of Rimbaud's poems is his most famous, *Le Bateau Ivre – The Drunken Boat* – it's so beautiful."

Henry picked up the strain. "The tale of a boat that breaks free of human society when its handlers are killed. At first thinking that it drifts where it wills, it soon realizes it's being guided. It sees visions both magnificent and terrible. It ends floating, washed clean, wishing only to sink and become one with the sea."

"I also love *Le Soleil Était Encore Chaud* and *Une Saison en Enfer*," Mercedes added. "Picasso, Nabokov, and so many others have been influenced by Rimbaud's poetry and life."

"Paul Valéry declared that all known literature is written in the language of common sense, except Rimbaud's," Henry said.

While we were on the subject of French poetry, I mentioned I had recently found, among my papers, a poem by another 19th century poet, Alfred de Vigny, "*La Mort du Loup*, which I studied in a course I took at Vassar. I was surprised I had typed out the entire poem. Not sure why I went to all that trouble."

"You must have had a special liking for it," Henry pointed out.

"Yes, at the time, but I had forgotten about it – and de Vigny."

"Poor sonovabitch," Henry said, "I think it was his destiny to be forgotten. Like so many other 19th century writers and artists, he led a sad life, a life full of disappointment. He was the product of an aristocratic family whose fortunes had declined. His marriage was unhappy; his wife, an Englishwoman who never learned French, became a semi invalid; they had no children; and his father-in-law remarried, depriving him and his wife of their expected inheritance. De Vigny's historical novel, *Cinq-Mars* was very popular, but his fame as a writer in the Romantic category was supplanted by Victor Hugo, who stole his thunder, you might say. It took de Vigny several attempts to be elected to the Académie Française. And so on – obstacles and difficulties all the way.

"For several years, he was the lover of Marie Dorval, a popular actress of the day who had many successes at the Odéon.

For her, he wrote and produced a play on Thomas Chatterton, which is considered one of the best of the French romantic dramas. But the affair had its emotional ups and downs. George Sand entered the picture, which turned into something of a scandal. De Vigny was interested in Buddhism, common among French writers and intellectuals of that period.

"A pessimist and stoic, he endured his disappointments, illness, physical and emotional pain with stoicism."

"That's very much evident in *La Mort du Loup*," I said. "It's the only poem that ever made me cry."

"Why do you suppose that is?" Henry asked, a fresh cigarette poised between his yellow-tipped, nicotine stained fingers. "What is it about the poem that caused that reaction? Why did it make you cry?"

"It's so graphic," I said. "Preparing the knives, hiding the guns, perceiving the wolf's eyes, sighting the wolf's children dancing under the moon, playing together in silence; the claws, how the wolf knew he was lost, his retreat cut off ... the knife penetrating his entrails, the wolf bathed in blood just looking at them, licking his wounds, closing his eyes, dying without uttering a single cry ... the poet's shame and his addressing the animal, 'the sublime animal,' he calls it... he says the animal knows how to leave this world and all its ills, to see all one did on earth that one is leaving behind; he says only silence is great, all the rest is weakness. He tells the wolf I understand you well, savage voyager, and your last look went straight to my heart. The wolf taught him a great lesson, that his soul should arrive at this high a degree of stoicism, that to cry and to pray are equally cowardly; and then he concludes that like the wolf, he too should suffer and die without speaking."

"Of course, it's so much better in French!" Henry said.

"Definitely. Maybe because I'm such an animal lover ..."

"You, St. Francis of Assisi, and Isaac Bashevics Singer," Henry said

"You're right about French, Henry," I said. "The poem is so moving in French."

"*La Mort du Loup* is certainly one of his finest works," Henry agreed.

Mercedes discovered to her utter despair that she had competition. She was crushed to learn Henry had "four, maybe even as many as six women on the string." Even worse, someone had told her Henry had a decided preference for Asian women.

Hating to see her so totally devastated, I hastened to reassure her. "A man of Henry's age can't handle that many women," I said. "He can have them as friends or as fans, but not as serious lovers. And as for the Asians, don't forget, he's married several Caucasians."

"I just want to be unique to him. I know I can be unique," she said plaintively. "If I can't be uniquely Henry's, I will die!"

Again I tried to make light of Henry's alleged four to six women on the string. Mercedes was not assuaged. "I understand Henry's suffering," she said. "That's why he identifies so much with Rimbaud. But I want to help Henry. I want to make him happy. I want to give him all the love in my heart, so he will never suffer again. I want to share all and everything with him, I want to be his. Henry is a living god! What an incredible man!"

Mercedes talked about Henry nonstop, constantly, incessantly. On one level, her obsession with him seemed like an advanced case of hero worship. In a way, it was not unlike Henry's fantasizing of women, dreaming the impossible dream. But unlike Mercedes who wanted something concrete, Henry could content himself with his imagination of what might be in an alternate universe. He didn't have to admit to himself his fantasies were all in his head, unrealistic, unrealizable. He didn't seem to care; he lived for the fantasy nonetheless; it kept him going. Henry's psyche thrived on teasing his own mind with the scenarios it created, no matter how impossible. All he wanted was the other person to participate, which as Maria Graciette had described, was almost like phone sex.

Mercedes was thrilled. We were invited to Henry's house for dinner. Henry lived at 444 Ocampo Drive in Pacific Palisades. When I turned the car onto his street, Mercedes became ecstatic. "Oh, my God!" she exclaimed, "Henry lives on Ocampo Drive! Oh, my God, this is too much! I can't believe it!"

"Believe what?"

"I must tell Henry about this. Oh, this is such a sign!"

I waited for an explanation. Mercedes, silent a moment, finally said in a soft voice, "Victoria Ocampo is one of the most renowned and revered women in all Latin America. The fact that Henry lives on a street named for her is so meaningful to me.

Victoria Ocampo is one of my great heroes."

Someone other than Henry, a person who was never properly introduced, opened the front door, and ushered us into a hallway with staircase to the right. We walked past a space containing lots of writing and drawings on a long white wall, to a room dominated by a ping pong table, a piano and an L shaped desk. The desk was neat and orderly; the entire house was neat and orderly. My eyes skimmed over a patio directly outside glass doors at the end of the room, with a pool beyond. Henry was playing ping pong, a game he loved, with Joe Grey. Seeing us, Henry put down his paddle, the game apparently over, and greeted us warmly. He was wearing a pink shirt with a beige sweater vest. Mercedes immediately told him how excited she was about his Ocampo address.

Henry lit a cigarette. "You're right about the eponymous street name," he said to Mercedes, "and by the way, Jeanne, Victoria Ocampo is an Aries like you." He elaborated. "She's a fabulous person, a writer, an editor, a publisher, a feminist, one of the most remarkable women of the entire twentieth century. She first started publishing her magazine, *Sur*, about thirty years ago. *Sur* is the most important literary magazine in South America. She also founded a publishing house of the same name as well. She's published the world's most important writers – Federico García Lorca, Jorge Luis Borges, Ortega y Gasset, Carl Jung, Camus, Sartre, Virginia Woolf, Kerouac, Gabriela Mistral, Andre Gide, Thomas Mann, T. S. Eliot, André Malraux, Octavio Paz ..."

"And Henry Miller!" Joe finished.

"Yas, yaz," Henry said, circling his cigarette in the air. "Henry Miller too, that's right, Joe." Henry took a drag and continued, "Victoria was raised at a certain time and in a certain class which restricted her life in the extreme. She couldn't go anywhere without a *dueña*, a chaperone. She wasn't allowed to go to school, but had to be educated by tutors. Her first language was French, her first book, on Dante, was written in French. She was also fluent in English and Spanish. Forced into an unhappy arranged marriage, for years, unsuspected by anyone, she had a secret lover. She came from great wealth on both sides of the family, and was known for helping a number of authors and poets financially. She hosted Nobel Prize winner Rabindranath Tagore during his stay in Argentina, and at that time, Tagore was even more worshiped than Krishnamurti."

My eyes were drawn to photos that covered the walls everywhere. Mercedes wandered around as if in a trance, overjoyed at seeing everything in the house, as if its entire contents were sacred, as if she were on holy ground. Henry's L shaped desk was sacrosanct, as was his remarkable bathroom. "He has photos of his friends everywhere," Mercedes rhapsodized to me. "His bathroom has pictures of Ludwig of Bavaria's castle, of Lao Tsu." To Henry, she said, "Henry, your bathroom photos made me want to stay there forever."

Of Lao Tsu, Henry said, "Popular legends tell of his conception, when his mother gazed upon a falling star, how he stayed in the womb for sixty-two years, and was born when his mother leaned against a plum tree. He then emerged a grown man with a full grey beard and long earlobes, symbols of wisdom and long life. He was reborn in many incarnations. In his last incarnation as Lao Tsu, he lived to nine hundred and ninety years. Some legends say he was the teacher of the Siddartha Gautama, or was even the Buddha himself."

Mercedes and I each played ping pong singles with Henry, then doubles with him and Joe. Naturally, they beat us. After that, dinner was served at a long table. As we finished eating and were drinking more wine, the name arose of a precocious child prodigy whose achievements throughout his short life were legendary. Henry began talking about this man, a "Blaise" of great fame, not Blaise Cendrars but Blaise Pascal, saying here was a truly phenomenal genius, another one who died young. "Pascal was born in Clermont-Ferrand, Auvergne. He made important contributions in the areas of theology, mathematics, philosophy and physics. He was also an inventor."

Mercedes said Pascal was one of her favorite 17th century figures. From his omnipresent notebook, always within reach, Joe read, "Pascal invented the first bus line, which moved passengers within Paris. He introduced a primitive form of roulette and the roulette wheel in his search for a perpetual motion machine. He invented the hydraulic press and the syringe. Pascal's Wager, Pascal's Triangle, Pascal's Law, Pascal's Theorem — all these he's known by today, centuries later. As a teenager, he did pioneering work on calculating machines; he invented the mechanical calculator that did addition and subtraction, called the Pascaline

"And that's not all. Pascal wrote a brilliant treatise on projective geometry at the age of 16. He produced a treatise on the hexagram; his essay on conics is still known today as Pascal's Theorem. He wrote an important treatise on the triangle, known as Pascal's Triangle. He wrote on the volume of solids. He refuted Aristotle's claim that nature abhors a vacuum. He wrote the mathematical theory of probabilities. Originally applied to gambling, today it's extremely important in economics. Pascal's work was so precocious that Descartes was convinced Pascal's father had written it.

"In *Pensées*, Pascal surveys philosophical paradoxes: infinity and nothing, faith and reason, soul and matter, death and life, meaning and vanity. From this, he develops Pascal's Wager, which he uses to justify belief in God. He asserts empiricism is insufficient for determining major truths; first principles can't be reached, he says; there's no way to know assumed principles are true. Pascal wrote on the subject of axioms upon which conclusions are based. He says the ends of things and their beginnings are concealed from us in an impenetrable secret. He agrees with Montaigne that achieving certainty through human methods is impossible. First principles, he said, can only be grasped through intuition. He said that man is equally incapable of seeing the nothingness out of which he was drawn and the infinite in which he is engulfed."

Henry continued, "Below the quantum level is a subquantum world, if you will, and below that, the levels are endless. Ultimate truths are forever beyond our grasp, do you see? Pascal was a proponent of a splinter group from the main body of Catholicism known as Jansenism, a precursor of existentialism, which got him in hot water more than once."

Mercedes said, "Pascal is regarded as one of the most important authors of the French classical period, and is one of the greatest masters of French prose."

Joe, still reading from his notebook, said, "T. S. Eliot described him as a man of the world among ascetics, and an ascetic among men of the world."

Henry said, "Pascal had poor health and died at only 39. Just think, if he had lived longer what more he might have accomplished."

"Add him to the list of lives cut short by early deaths," Joe said.

"Joe likes Pascal; he's also a big fan of another 'P'– Proust, that is," Henry was saying. "Joe, what can you tell us about Proust?"

"Proust wrote the ultimate memoir, a memoir to end all memoirs," Joe said. "*In Search of Lost Time*, also known as *Remembrance of Things Past*, has more than 2,000 characters. Graham Greene called Proust the greatest novelist of the 20th century, and Somerset Maugham said his chef d'oeuvre is the greatest fiction to date."

"Proust was a dilettante and a social climber," Henry said. "Through his school mates, he had access to the salons of society, the salons of the widow of Georges Bizet and others, which provided him with his literary material."

"Proust had a close relationship with his mother," Joe said. "He was a closet homosexual, and one of his lovers was Reynaldo Hahn."

Mercedes said, "Proust spent several years reading Carlyle, Emerson, and Ruskin. He translated Ruskin's *Sesame and Lilies*."

"Then we have his *Contre Sainte-Beuve*," Henry said. "Sainte-Beuve, the celebrated 19th century literary critic, became friendly with Victor Hugo, doncha know, and had an affair with Hugo's wife, which resulted in their estrangement. Then, as fate would have it, when Sainte-Beuve was made a member of the French Academy, wouldn't you know, it was Victor Hugo who had to give the reception speech."

Oddly enough, it was the Siegels's teenage son Lee who told me Victor Hugo continued to have sex with his wife three times a day when he was into his 80's. That wife of his must have been pretty busy if she was also having an affair with Sainte-Beuve.

"*Port-Royal* is Sainte-Beuve 's masterpiece – a history of the Jansenist abbey of Port-Royal des Champs, near Paris," Henry said.

"With which Pascal was associated," Mercedes said.

The long white wall with writing and drawings in Henry's home doubled as a guest book. Here, visitors could become creative, take felt tipped pen in hand, write gushing compliments to Henry, aphorisms from poets and philosophers, and either express their own original thoughts or draw amusing pictures and cartoons. I believe utilizing the wall in this manner was an inspiration Henry derived from Caresse Crosby, whose wall at her home in France, Le Moulin du Soleil, was similarly dedicated. After the war, Caresse was upset to learn Nazi troops who had set up base in her home had painted over her guest book wall. Along with covering over the signatures of Salvador Dali and D.H. Lawrence, the Nazis covered the signature of Hitler's beloved, Eva Braun, who had signed her name when she visited the Crosbys with an Austrian big game hunter she was dating. Henry's wall contained many entries, including numerous quotes from Montaigne written by Joe. At Henry's request, Mercedes and I both wrote something that night, mine in French.

Henry often used to ask me, in French, about my cats, using the double entendre *ta chatte*, meaning both "your cat" (female) and "your pussy." This was enough to convince me that Henry would be happy to go all out in my direction, if given the chance. Henry was an incredible, utterly delightful man, but as I told Maria Graciette, I did not want to encourage him on a romantic basis or, in fact, as someone with whom to engage in sexual banter. Had he been a few decades younger or I a few decades older, it might have been a different story, but since we were born more than forty years apart and I was not into elderly men, end of story. I tried to be careful not to give any indication of having romantic inclinations toward Henry, making it a point not to respond to suggestive remarks that might lead where I didn't want them to, deliberately ignoring any hints in that direction Henry made toward me. When Henry would ask, with a glint in his eye, how was my "*petite chatte*." I would dismiss the obvious and play it straight with some silly answer, like, "I just took my cats to the vet this week."

Saying that Céline was a great cat lover or that Edgar Allen Poe had a cat named Caterina who perched on his shoulder while he wrote would somehow end up as a prelude, so that "*ta chatte*" or "*ta petite chatte*" would be contained in Henry's next line. At the back of my mind was always the fear that Henry could have designs on me, if for no other reason than for his need for fantasy, and to push the envelope to see just how far he could take things.

Something strange was afoot, only I didn't immediately suspect it. Henry was beckoning me to the back of the house. He got me alone there on some pretext and quickly made a grab. I hadn't seen it coming, but before I knew what was happening, Henry had made his moves. He was eager and aroused, and I was mortified and intimidated, uncomfortable because I didn't want to hurt Henry's feelings. But I didn't want this. Didn't Henry know that? Couldn't he pick up the signals I'd been sending out?

I was wearing five inch platform clogs. Henry was not that tall, and in the clogs, I towered over him. Still, he found my mouth. It felt like I was bending over in a very awkward position. This couldn't be happening, but it was, and there was no way I could escape gracefully. So against my will, I ended up kissing Henry. To this day I remember that kiss. A tremendous amount of saliva just poured thickly out of Henry's mouth. When I broke away, Henry's mouth was frothy and wet with it and so was mine. Anaïs Nin said of Henry, "He knows the technique of kissing better than anyone I've met." This was not my experience kissing Henry.

Neither of us ever mentioned the incident after that. I felt guilty because of Mercedes, knowing how utterly in love with Henry she was. Why had Henry not chosen to corner her instead of me? She was in the next room and I didn't want to hurt her feelings either. I thought how upset she would be if she knew Henry had made a pass at me.

I recalled a line from Edmund Wilson. In one of his books, Wilson describes a character in upstate New York who gives the impression he was "ashamed of being old." The words went through my head because there was no shame in Henry; he never felt old in his mind, he was eternally young in that part of his being, willing himself at seventy-something to be the equivalent of a young man of thirty or forty at most. In his mind, this was how Henry saw himself. He had to know, but pretended otherwise. He didn't want the truth. He wanted fantasy at all costs. Another line went through my mind, a line from George Bernard Shaw's *Heatbreak House*: "Old men are dangerous." I should have thought of that earlier and been prepared.

I hoped Mercedes would never know about that kiss that I never wanted in the first place.

It may have been that night or perhaps another night at Henry's for dinner, when Henry gifted me with two of his lithographs and autographed them, suggestively, in French. One contained the line *"molle à la fesse, folle à la messe"* (crazy at mass, soft in the ass), which, being in French, I mistakenly supposed must have been written especially for me, but later discovered was a line Henry used with any number of women, including those who spoke no French. The other inscription, also in French, probably was directed uniquely at me, in which Henry told me to be sure to take care of myself, *"toi et ta petite chatte."* I had both lithographs framed.

During the sixties and seventies, I was making frequent trips to New York and Europe, where I would sometimes stay several weeks or as much as three and four months at a time. While visiting my parents weekends at their home in Mill Neck, Long Island and staying in the city at Norman Hickman's during the week, from time to time, I often wondered how Mercedes and Henry were interacting.

Norman, a Navy PT boat commander in World War II, recipient of the Distinguished Service Cross by Great Britain and the Bronze Star by the United States, was crazy about the TV show *McHale's Navy* and never missed it whenever it was aired. Together, we watched an episode I was appearing in, *"It's a Mad, Mad, Mad, Mad World,"* in which the entire naval crew faces courtmartial unless they can locate a girl with a heart-shaped beauty mark on her ankle. *Moi.* That evening, we enjoyed dinner in Norman's huge dining room overlooking the East River, served by Norman's devoted Irish maids Molly and Mary, who had been in the employ of Norman's parents and regarded Norman as their surrogate son. Molly and Mary, both dyed redheads, were now quite elderly and arthritic, but each day they still faithfully trudged at the crack of dawn to early mass at St. Patrick's Cathedral.

I asked Norman, "You introduced me to Mercedes Ospina. What do you know about her?"

"I hardly know her at all," Norman replied. "She's a friend of a friend who asked me as a favor to see what I could do for her, since she wants to make it in acting. I introduced her to a few people in New York, but I met her only briefly and never got to know her."

"Can you tell me anything about her, her background, anything at all?"

"All I know is she is supposed to come from one of the best families in Colombia."

"I'm sure that's so. I've met her mother and one of her sisters, and they're lovely people. Well, I wanted to know, because I'm a bit concerned about Mercedes."

"Why?"

"Because she's in love with Henry Miller, and ..."

"Henry Miller, the writer? *Tropic of Cancer* Henry Miller?

"Yes."

"Good God, he's old enough to be her great-grandfather!" Norman sputtered.

Returning from my trip to the East coast, I was curious to find out what developments might have been taking place between Mercedes and Henry during the time I'd been away. I tried Mercedes' phone number, but found it wasn't working.

It was Dr. Siegel who gave me the shocking news that Mercedes Ospina was dead. Dead? Mercedes dead? At first I could not process it. How could that possibly be? How could Mercedes be dead? She was too young to be dead. Slowly, reality sank in. How? Why? What happened? When someone young dies, one immediately thinks suicide, accident, murder, drug overdose, malfeasance, anything but "natural causes." By way of explanation, most of those we knew in common said simply, "she passed away," and left it at that. But what was the cause of death? What did she die of? I asked Dr. Siegel, who gave the medical answer, "cardio-respiratory failure," which didn't satisfy my question as to underlying cause. Doesn't everyone who dies experience cardio-respiratory failure? What event prompted the cardio-respiratory failure? It seemed improbable that someone as vibrant as Mercedes could suddenly no longer be living. Mercedes had died September 22, 1965, the same day actor Charles Boyer's 21 year old son killed himself playing Russian roulette.

Henry was shocked as everyone was, touched by Mercedes' short life and tragic ending. Whether Henry realized the extent of her adoration of him and the importance he played in her life, I will never know. When I spoke to him about Mercedes, he just kept shaking his head, and said the word "tragic" several times. He was saddened, he said. But Mercedes' death seemed to be as much of a mystery to him as to everyone else who knew her.

While in New York, I had picked up a copy of the August 16, 1965 Spanish edition of *Life* magazine, which contained a cover story on the upcoming opening of the film *Un Alma Pura*. Pictured on the cover was a striking photo of Arabella Árbenz. I showed the magazine to Henry. "Beautiful!" he exclaimed. "This young lady surely has a big future ahead of her. She'll be a huge international star."

But there was more to come, another shocker, another young death. Arabella Árbenz, 24 years old, star of the film *Un Alma Pura*, committed suicide on October 5, 1965. It happened in a restaurant in South America, in Colombia. According to one newspaper account: "Arabella Árbenz, daughter of a former Guatemalan president, pulled a gun in a Bogotá restaurant after an argument with her bullfighter husband Monday and shot herself in the head, police said." The account was only partially accurate. Newspapers called Arabella a "Mexican actress," which she wasn't, nor was the bullfighter her husband.

As newspaper columnist Walter Winchell wrote: "She shot herself before the very eyes of bullfighter Jaime Bravo. Bravo was identified as her husband, which came as quite a shock to his American wife, actress Ann Robinson, mother of his two children. Miss Robinson was not aware that she had been divorced, or that Bravo had remarried... Jaime may be a great Romeo (he is supposed to have had four wives before Ann)..."

I asked Henry if he knew any details about Arabella's tragic suicide. He said, "It's hard to understand what could possibly have caused such a terrible event. I heard there's some speculation about her being into marijuana and LSD, but that's hardly an adequate explanation. Why does a beautiful young woman, especially one whose life is on the ascendant, take her own life? And in such a violent manner and in a public place. Can you beat it? Killing herself just a few weeks after a huge cover story on her appears in the Spanish edition of *Life* magazine. She had everything going for her, everything was coming her way. What could possibly have motivated her to do this?"

Carlos Fuentes was quoted as saying that all the girls in their circle were beautiful, but the most beautiful of all was the tragic, fragile "hothouse orchid," Arabella Árbenz. And now here were two young, beautiful women in their mid-twenties, Arabella and Mercedes, both appearing in the same movie, dead within two weeks of each other.

Only recently, so many years later, I found on YouTube a degraded old black and white copy of *The Life of Juanita Castro*. The quality is marred by a garish, greenish tint. Mercedes sits in the second row, right side, near center, wearing a light colored form fitting cap sleeve dress accessorized with a pendant on a long chain. Her hair is blunt cut, a length between chin and shoulder. I notice her square jaw, her determination, her melodious voice of compelling range and resonance. She frequently places a hand pensively on her chin; she lights, then smokes a series of cigars. She speaks both English and Spanish, in the latter gives a 15 minute impassioned speech in the Fidel vein. She is attentive, focused, intense, strong, dynamic, always in the moment. She is an exceptionally interesting listener. Although Marie Menken received top billing and was the more publicized actor, Mercedes' was the more important role. Further, Menken frequently blows her lines, seems drunk (which apparently she was), and swills beer throughout. I noticed how Mercedes was always in character, a true professional. Genuine, sincere, dedicated to her work

All these ensuing years, the why and how of Mercedes' death has remained elusive and incomprehensible. These ensuing decades, I have carried in my mind two images of Mercedes, always in her kelly green pant suit, one of her jumping in the air on the beach at Malibu, her mother and sister looking on; the other, lying dead on the beach, the ocean gently lapping ever closer to her motionless body. I could not shake the mental image of her being discovered on the beach, dead. After all the time that has passed, nearly 50 years, I don't know why I have that image of Mercedes lying dead on the beach. Was there any truth to it, or did my mind conjure it? Whatever the cause, her demise was unfathomable. I still often think of her mother and sisters, of the grief they must have felt. There is another Colombian actress by the name Mercedes Ospina who is not "our Mercedes." I wonder if she has any idea about the young woman who once carried her name.

I still ask myself: did Henry know any more than I did? And if he did, what wasn't he telling?

CHAPTER EIGHTEEN

Given our mutual musical backgrounds, Henry and I often spoke about music. Henry got a kick out of some of my childhood musical experiences, as for instance, in the fifth grade, when I founded the Lily Pons and Andre Kostelanetz Fan Club. I would write to the Bell Telephone Hour at NBC and to Pons' husband, Andre Kostelanetz's CBS radio show for free tickets, then organize my entire class to attend, en masse, with chaperones, of course. It was a big adventure for us kids, taking the Long Island Rail Road to Manhattan, then walking up the few city blocks to the RCA Building or the place from where the CBS shows were broadcast, followed by the actual radio concerts themselves. When Henry said, "You had an interesting childhood – conventional, yet unconventional," I thought he would appreciate hearing the following story (which he did):

Every Saturday, without fail, I listened to the Metropolitan Opera matinee performances on ABC Radio, station WJZ, "the blue network," sponsored by Texaco, hosted by Milton Cross. My distant cousin by marriage, Marcia Davenport, was often an intermission guest on the Opera Quiz section, along with Deems Taylor and Boris Goldovsky. I was a subscriber to *Opera News*, which cost something like $4 a year back then, and was lucky enough to be taken to any number of opera performances by my grandmother and Aunt Marie. But there was one important opera event I was eager to attend for which no adult supervision was available. What to do? How to get there?

Joan Fitzgerald and Alberta Barber, two classmates and I, devised a plan. Adding our ages together, we totaled thirty years. We then combined some letters of our surnames to arrive at a fictitious name for a fictitious thirty year old chaperone who, we told our parents, had agreed to accompany us to the city. The special event was the annual meeting of the Metropolitan Opera Guild, held at the Met's historic Broadway and 39th Street building. The meeting was spearheaded by noted society maven Mrs. August Belmont and retired diva, Spanish soprano Lucrezia Bori, who was reputed to be descended from the Borgias. The Met's General Manager, retired Canadian tenor Edward Johnson, put in an appearance to give a speech, and there was even some entertainment provided by the tall, dark-haired, comely Canadian mezzo Mona Paulee. Just walking through the Met's fabled lobby, its walls covered with framed black and white photos of opera greats past and present, being seated in the orchestra level and beholding the Met's famous gold curtain were thrills beyond compare. We were the only children present; everyone else, mostly women, looked old, even older than our mothers. We were in heaven, at least I, for sure was, transported to a magical world, made even more exciting after the meeting by approaching black clad, white haired Mrs. Belmont, who wore a big black hat, and diminutive, henna haired Madame Bori, glittering diamond (or possibly rhinestone) earrings adorning her small ears ... and actually engaging them in conversation! They must have wondered who the heck we were, three unchaperoned starry eyed ten year olds on the loose. These were indeed heady times. But the spell was not to last. When I got home, my parents had somehow discovered the truth, and I was spanked for having lied to them. This is the only time I can recall ever telling my parents a lie.

The story brought a big laugh from Henry.

Henry told us about a fascinating woman, Winnaretta Singer, the Princesse de Polignac. "Winaretta was a Capricorn, a renowned music patron," he said. "She was the twentieth of twenty-four children born to Isaac Singer."

"Isaac Bashevis Singer, the writer?" Joe asked.

"No, Isaac Singer, inventor of the sewing machine. She was an heiress to the sewing machine fortune Her mother was Singer's second wife, a Frenchwoman who was the model for the Statue of Liberty. Winaretta was born in Yonkers, New York, but spent most of her life in Europe."

"And she was a princess, you say?" Joe asked.

"She was twice a princess, having married two princes. The first marriage didn't work out, mainly because she was a lesbian and prince # 1 was straight, but she lucked out in marriage #2 to the Prince de Polignac, a gay composer. They had a wonderful union, albeit unconsummated, based on their mutual love of music," Henry said. "Winaretta was one of the greatest patrons of the arts who ever lived. She and the Prince de Polignac established a salon in Paris which was a haven for avant-garde music, ya know. She commissioned works by Stravinsky, Erik Satie, Darius Milhaud, Poulenc, Kurt Weill, Debussy, Fauré, and Ravel; she was a patron to

Nadia Boulanger, Arthur Rubinstein, Vladimir Horowitz, Ethel Smyth, the Ballets Russes, the Paris Opera, the Paris Symphony..."

"Winaretta, where were you when Henry needed you?" Joe asked dramatically.

Henry laughed, acknowledging Joe's remark. "Her salon was frequented by Isadora Duncan, Cocteau, Monet, Diaghilev, Colette and Proust. Winaretta was an accomplished musician herself, who performed as a pianist and organist, and she was an excellent painter who exhibited at the Académie des Beaux-Arts. She also led in the development of Paris public housing for the poor, commissioned Le Corbusier to construct shelters for the Salvation Army, worked with Madame Curie in World War I to convert private limousines into mobile radiology units serving wounded soldiers at the front. With Consuelo Vanderbilt Balsan, she helped construct the Hôpital Foch, which is one of the best hospitals in France, noted for renal transplants, and which includes a school of nursing."

"Didn't you ever meet her, Henry?" I asked. "You should have."

"No, I didn't. I certainly wish I had. Incidentally, her younger brother, Paris Singer, who had a child with Isadora Duncan, was one of the architects and financiers of Palm Beach, Florida, doncha know. And one of Winaretta's lesbian affairs was with a married woman whose biological father was King Edward VII."

"You just mentioned Ethel Smyth, Henry," Joe said. "I never heard of her. Who is she?"

"Dame Ethel Smyth? British composer and women's suffragette. She's another musician who lost her hearing, along with Fauré and of course Beethoven. After she became deaf, she gave up composing and wrote and published ten successful books."

"Fauré went deaf too?"

"Fauré not only went completely deaf, but leading up to it, sounds became distorted, so that high and low notes sounded painfully out of tune to him. An unprecedented national musical tribute was held for him at the Sorbonne, headed by the president of France, in which his own works were performed, but he was unable to hear a note."

Henry knew one of the favorite chansons in my repertoire was Fauré's *Après un Rêve*, based on Baudelaire's poem of the same name. "Fauré was the leading French composer of his day," Henry said. "He was the organist at the Madeleine and director of the Paris Conservatoire. He taught many composers who became well known – Ravel, Koechlin, Nadia Boulanger. He had a romantic attachment for several years to the singer Emma Bardac. His *Dolly Suite* piano duet was dedicated to Bardac's daughter Dolly. After Bardac, his mistress for the rest of his life was the pianist Marguerite Hasselmans, daughter of Alphonse Hasselmans."

"These creative and artistic people in times past always seemed to have interesting love lives. Much more interesting than those of today," Joe said.

"Give it a few more decades and you'll be reading things about our contemporaries that sound that way too," Henry replied.

"Did you ever play some of his piano pieces, Henry?" I asked.

"No, they're difficult to play; even Liszt found them challenging. The fingering is more suited to an organist, which Fauré was, than to a pianist," Henry said, adding, "Fauré was extremely attractive to women. It was rumored in Parisian musical circles that some of his most talented pupils were his illegitimate children."

One of the composers Henry and I shared a passion for was Eric Satie. "In addition to being a composer, Satie also did a remarkable amount of writing, doncha know – he wrote for several dadaist publications and also for the American magazine *Vanity Fair*," Henry said.

"Satie was an eccentric, all right, he made some, in my opinion, unfortunate decisions. We all make our share of poor choices, isn't that right? But Satie's were more life altering than most, some bound up with his stubbornness, his rigid character. He was a bit strange, in a manner of speaking... hmmm ... hmmmm... he was the official composer and chapel-master of the Rosicrucian Order, the Ordre de la Rose-Croix Catholique du Temple et du Graal. He founded a church of which he was the sole member, the Église Métropolitaine d'Art de Jésus Conducteurm, and named himself Maître de Chapelle.

"Satie wrote several religious works, but his bread and butter money was made as a cabaret pianist, composing and adapting hundreds of popular music pieces for piano and voice, many of which have been lost. He later repudiated all that music as trash, beneath him, just something he did for the money."

"Like Henry writing porn for that fabled oil baron," Joe said.

"Paris was the artistic capital of the world then," Henry said, "and continued to be when I was there, which was a good part of the reason I wanted to be there in the first place – Paris was the place to be.

"My friend Blaise Cendrars put on concerts at the studio of the painter Émile Lejeune, whose walls were decorated with canvases by Picasso, Matisse, Léger, and Modigliani. They would play music by Satie, Hönegger, Auric and Durey. These concerts gave Satie the idea of assembling a group of composers around himself devoted to avant garde music, which came to be known as Les Nouveaux Jeunes. They were the forerunners of Les Six."

"Les Six?" Joe asked.

"Les Six was a group of six Montparnassian composers," Henry said, "Auric, Durey, Hönegger, Milhaud, Poulenc, and the one woman, Germaine Tailleferre."

"Tailleferre and I share the same birthday," I interjected, "April 19."

"Satie abandoned the Nouveaux Jeunes less than a year after starting it, and Cocteau, who had maneuvered his way in, took over. Satie worked with Cocteau on a few productions. Through Picasso, he mingled with Cubists like Braque, with whom he also worked on projects. Satie knew several of the Dadaists – Marcel Duchamp, Man Ray ..."

"Who influenced you more, Henry, the Surrealists or the Dadaists?" Joe asked.

"Both, of course, but more so Dadaism. The Dadaist movement was truly revolutionary, it showed the insanity, the absurdity and the worthlessness of life. The Dadaists were an incredible bunch.

"Satie and Suzanne Valadon, mother of Maurice Utrillo, had an affair. Satie was devastated when she left him. That may have led to his alcoholism. He was a heavy drinker, died of cirrhosis of the liver, ya know. He led a sad life – he was a loner, an eccentric, a genius who set himself apart."

"You mentioned Darius Milhaud, Henry," Joe began.

Henry said, "Yes, Milhaud was a member of Les Six, and is one of the most prolific composers of the 20th century. Milhaud left France around the same time we all did at the start of the war, and came here to the United States, where he's been teaching at Mills College ever since. He's taught several students who've made their mark – Burt Bacharach, Dave Brubeck, and others."

I told Henry some of Milhaud's songs were in my repertoire: "*À une fontaine, À Cupidon, Tais-toi, babillarde, Dieu vous garde ...*"

"Ah, Ronsard!" Henry exclaimed, recognizing the works, "*Les Chansons de Ronsard.*"

I was surprised Henry knew these vocal pieces, but really, why should I have been? He knew something about just about everything. I said, "Milhaud wrote the *Chansons de Ronsard* for Lily Pons, my childhood idol. I heard her perform them at Carnegie Hall when I was about ten years old."

"Those Milhaud Ronsard chansons are utterly charming."

When Henry mentioned something about the house Anaïs had in Louveciennes just outside Paris that had been owned by Madame du Barry, I asked him if perchance he knew the *Chanson de Marie-Antoinette*.

"Do you sing that too?" he asked.

"Supposedly written by Marie Antoinette, who many don't know was a talented musician, and yes, I do sing it."

"It ends on a high note," Henry said.

"An F above high C."

"You have that range?"

"It's a very brief note, sung for an instant of an instant. I can get there, although I couldn't handle a *sostenuto* – not yet, anyway."

Henry wanted to know more about my repertoire. I told him, "I sing chansons, lieder, operatic arias...."

"What voice classification are you?"

"Lirico spinto. As a child, I sang along with my Lily Pons records and fancied myself a coloratura, but I'm classified a spinto now."

"So from the operatic standpoint, you do *Bohème, Turandot, Butterfly, Gianni Schicchi* ...."

"All of the above."

"Henry said. "Ya know, Gianni Schicchi's daughter is named Lauretta, which is my sister's name ... hmmmm ... hmmm.... Schicchi was an actual historical character, doncha know. He's referred to in Dante's *Inferno*, where Dante visits the Circle of Impersonators. Puccini's opera is based on an actual incident that took place in 13th century Florence."

Henry said he had been at the Met to hear Giuseppe De Luca sing Gianni with Florence Easton as Lauretta back in the 20's. Since the group had not heard of Florence Easton, Henry told us about her: "Florence Easton was a popular English soprano, one of the most versatile singers of all time. She sang more than 100 roles from Mozart, Meyerbeer, Gounod, Verdi, Wagner, Puccini, Strauss, you name it. In Wagner she sang virtually every soprano role except the *Götterdämmerung* Brünnhilde. She sang everything, in every range, from light coloratura to the Hochdramatische. She was the first ever to sing *O Mio Babbino Caro*, personally chosen by Puccini to create Lauretta. She held the world record for having sung Butterfly the most of any singer – over 300 times."

Henry asked what I was singing at present in my lessons with Maria Martino. I named some pieces, including a Fauré chanson, the words which were from one of Verlaine's poems, *Mandoline*: *"Les donneurs de sérénades / Et les belles écouteuses / Échangent des propos fades / Sous les ramures chanteuses,"* I quoted.

"But you have to sing it, not recite it," Henry urged.

"All right, if you'll be my accompanist."

"I'd love to be your accompanist," Henry said, a wicked gleam in his eye.

Henry hadn't forgotten Marianne, and asked about her frequently. He was always interested in hearing news about her. "We should get together," he said. "You girls should come over for dinner."

"Thank you, Henry. I'm sure Marianne would enjoy that, but right now, she's staying home, cooking, catering to Myron. She's on her best behavior, trying to get Myron to agree to marry her."

"Why is he so reluctant?" Henry was puzzled. "She's a fantastic girl. This Myron sounds like a prize jerk."

"He's been married once and is very anti-marriage."

"Sounds like your friend, what's his name, the Harvard man?"

"Andy."

"Is he still in the picture?"

"Andy? No. He's history."

"Well, you saw that one coming," Henry remarked.

As Myron continued fighting marriage, things reached critical mass between him and Marianne, resulting in a temporary breakup, during which Marianne came to stay with me. She was very upset and was crying day and night.

"This man of hers isn't worth it," Henry declared firmly. "You say she's staying with you. Why didn't she come with you today?"

"Because she's so miserable. She can't stop crying, her eyes are all swollen, all yellow, purple and green and horrible. The emotional upheaval has taken a terrible toll."

"All that suffering." Henry shook his head. "It's not worth it." And, he said, alluding to his own past, looking back on all the suffering he did over June, it seemed like a million years ago, "and you ask yourself, in time, what was that all about? It will be the same for Marianne," he predicted.

Not long after Marianne moving in with me, Myron missed her, wanted her back, so finally agreed to her terms: marriage.

"Really?" Henry said. "My guess is he misses having his meals cooked, his bed made, his dishes washed, his shirts ironed, the apartment vacuumed ...he needs a maid."

In a matter of only a week or so, I conveyed the news to Henry, "They got married."

"So it finally came off. She talked the reluctant bridegroom into marriage. My congratulations."

I nodded. "It's official. They're man and wife. Marianne called the day after to tell me."

"Weren't you invited to the wedding?"

"Nobody was. It wasn't a real wedding-wedding. It was just the two of them and some witness they were able to round up. But there was a party, a sort of reception last night at their apartment, and I was invited to that."

"I hope for her sake she didn't have to twist his arm too much."

"I think she did."

"Too bad, too bad. She's a lovely woman. She deserves a man who honors her, who treats her as she deserves to be treated. If she had to fight so hard to get this fellow to marry her, how secure will she ever feel in the marriage?" Henry shook his head. "I never understood why men resist marriage. Maybe we should ask Joe – he's resisted. Joe, what can you tell us about the subject?"

CHAPTER NINETEEN

Actress Eve Bruce was a gorgeous, curvaceous, shade under 6 foot tall blond of stunning presence who was like a sister to me. She lived across the hall in the same apartment building as I, at 1226 North Havenhurst Avenue, West Hollywood. (I had moved there from my house on Larrabee). I later based the character description of Calista in my novel *Odalisque at the Spa* on Eve: "voluptuous, junoesque ... stately caryatid of a woman ... magnificent glamazon, commanding and radiant ... prototype of the Greek goddess."

Eve was the epitome of Hollywood glamour. Her weakness was gurus. She met, became intimate friends with, sometimes the lover of, and in some cases was even responsible for the rise and fame of the likes of Peter Hurkos, Uri Geller, Neville, Werner Ehrhard (EST), Bruh Joy, pyramidologist Pat Flanagan (whom she briefly married), John Lilley, Jose Silva, Jess Stern, Jim Jones (embarrassingly!), who later led hundreds of people to their deaths in Belize, and many others. She knew some of these long before they were recognized by the world, and was such an enthusiastic organizer she could rally half the Hollywood community on their behalf. In New York, prior to her move back to her native Hollywood, Eve had been involved in Scientology and Gurdjieff's Work, as well as with another guru named Abdo, whom she thought had controlled her mind. Eve was a seeker who discovered every spiritual path, every spiritual class and seminar, every spiritual leader, every spiritual healer and every health food expert in New York and Los Angeles before anybody else had heard about them. Eve and Joe Grey were friends, having worked in a couple of films together. Like Joe Grey's, Eve's apartment shelves were stocked with every kind of teas, vitamins, tinctures, elixirs, oils, and essences known to man.

Whenever Eve and I were free, we frequented all the Hollywood natural food restaurants together. Every now and then, we'd see Joe Grey at various health food stores, particularly at Patton's on Melrose. Patton's, which Jacobina had introduced me to, was run by two enterprising black men, Prince Forte and Rudy Marshall, who later opened a great place we also often went to for dinner, the Nucleus Nuance. Patton's not only had excellent food, but was a store where you could buy vitamins and other health food supplies. It was said Howard Hughes was a regular customer at the Patton's luncheon counter, although I never saw him there.

Joe, health food aficionado like Eve, was an advocate of Dr. Bieler, Dr. Bernard Jensen, and others of their ilk. Joe was on Eve's list. Whenever she would hear about a new holistic doctor or revolutionary new remedy, she would call everyone on the list and let them know about it. Eve introduced Joe to Dr. Peter Rothschild, a protégé of Dr. Anna Aslen, who gave youth shots both in LA and at his clinic in the Caribbean, and to Dr. Peter Bruch, who was from Bad Homburg, Germany, who also came to L.A and administered youth shots. There were a couple of Mexican doctors aboard as well. Everyone bought in. For a few hundred dollars, your agelessness was guaranteed forever. You didn't have to go to Switzerland for those sheep embryo injections prized by Konrad Adenaur, Charles De Gaulle and all the movie stars, you could prolong your youth right here in Hollywood if you knew Eve Bruce.

One time Eve and I ran into Joe shopping for vitamins at Patton's, Henry happened to be outside, waiting in the car. Henry didn't want to come in; he loathed everything to do with health foods. "Come out and say hello to Henry," Joe invited.

We did. It was Henry's first glimpse of the magnificent Eve. It was just a brief one, but more than enough to arouse Henry's curiosity and interest. Henry was entranced, likening Eve to Ursula Andress, only better. He wanted to know more, everything.

"If I were to write a book about Eve, it would have to be endlessly long, yet nothing I could say would adequately explain her," I said. "Her family, her career, her experiences as a seeker, and especially her relationship with her eccentric mother."

"Her mother," Henry repeated. "Oh, don't tell me. Not another one with a bad mother."

"I'm afraid so. Eve has a terrible mother. Her mother drives Eve crazy. She says her mother will be the death of her."

"I can certainly relate to that, speaking as someone who had a bitch of a mother," Henry said. "Why don't you bring her here sometime? I'd like to talk to her."

"I'll ask her, but I doubt she'll come. She usually has other plans Sundays."

"What kind of plans? What does she do Sundays?"

"She's very good friends with Zsa Zsa Gabor, Ann Miller,

and Kathryn Grayson. They all get together once a week for a hen session Sunday afternoons."

"Eve is much younger than those women," Henry pointed out.

"I know. They've adopted her. She's like a daughter to them; they're substitute mothers for her. They all want to mother her."

"What's her own mother like?" Henry wanted to know.

"Unlike your mother, Henry, Eve's mother isn't a bitch. Her problem is she's nuttier than a fruitcake, she's totally bats. She's also a hypochondriac who goes to doctors all the time, shows them pictures of Eve, 'her little bubba,' she calls her, and asks the doctor if he wants to be fixed up with her sexy daughter whom she's sure would be happy to go to bed with the doctor."

"That's one thing my mother wasn't guilty of," Henry said. "Although it might have been a saving grace if she were."

"Eve's mother is very rich, but very cheap. She burns the lowest wattage light bulbs and buys bargain basement house dresses on sale at Sears. She embarrasses Eve all the time by speaking out of turn."

"Hmmm... hmmm... I see what you mean."

"When Eve was growing up, her mother didn't feed her properly. She would go off somewhere with her boyfriend, whose name was Herbie, and leave ten year old Eve a bag of potato chips and a chocolate bar for dinner. So later, as an adult, Eve became obsessive about food. She has a lot of allergies, or thinks she does. Her mother is very short, by the way. She's barely five feet tall, and five feet wide at least. She must weigh about 350 pounds, maybe more."

"With such a tall daughter – Eve must be a good 6 feet tall. And perfectly shaped, I might add. Hmmm... hmmm... Gorgeous, gorgeous. It's hard to believe a woman such as you describe could have spawned a daughter the likes of Eve. What kind of father did she – does she have?"

"Eve never knew her father. Her mother told Eve he was a big Swede."

"So that's where the height and the Nordic features come from."

"Eve's mother has a peculiar, very unusual gift. She can guess anybody's middle name."

"Oh, she's an idiot savant, then?"

"I was amazed when she guessed my middle name, which is my maternal grandmother's maiden name, Allyn. I never use it and nobody knows it."

"Sadie Allyn Wright," Henry said, remembering my grandmother's name.

"Henry, you have a phenomenally retentive mind!"

Continuing our discussion of Eve Bruce, I told Henry, "She's done several films, but she hasn't been able to break out of the dumb blond category. Eve wants to really act, to be known as a serious actress, not an empty-headed trophy, a sex object."

"Eve is a magnificent woman, a woman all men should worship. She has that goddess quality, shall I say?"

"Yes, she commands attention wherever she goes, and she has a million men after her."

"That I can believe... hmmm ... hmmm...."

"She was propositioned by President Kennedy's pimp – or one of them. I assume he had more than one."

"Did she take him up on it?"

"No way. Eve really resents that type of thing. She hates being thought of in that kind of a light."

"I'll bet she's had some interesting experiences with men, though," Henry speculated.

"For sure. You wouldn't believe some of them," I said.

"Try me and see," Henry invited.

"Eve's dating life alone would make an incredible book. She's been pursued by Hollywood's most important figures."

"By whom, for instance?"

"You'd know them if I told you their names. One in particular, who happens to be one of the biggest stars in Hollywood, got out his checkbook, waved it at her and asked, how much for one night with you? Five thousand? Ten thousand? Eve told me this guy wears a corset, by the way."

"Oh, so she took him up on the offer, then? How much did he pay her?"

"She didn't take him up on the offer. She turned him down."

"Then how did she know he wore a corset?"

"You would ask that, Henry. I'm not sure how."

"I guess there are other ways of finding that out." Henry allowed. "But I don't blame him for offering. Any man who's accustomed to paying tributes to beautiful women, any man who could afford it would do the same thing."

"But this is something Eve doesn't want. Yet I have to admit that on the one hand, she feeds off it, because it brings attention, it highlights her importance. But the main thing is, she doesn't want this to be the way she's identified."

"Yet she can't avoid it."

"One very famous star who begged her to be his mistress gave his wife gonorrhea. Another one who was after her is notorious for giving women hemorrhoids."

"Hopefully, she passed on those two."

"She passes on just about all the offers that come her way. Eve is very independent, and she's independently wealthy, which a lot of men don't realize when they think she can be bought. But she can't be. Eve is an heiress, by the way."

"An heiress to what?"

"Her ancestor Malcolm Bruce – he was from Virginia – was the largest slave holder in the United States at the time of the Civil War. All her relatives are important diplomats. One of her relatives is David Bruce."

"The David Bruce who was Ambassador to France and the UK? David K.E. Bruce?"

"That's right, and she's also part of the Fisher Body family. Eve doesn't need any financial help from anybody. She has a trust fund from her grandfather that takes care of everything."

"Lucky for her. Or unlucky, as the case may be."

"She has no unmet needs. In addition to her income, anything extra she covets, it's there. If she wants a new car, it's hers. She wants to take a trip? No problem. But she doesn't have control of the trust fund. The bank controls it and she can't get her hands on the principal to invest as she sees fit. The bank will listen to her ideas, but won't give her authority."

"When she dies, what happens to the trust fund?"

"If she doesn't produce an heir, the money goes to twin cousins she's never met."

"Oh, is she trying to produce an heir, then?"

"No, not at all. First of all, she's very conventional and would never do it out of wedlock. Secondly, it's doubtful she'd ever do it, period. She's not motherhood material."

"Every woman is motherhood material, potentially."

"Not Eve. She has no interest in being a mother, raising kids."

"What is she interested in?"

"Aside from acting, spiritual evolution, higher consciousness, primarily."

"Motherhood would do that for her. Just ask our beautiful Noreen, the mother in our midst. Isn't that so, Noreen?"

"Absolutely," Noreen replied. "I highly recommend motherhood to any woman as being spiritually fulfilling."

"Well, the only way Eve could get authority on the trust would possibly be if she would produce that heir. The bank says they might be able to reconsider, but only under those circumstances."

"Well, what's she waiting for? I'm available. I'll give her an heir," Henry volunteered.

"Tell me more about your friend Eve. She intrigues me," Henry said.

"Well, she dated Elvis Presley," I began, "and she speaks highly of Elvis, says he's a real gentleman. You know, Eve is a fabulous person. Everybody likes her. She's one of the most well-liked people I know."

"I can see why. She's a lovely girl, enchanting, with great charm. I met her only briefly, but you can see this instantly. Very warm, very sweet." Henry asked, "What motion pictures has she done? I don't go to movies that often anymore, because I don't like the products they're putting out these days. I'd rather watch the wrestling matches on television, doncha know. But should I be aware of anything she's in?"

"She's been featured in several films with Dean Martin, James Colburn, Henry Fonda, Elvis Presley, and with Joe Grey!" I said. "*In Like Flint, Yours, Mine and Ours, Cactus Flower, The Love Machine, Tickle Me, It Takes a Thief, The Family Jewels, How Sweet it Is...*"

Eve had confided to Joe on the set of a recent film they'd done together that she was being plagued by severe sleep problems. She was convinced her mind was being invaded by thought waves sent by an ex-boyfriend named Bobby, who was in prison in Nevada for murdering an oil heiress named Barbara, because Eve had given him the ultimatum "it's either her or me." Eve didn't want to share Bobby, but she had certainly never imagined he would take a gun and shoot her rival in cold blood.

"Barbara, whose last name escapes me, was the daughter of a wealthy California oil man whose name you would recognize."

"What happened?" Henry asked.

"Eve told Bobby she didn't want to see him anymore if he continued seeing Barbara."

"So she said one of us has to go?"

"Right, so Bobby shot and killed Barbara. Leading to Eve's bad dreams and nightmares. Eve is convinced Bobby knows how to astrally project and disturb her sleep."

"Must be guilt that's giving her these sleep problems," Joe concluded.

There used to be a French restaurant in Westwood not far from the UCLA campus, where Eve and I frequently dined together. Wish I could remember the name. Eve discovered the place. The French couple who ran it were into some unusual religion or cult with headquarters in France, somewhere in the Massif Central, I think. The cult had a guru revered by this couple who thought of him as the new world messiah. I bought a series of their books but never got around to reading them. Eve and I ran into Henry and Joe there a few times. The first time, we were already seated and had placed our orders when Henry and Joe entered and took the table next to us.

Eve had been in Gurdjieff's Work in both New York and L.A. for several years, but by the mid-sixties was finished with it. Henry said he thought nobody understood Gurdjieff, including himself.

"I know what you're saying, Henry, and many people would agree with you," Eve said. "The fact is, you have to actually be in The Work to fully understand what it is. You can't just read about it, you have to experience it, interact with the group."

Henry said, "That Institute of his – for the Harmonious Development of Man – I can't subscribe to the idea that spiritual development is harmonious."

"But it is," Eve disagreed, "or rather, it should be."

"Should be, but isn't," Henry said, "therefore, impossible."

"You're wrong about that, Henry," Eve maintained. "Actually, the whole point is that it's a possibility – it's 'man's possible evolution.' Harmonious is an ideal, not an attainment already reached, but one to aspire to and work toward."

"Hmmm... hmmm... I approve that Gurdjieff's didn't consider himself holy, doncha know, and that's a lot more than some gurus do," Henry said, "but I simply don't believe man is meant to ever lead a harmonious life, that it's possible."

Eve said, "When Gurdjieff talks about the harmonious development of man, he means integration, the balancing of the three centers: the will, the emotions, and the intellect. Gurdjieff says only one of the person's three dimensions— either the emotions, the physical body or the mind – develops at the expense of the other two centers. Instead of working on these separately, Gurdjieff's discipline tackles all of them at once, to promote balanced development."

"But does it really?" Henry asked.

Eve said, "To achieve it takes conscious effort. Gurdjieff believed the practice of self-remembering with self-observation and not expressing negative emotions are the three things necessary to create higher consciousness. He used exercises such as the stop exercise and sacred dances, movements to this purpose."

"Did you do these movements?" Henry asked.

"I did. That is, I tried, I made efforts. The movements aren't easy to do, and I wasn't good at it. After several years of trying, I still struggled, still didn't get it right. Those exercises are so complicated. One of your limbs is doing one thing, your hand is doing another, your head another."

"Yes, that would be a challenge. And frustrating, besides, having to go contrary to all your usual habits."

"Gurdjieff said, though, it's absolutely necessary to learn to feel and think at the same time in everything you do ... for instance, be able to read with your three centers. You do the exercises as an obligation, not for results. He says that we have to act with intention, not for personal reward but for our Being."

Henry said, "I know Gurdjieff says the majority of humanity lives in a state of hypnotic waking sleep, that it's possible to wake up, and that his method is called the Fourth Way. At one point he described his teaching as esoteric Christianity."

"The Fourth Way predates all Western teachings," Eve said,

"and Christianity is derived from the Fourth Way— not vice versa."

"That's quite a claim."

"Yes, it is. Gurdjieff said Christianity was taken in already existing form from prehistoric Egypt."

"Oh, yes, didn't he mention having seen a map of pre-sand Egypt that led him to study with an esoteric group..."

"The Sarmoun Brotherhood."

"Gurdjieff was looking to find knowledge which existed in Egypt and Babylon a couple of thousand years before Christ, isn't that right?" Henry asked, "What is true Christianity? How does Gurdjieff define it?"

"He says so many distortions exist that we get everything not even fifth hand, but twenty-fifth hand, so everything really essential was lost long ago. The Gospels have been copied and translated by so many different hands that they're completely watered down, distorted by now."

"I've always maintained that," Henry said. "It makes perfect sense, isn't that so? Just like when you have a group of people, you whisper a story into the person's ear next to you, and the story gets passed on down to the end of the line, until at the end, it's unrecognizable."

"Gurdjieff said spiritual tradition on Earth lost connection with its original meaning, so that humans are susceptible to falling into mass psychosis. Ouspensky explains all this in his tract on conscience."

"Ah, Ouspensky," Henry said, "he writes far clearer, cleaner prose than Gurdjieff. I've read most all of Ouspensky's books: *The Fourth Dimension, Tertium Organum, A New Model of the Universe,* his interesting novel *The Strange Life of Ivan Osokin,* which explores the concept of recurrence, eternal return; *Fragments of an Unknown Teaching, In Search of the Miraculous...*"

"So you know that Gurdjieff said self-remembering was the missing link to everything else."

"Yas, yaz ... hmmm.... hmmm... But just how is this self-remembering accomplished?" Henry asked. "And how would you even begin to describe it?"

"It's one part of attention, so that you're simultaneously aware of what's going on in the exterior world as well as inside yourself, in the interior, and the division is separate but unified."

Henry was thoughtful. "All that business Gurdjieff writes about – self-observation, the permanent I, the permanent center of gravity, identifying, essence vs. personality ... I'm not sure exactly to what degree all that really worked for his students."

"That's for each to decide."

"Sure, sure. Now Fritz Peters – you're familiar with him, aren't you?"

"Yes, I've read his two books on Gurdjieff."

"When he was nine years old, Fritz's mother, Louise Peters, had a nervous breakdown. His mother's sister was Margaret Anderson. Margaret and her companion Jane Heap adopted Fritz and his brother. When Margaret and Jane returned to New York, Gertrude Stein and Alice B. Toklas raised the boys," Henry said. "In simple, homey ways, Gurdjieff had solid answers for the boy Fritz. Gurdjieff spoke most profoundly about small things, doncha know. When he went for the large concepts, and when he used all those Armenian words, he lost me, not just because I don't speak Armenian. Fritz Peters' books portray the heart and soul of Gurdjieff in a way nothing else does. Fritz's books speak to me," Henry said, "they say a great deal about Gurdjieff, in a manner of speaking."

Eve said, "You know, when Fritz Peters was a grown man, he visited Gurdjieff in Paris. Gurdjieff filled him with 'a violent, electric blue light,' which Gurdjieff called his *hanbledzoin*, to recharge Fritz's energy. Fritz Peters said everything instantaneously took on a new shape."

"*Hanbledzoin* ... there's another of those Armenian words," Henry said, shaking his head. "Reminds me, shall I say, of the word for the New Jersey harness race, the Hambiltonian."

"Very important race," Joe put in.

Henry asked, "And Gurdjieff's *hanbledzoin* is...?"

"The 'blood' of the Kesdjan body, to nourish and perfect the body Kesdjan."

"Kesdjan body," Henry said, "It's not a term one often hears, other than from the Gurdjieff people, but one assumes it's similar to the subtle body of Eastern religions."

"You could describe it that way," Eve said.

"And how about that other Armenian word Gurdjieff used, a word that begins with 't.'"

"Oh, you mean *tzvarnoharrno*," Eve said. "Yes, that's one of

Gurdjieff's legomanisms, a word allegedly coined by King Solomon."

"King Solomon, son of King David," Henry mused. "One would never guess he spoke Armenian."

"I suppose it must have been translated from the original ancient Hebrew," Eve suggested, shrugging and laughing.

"It just goes to show how much can be lost in translation. So, back to Fritz Peters...."

"Fritz was a member of the Chicago and New York groups, and was dissatisfied with both of them," Eve said. "He thought they were phony. Like his mother, he had several nervous breakdowns."

Inspired by my friendship with Eve, I read everything available about Gurdjieff, who was one of my biggest interests. I told Henry, "I wanted to be in the Work, but I was turned down by the woman who's the head of it in L.A."

"On what basis? What was the reason?"

"Because I refused to say I'd gotten nothing out of my previous searching. They want you to be desperate. They want their path to be the only answer, that you absolutely must have this, you've tried everything else, and nothing has helped. I couldn't say I got nothing out of all the other paths I've studied.

"The interviewer, this woman, kept trying to get me to say I'd tried everything under the sun looking for answers, but nothing worked, that I was at the end of my rope and truly believed Gurdjieff's Work was the one thing that could possibly save my life. I couldn't say what wasn't so. This woman kept throwing out leading questions to get me to admit what she wanted me to say. She didn't like the fact that in my seeking, I'd found other paths useful, that everything I had come across had made me a richer person."

"Sure, sure, of course they all contribute something, they lead you somewhere, help your growth and understanding," Henry said. "I don't blame you. This woman was trying to manipulate you, to bend you to her way of thinking. I wouldn't have gone for that line of questioning either."

"Despite that experience, I still think there's a lot to be said for Gurdjieff. I have every book that's ever been written by him or about him and his teaching. I bought some of them in London and Paris that are in French and haven't been translated yet or published here."

Henry said, "There are no panaceas. We can take it all in,

assimilate, absorb, rearrange and come out with a synthesis that makes sense to us, if you will. And what was meaningful a decade or three, four decades ago, no longer is today. We get to new levels, experience new apotheoses, we make sense in renewed aspects. The important thing is moving ahead. Of course everything we've seen and done makes a difference. As Tennyson said, I am a part of all I have met."

Joe and Henry often dined at Henry's favorite Japanese restaurant, the Imperial Gardens, which was located on Sunset below the fabled Château Marmont. (The Imperial Gardens pianist, Hoki, would become Henry's fifth wife). Saying Henry and he were at the Imperial Gardens "all the time," Joe extended a casual invitation to Eve and me to meet them there on a particular night at a particular time. The restaurant was only about a five minute drive from the apartment building where Eve and I lived.

Eve and I dressed up more than usual for that dinner date, but Henry and Joe never appeared. I had that same desolate feeling I'd had in Big Sur and Rome, Paris as well, that feeling of something being missing, cities empty of Henry. He had long ago abandoned Paris and Paris had never been the same; Bricktop was empty and Henry belonged there. His aura hung over Big Sur. And his not being at the Imperial Gardens that night made me feel his absence keenly.

Apprized of the mixup, Henry wanted to make it up to us, so he invited us to dinner another time. He and Joe did show, and we had another discussion about Gurdjieff

"Some people can't figure if he was a phony con artist or an enlightened genius," Eve said.

"And you?"

"I've struggled with who he was. I have trouble accepting him 100 %."

"Maybe a combination of both?" Henry suggested. "Well, this is one of my reservations about him, doncha know. He supposedly inspired his students to higher consciousness, but at the same time, it's clear he manipulated them. There's the question of how he exerted such influence, whether he essentially hypnotized his students. Grown men of accomplishment like Orage, Ouspensky, J.G. Bennett, Thomas de Hartman and others, were in thrall. And the women who followed him..."

"Yes, lots of women."

"There was that group of lesbians, including Katherine Hulme, who wrote *The Nun's Story*. He had all these ladies mesmerized as well. There was the opera singer who was the mistress of Maurice Maeterlink, Georgette LeBlanc; there was Solita Solano, whom I believe was the lover of Janet Flanner, Gênet of *The New Yorker*; Dorothy Caruso, the widow of Enrico Caruso..."

"Margaret Anderson was one of his most devoted students," Eve said.

"Margaret's literary magazine, *The Little Review*, introduced some of the finest new writers in the English language – T. S. Eliot, Hemingway, Joyce, Pound, Yeats, Gertrude Stein... Margaret was the first person to publish James Joyce, doncha know, and ended up being tried and convicted of obscenity for that. Ya know, Ben Hecht was very taken with Margaret. He wrote that he forgave Margaret her chastity because she was a genius. What Ben didn't realize is Margaret is a lesbian."

"The women you're talking about, the lesbians, were known as the Ladies of the Rope," Eve said.

"In addition to these ladies, so many powerful men of achievement, Gurdjieff followers, were seeking validation," Henry said. "Orage was a brilliant British intellectual, he studied theosophy, he corresponded with Harry Houdini on esoteric subjects, including the afterlife. He attended Ouspensky's lectures in London. Ouspensky introduced him to Gurdjieff. Orage moved to France to study at Gurdjieff's Institute."

Eve said, "All of these accomplished men keenly felt something was missing ...it points up the feeling of inadequacy and the search for the missing essence in man."

"The point is, Gurdjieff capitalized on this, played it for all it was worth," Henry said. "Hmmm... hmmm ... He did make two most interesting observations about mankind that I think are quite true: people always have the need to be right, and they are always looking for an authority beyond the self. That last statement, I think is a clue why these accomplished men embraced him to the extent they did. They believed he had answers, answers to why are we here, who are we, where did we come from, where are we going, what is the purpose of life on earth, what will happen to us after we die?"

"The eternal questions," Eve said.

Henry said, "It's interesting that the Old Testament has seventy-two words for God, while in English, we use just the one. According to the Bible, one of the three most important of these seventy-two words we translate as God is Elohim. The Bible is explicit in saying the Elohim created humans. One interpretation of the Elohim is the Elohim is not one entity or being, but consists of twelve female deities, doncha know."

"So twelve females created us," Joe said.

"Well, as you know, I've always maintained women are the stronger sex," Henry said.

Henry asked Eve pointedly, "Why did you leave the Work?"

"It's complicated, Henry. I ask myself that question a lot," Eve replied. "I'm not totally sure I know, although I have my theories."

"Which are?"

Eve took a deep breath. "There are things I didn't like about the Work and how they run the groups. There's no doubt in my mind that Gurdjieff's teaching is an authentic teaching. But I felt the people in the New York and California groups were not at a level of consciousness I could profit from. I was dominated and overruled by them, and it wasn't working for me."

"Weren't you supposed to accept the group for better or for worse, to use it to work on your own reactions – or something to that effect?" Henry asked. "Isn't that how it works?"

"True enough, but there came a point where I asked myself, is this constructive? Haven't I given this more than enough time to know whether it's to my benefit or not?"

"I suppose the rest of the group would have disapproved, would have been critical of your decision to leave."

"You're right, Henry. I had to contend with that. But I realized I was surrendering my power to others, that their will was taking precedent over mine. Who is to say I have to keep deferring to someone else, that I should have to stick things out till the bitter end?"

"No, of course that's not a healthy condition. It's something we all face at one time or another, in one life situation or another," Henry said, "Still, didn't Gurdjieff say we should thank anyone who gives us the opportunity to see ourselves, to see what he called the 'little i'?"

"He did say that."

There was more to Eve's disillusion with the Work. Eve had told me about her run-ins with Lord Pentland, President of the Gurdjieff Foundations in New York and California. I spoke up. "Lord Pentland is highly respected in the Work," I said, "but he showed a different face to Eve, and it turned her off."

"How is that? What did this man do?" Henry wanted to know.

"He went after me relentlessly," Eve said. "He was making unwelcome passes, pushing, insisting, being obnoxious. I made it clear I wanted him to stop, but he refused to take no for an answer, he just wouldn't quit. How much crap am I supposed to take, when I keep saying no and he still doesn't get it? Here's Lord Pentland, the biggest, most important man in the whole Gurdjieff movement, and he's way, way out of line."

"You would expect a man in his position to – what?"

"This guy should not have been acting like any ordinary middle aged man in heat!" Eve protested. "His ego got the better of him, he had no control over that outsized ego of his. He should have recognized he was out of line and stopped, already. But he kept saying, 'Miss Bruce, Miss Bruce, I've got to have you!'"

"Isn't that the same line some friend of Jeanne's used?"

"Yes," I answered, "Myron, Marianne's husband used that very same line on me."

"These men who go with that approach, the 'I've got to have you' approach – do you think some women must find that effective?" Henry asked.

"No!" Eve and I exclaimed in unison. Then Eve said, "Here's Lord Pentland chasing me around the room, around the furniture. It was so undignified of him. He looked ridiculous. I was disgusted. I felt that a man who'd been a student of both Ouspensky and Gurdjieff, who was personally chosen by Gurdjieff to lead the American groups, a man of such an exalted position and experience should not be behaving as he did with me."

"But this man, after all, is just a man."

"That's no excuse, Henry. Men, no matter who they are, no matter what their position, or especially in their position, need to know the rules. And imagine, after working the Fourth Way as extensively as he had. I guess we could get into an argument here on a woman having the right to say no, but having her wishes violated, and the man just assuming his are the desires that ought to prevail, not hers."

"Could it be he was demonstrating something, deliberately enacting a scenario in creating a situation he thought you needed for your development?"

"That would be according him too much power, that he has the right to assume a godlike position over me. Face it, Lord Pentland was on a power trip. That's one of the main things that turned me off of the Work."

"You refer to this man as Lord Pentland. He's a British lord?"

"That's right, a member of the House of Lords. He was born Henry Sinclair and inherited the title."

"Does something of what you gained in the Work stay with you now?" Henry asked. "After leaving, do you feel that overall, your years there were still worthwhile?"

"There's no question but that I gained something. You gain through making efforts. Nothing is ever wasted or lost. It all counts – toward something. It's just that my association with the Work had to come to an end; it couldn't continue."

"Yas, yaz." Henry said, "Hmmm ... hmmm.... I understand."

The next time I saw Henry at the Siegels', he said, "You know, although Eve is a tall, imposing woman, although she's cheerful and outgoing, I sense a sadness, almost a helplessness in her. She is so open, so delightful, so giving of herself; people think of her as strong, doncha know, but inside she's like a little girl, afraid to dream her dream and afraid she'll never find it."

When I told Eve what Henry had said, she was touched.

Another time at the Westwood French restaurant, the four of us entered within minutes of each other and ended up sharing a table together. Eve was saying, "Gurdjieff stated that everyone should constantly sense and acknowledge the inevitability of their own death, as well as of the death of everyone else in the world."

"I recall Gurdjieff said it was important to live as long as you can, not to die a sudden death," Henry said, "but to try to linger if you can, even if you're sick; it's preferable to an early or sudden death."

"Well, he lived fairly long, and he lingered, I'd say, being ill for some time. He always said not to die like a dog, and in my opinion, he died like a dog. A lot of his followers don't acknowledge that. He almost died from an auto accident, from which they say he never fully recovered. The cause of death, eventually, officially, was cancer. Isn't that dying like a dog? It's a miserable death. In my opinion, Gurdjieff died like a dog."

"It depends," Henry said. "It could be called a noble death, too – all depending on how it was faced."

Eve said, "Henry, you're right. I never thought of it that way. And his doctor, William Welsh, said he died like a king – so maybe you're onto something there."

"Henry's always onto something," Joe said. "That's what Henry's all about."

Joe Grey was part of another group that often met Sunday evenings at actor/ restauranteur Nicky Blair's digs, where Nicky cooked and served delicious buffet style Italian food featuring his Italian mamma's recipes to a dozen or more, perhaps up to as many as twenty guests. Eve and I sometimes attended Nicky's dinners, as did Henry and Joe, the latter who was a longtime friend of Nicky's.

Nicky Blair was co-owner of Stefanino's, a popular restaurant on the Sunset Strip where Henry and Joe frequently dined. Nicky's partner in that venture was Steve Crane, one of Lana Turner's ex-husbands, who also owned the Luau in Beverly Hills, another high profile hangout. A few years later, Nicky would open his own eatery on the Strip called – what else? Nicky Blair. Later yet, he would open a branch in Las Vegas. Nicky's film star cronies Dean Martin, Frank Sinatra, Milton Berle, George Burns, Tony Curtis, Sylvester Stallone, Clint Eastwood, and others were devoted regulars at Nicky's restaurants.

Nicky and Joe's movie star buddies cast them in their films and TV shows, making sure Nicky and Joe always had work. Nicky's biggest movie role was as Elvis Presley's sidekick in *Viva Las Vegas*. He played in scores of other flicks, a few of them with Eve, *In Like Flint*, *The Love Machine*, *The Manchurian Candidate*, *Birdman of Alcatraz*, *Breakfast at Tiffany's*, *Ocean's Eleven*, *Sweet Smell of Success* (along with Joe Grey), and others.

One reason other men liked to be around Nicky Blair and Joe

Grey was that Nicky and Joe attracted a steady supply of pretty girls whom they generously shared with their cronies. Two single men, Nicky and Joe were blessed with a seemingly infinite supply of toothsome lovelies. Neither Joe nor Nicky ever seemed to have a real girlfriend, but both enjoyed producing the constantly rotating contingent of beauties on demand. Sometimes a guest might get lucky and make it back to the apartment of one of the girls he met at Nicky's, but that wasn't the main goal of these bashes; chiefly, the guys just wanted to let their hair down and relax around some adoring females. If sex should enter into the picture, it was a welcome lagniappe, but would usually only amount to no more than a short lived flirtation.

Henry gave the Blair gatherings cachet, an intellectual, highbrow, literary note they would otherwise have lacked. In fact, Henry, whenever he appeared, instantly became the stellar attraction at Nicky's parties. Women were always charmed by Henry, who had more young ladies worshiping at his feet than Sinatra, Martin, and the other big names combined. Women loved being around Henry because of his gift of gab, because he was such a stimulating conversationalist, because of the optimism and good humor he radiated, because of his ability to hold an audience spellbound and make everyone laugh. His enormous curiosity and interest in others always led to fascinating dialog. Compared to Henry, other males at Nicky Blair's were dullards; Henry's fascination by far outpaced all the rest.

Should the subject of sex arise at the Siegels, Henry would couch his comments in the most careful and discreet terms, whereas at Nicky Blair's, he was more open on the subject. Joe showed no restraint whatsoever, never hesitating to use four letter words. Joe was saying something about a friend of his "who has an enormous prick. If you want to see it, he'll gladly take it out and place it in your hand."

I knew the person Joe was talking about, although I had never met him, but had heard many stories about him. I knew his name was Freddie, that his sobriquet was "Okay Freddie," and that he was a popular guest at Hollywood stag parties, where those present always asked to see his penis, to which Freddie's invariably good natured reply was, "Okay," whereupon he would whip out the engorged organ for inspection. Thus did he become known as "Okay

Freddie," widely celebrated for his ability to serve a tray full of drinks perfectly balanced on his erect phallus.

Another "Fred" Joe knew was the rather notorious private detective Fred Otash. Eve and I sometimes went to Fred Otash's parties at his apartment on the Sunset Strip. Fred Otash was said to have tapped Marilyn Monroe's phone, and to have in his possession dynamite tapes of her final hours.

Dean Martin, with whom I had doubled when I was dating his agent, Mort Viner, noticed my lips were shiny. I told him it was due to Viks Vapo Rub I was using on them. Dean said he was going to send me a case of Viks. And he did just that the very next day. This reminded me of the time in New York when my friend, designer Oleg Cassini, sent over his Hollywood actor pal Kirk Douglas to the garden apartment I was sharing with two other girls. Kirk thought our apartment was such a great place he wanted to give a party there. The next day, several cases of scotch, gin, rye, vodka, bourbon, you name it, all arrived, plus three huge jeroboams of champagne. Kirk invited all his friends to the party – but never showed up himself.

A particular night at Nicky's when Marianne's husband Myron was otherwise occupied attending a bachelor party, Marianne made one of her rare appearances. That same evening, another drop dead gorgeous actress/model and close friend, Judy Carrol, who had been a fellow "Away We Go Girl" with me a season on the *Jackie Gleason Show* in New York, also was there. It was an embarrassment of riches for Henry, surrounded by Eve, Marianne, Judy and me, all of us his devoted acolytes.

Myron had decided that he and Marianne should join the Peace Corps, they had been accepted, and Marianne was studying Woloff in preparation for their tour of duty.

"Woloff. That's an African language, isn't it?" Henry said.

"Yes, not many people know that." (Of course, Henry would know). Marianne said, "It's the native language of Sénégal. Myron is learning French. They speak that in Sénégal as well."

"Oh, so now he'll be able to talk to you in your mother tongue," Henry pondered. "Hmmm .... hmmm."

Marianne, never one for inhibitions, brought up a subject I had told her about. "Jeanne told me her friend in Italy, Charlie Fawcett, told her about something very esoteric he called a 'Chinese trick,' and you, Henry, knowing so much about Asian women, I wondered if you knew anything about this so-called trick," Marianne asked.

"What trick is that?" Henry wanted to know.

Marianne said, "Well, from what Charlie told Jeanne, he had gone to the Far East as a young man, where he fell madly in love with a Chinese girl. The girl's mother took him aside. She was very concerned about her daughter's virginity. So she told Charlie, 'I'm going to show you something special that you will not learn anywhere else. I want you to do this with my daughter. My daughter's maidenhead must be protected at all costs. If you practice with my daughter what I am going to show you, my daughter will not crave intercourse, her pleasure will be so great that her purity will be intact. And as for yourself, your pleasure will be so intense that you will be satisfied as never before in your life."

"And did Charlie do as he was instructed?" Henry asked.

"He certainly did. According to what Charlie told Jeanne, this esoteric practice was utterly incredible, the Chinese mother was right about that. And it was unique, because Charlie never found anyone else who knew about this in all his travels around the world and all the women he knew over the years."

"Well, I can't imagine what that would be," Henry mused, scratching his head.

Marianne asked, "Is it true, Henry, that Chinese women have double vaginas?"

Henry laughed. "I've heard some do, although in all honesty, I've never come across one. But I have heard that Diamond Jim Brady had a double stomach."

"A double stomach? How is that possible?"

"Well, maybe not technically, exactly a double stomach,' Henry conceded. "But when he died, an autopsy revealed the size of his stomach was six times that of a normal one."

"My God, how did Lillian Russell manage to have sex with him?" Marianne wondered.

"Yes, Diamond Jim was a very large man," Henry said. "Hmmmm ... hmmmm..."

The conversation shifted once more to Gurdjieff. Eve said, "Critics have called Gurdjieff a charlatan, and made a case for his being a con man who controlled his followers. People would unquestioningly do exactly what he told them to; they followed his orders like sheep. And he could have any woman he wanted."

"That's what I heard, too," Henry said. "Reportedly, Gurdjieff was supposed to have fathered a whole flock of bastards."

"Gurdjieff lived in Paris during the Occupation and continued to teach throughout World War II," Eve said. "The dinners he gave at his apartment are legendary. There was always plenty of Armagnac, his favorite drink."

"Oh, yes," Henry chimed in. "And those famous idiot toasts – where he made everyone be an animal, doncha know. And they had to drink. He insisted. Some of them had health problems and shouldn't have been drinking, but he forced them to, anyway. Some got sick or drunk. And if they couldn't take the drinking, he belittled them."

Eve nodded. "He had them groveling."

Henry wanted to know about a trip Eve had recently taken to Egypt which was written up as a feature story in *Esquire* magazine. Eventually Eve would marry and divorce the 5 foot 2 inch pyramidologist Pat Flanagan, who accompanied her on the trip. Together, they had spent the night in the Pyramid of Giza.

Eve said, "Seeing the Sphinx, the Great Pyramid, going up the Nile, seeing the Luxor temple, the Valley of the Kings ... I was awed by the huge scale, the esoteric understanding that had to have existed to create these wonders. We visited the Temple of Edfu, which is about 30 miles up the Nile from Thebes. The walls there date way back, and tell us about Seven Sages who came from the homeland of the Primeval Ones, an island that sank during a catastrophic flood. The Seven Sages introduced religion to Egypt. Its focus was on Being and self-transformation, which jibes with what Gurdjieff says about the Fourth Way."

Later turning his attention once more to Judy Carrol, Henry invited, "Why don't you join us next Sunday at the Siegels'?"

"That sounds like fun," Judy said politely. But Judy was seldom free. She had a young daughter, Micheline Pierrette Berry, to whom her weekend time was usually devoted. After that, quite taken with Judy, Henry mentioned her often, and asked several questions about her. For one thing, he wanted to know if she had a boyfriend. I said, "Judy always has a boyfriend or a reasonable facsimile thereof. She's never without."

"Which makes perfect sense," Henry said. "Charming girl. Very beautiful."

Replying to Henry's further probing questions about Judy, I told him, "Judy was orphaned in childhood and was raised by an aunt. She had been looking forward to going to college, but then her aunt got married and had a baby, and college was out of the question. So Judy went to New York and became a model and actress. She played on Broadway in a Norman Lear play, *Come Blow Your Horn*, she starred in a TV series. We were on Jackie Gleason together for a year. She's one of the sweetest people you'll ever meet."

"All your friends are lovely, sweet girls, Henry said. "And all beautiful, too. You have these very interesting and attractive women friends who are involved in endeavors spread out all over the place, who are all so busy all the time."

CHAPTER TWENTY

Lee Merrin, the fabulous Hollywood public relations woman and a great friend, reminded me that she and I had gone to Henry's home together, when on Facebook, Lee wrote: "Never forget your taking me to visit his home. The great Henry Miller delighted in requesting you to 'autograph' his special art wall!"

I had sold my novel about the modeling industry, *The Beauty Trap*, to Trident Press, a division of Simon and Schuster. Thanks to a huge media blitz, to the all out efforts of the Simon and Schuster sales force and the brilliant masterminding of P.R. geniuses Lee Merrin and partner Gene Shefrin, exposure for *The Beauty Trap* was incredible – a four page article in *Life* magazine, three page *Playboy* nude spread, full page ads in the *New York Times* and *Los Angeles Times*, feature stories in newspapers throughout the world, radio and TV bookings, appearances in twenty-two cities in the United States, followed by tours of several foreign countries in Europe and Asia. *The Beauty Trap* sold over one million copies and became Simon & Schuster's fourth most profitable book of the year. A friend of Sylvia and Irving Wallace, Hollywood producer Frank Rosenberg, took the book to Joseph E. Levine of Avco-Embassy, who bought the film rights outright for a six figure sum, considered large at the time.

"I hope you have better luck with Joe Levine than I did," Henry said. "I signed a contract with him a few years back for *Tropic of Cancer*, and I'm still waiting for the movie to be made."

The Beauty Trap was an enormous commercial success, but in another sense, despite garnering its share of glowing reviews, I was also pilloried by a number of media people for having dared to write "a dirty book," which "obviously she wrote to make money"– a big no no at the time. The book that had been so highly praised by fellow students at the UCLA Leonardo Bercovici Workshop in the Novel, as well as by Bercovici himself, was now too often ridiculed. A good deal of *The Beauty Trap* criticism faulted the book for bordering on pornography, so much so that my family was scandalized and wanted me to change my name, my dad's uncle disinherited him, and my Aunt Helen had to quit her bowling club in shame.

This all happened before the media had gotten used to women writing about sex. I was one of the three or four women who, in 1969, were pioneers, the female Henry Millers of the late 60's. Along with fellow "dirty book writers/ naughty ladies" Jackie Susann and Gwen Davis, I was singled out for scorn. It was fine for the likes of John Updike in *Couples* or Philip Roth in *Portnoy's Complaint* to open the bedroom door – they were men, after all -- but it was not okay for women to do the same thing. So I had to face headlines like "Girl Sex Novelist with Angel Face," 'Naughty Lady of Letters," "Beauty is a Detriment, Says Author of Sex Sizzler," "Beautiful Model's Sexy Book Just What Happens, She Says;" "Author Hits 'Dirty' Label Put on Book," "The Dénouement of the Dirty Book," "Is it Reality, or Just a Dirty Book?" "Her Hot Book Earns Cold Cash," "Girl Writes Dirty Novel," and others in that vein.

It was hard to believe that according to these media arbiters of taste and mores, women were not supposed to even know four letter words, let alone be vulgar enough to use them. "Obviously, these writers have little acquaintance with show business, an ambiance where women have been using these words since before I was born," I complained to Henry. "They also have never been in a dorm at Vassar."

When Lee pointed out to Henry that both male and female critics and feature writers seemed jealous, Henry commented, "Sure, sure, because they can't grace their own book cover (a novelty at the time), and because nobody asked them to pose in the nude ... they think you're taking unfair advantage, promoting yourself by doing something other authors can't do. I'm not holding my breath till somebody asks me to be photographed naked."

An article headlined "Beauty and the Beasts" called *The Beauty Trap* "a horribly cautionary tale ... said to be admired by Henry Miller." Lee, defending me (and Henry), said: "*The Beauty Trap* contains some pioneering ideas that have never been seen in print before in the West. Among the firsts: blue balls, tai chi, tantra yoga, acupuncture..." In New York, they hadn't yet heard of these things.

"But my book is not a dirty book," I insisted over and over. "It's a true picture of the modeling world."

Continuing to stick up for me, Lee insisted, "As the critic for the *Literary Times* said, '*The Beauty Trap* is possibly the most honest book by a female writer in the past decade.'"

Honesty. That was what the put down artists of critical bent couldn't get used to – honesty. Nor could the critics reconcile my profile as "Vassar graduate" or the fact that I was a Mayflower descendent, eligible for the Colonial Dames and the Daughters of the American Revolution, descendent of a signer of the Declaration of Independence, being fluent in foreign languages, being cultured, having an elitist "blue stocking background." Actually, *The Beauty Trap* was tame by today's standards, and I was gratified that when *Playboy* published my personality piece, that even though I was nude, I was portrayed respectfully as serious writer and intellectual.

As author Irving Wallace's wife Sylvia recommended, accept it, be grateful you're noticed, and use it. Still, it bothered me. I hadn't expected the kind of publicity I received. I was ashamed of it, as if the critics professed to know me better than I knew myself, seizing the pulpit and defining me in a way that I didn't see myself at all.

Much was made about the two dogs in the book, named Warren and Kurt, named after two men who had played prominent romantic roles in my life, Kurt Frings and Warren Beatty, the latter relationship which spanned cities on two continents during more than half a decade and has since been chronicled in Suzanne Finstad's biography, *Warren Beatty, a Private Man*. When Henry expressed curiosity about Warren and me, Lee referred him to a three page *Screentime* magazine spread headlined "I was Warren Beatty's Girl and Lived to Tell About It." The human counterparts of the two canines laughed together about their being named as dogs, and I think they may have been secretly flattered.

Henry was invited to my fabulous, widely publicized *Beauty Trap* Hollywood party, given by my friends industrialist /venture capitalist / IBM scion / renaissance man Sherman Fairchild and the lovely, multi-talented actress/model Diahn Williams (who later became New York attorney Diahn McGrath), and of course the Wallaces and the Siegels were there, too. "You've had quite a life, haven't you?" Henry remarked. I hadn't remembered his saying that until I ran across it again not long ago in an article in one of the San Francisco newspapers, the same one that referred to me as a "sex book machine."

Lee Merrin arranged for me to appear on Chuck Barris' TV show *The Dating Game*, where I won a trip to Hong Kong with my date, actor Tab Hunter. Tab and I stabled our horses at the same place, Pepper Tree Ranch in Glendale. At virtually the last minute,

Tab announced he needed to cancel as my escort. It turned out none of the males of my acquaintance was free to take off on such short notice, but fairy godmother Lee Merrin came to my rescue by lassoing Major Daniel Boone, a descendent of *the* Daniel Boone, to accompany me.

After Hong Kong, we rerouted our flights to India, Pakistan, Afghanistan, Iran, Turkey and Israel, where I sought out mystics referred to in Rafael Lefort's book *The Teachers of Gurdjieff*, information which I used in my second novel, *The Motion and the Act*. During the trip, I stayed in touch with Henry, sending him post cards along the way, including from subsequent stops in London and New York.

Lee had a great deal of telephone contact with Henry during the whole Beauty Trap period. She chatted with Henry about my nude shoot for *Playboy*, lensed by celebrated glamour photographer Don Ornitz.

"That, I want to see," Henry said. "When is it coming out?"

"The January issue."

"I'll be sure to get that one. Jeanne in the nude ...hmmm ... hmmm ..."

Lee said, "We've gotten tremendous coverage for the book, and Simon and Schuster has been very cooperative. The book is in its fourth printing now. Sales are going great."

"As well they should," Henry said, "with the kind of sendoff the book is getting."

"You got your autographed copy we sent?"

"Yes, yes, thank you. Striking book jacket. Jeanne's picture on the front and back covers both. But fully clothed ... hmmmm.... hmmm."

I had been hoping that Henry would read *The Beauty Trap*, but his eye problems had worsened, he said, apologizing. I wondered if this was just an excuse. Henry had been through his own fiery furnace, his trials and tribulations, and had a long history of being ostracized and persecuted for writing "dirty books." I could understand he would be apprehensive and would wish to back off from endorsing someone else who was being branded a pornographic author. My situation was not that far from what Henry himself had faced, lauded on the one hand, condemned on the other. Finally, Lee convinced Henry that any condemnation presented a far from true picture of my book, and she was able to persuade him to agree to be photographed with best selling novelist Irving Wallace (whom Henry referred to as "Wallace Irving") and me in a publicity shoot on my book for *Life* magazine.

CHAPTER TWENTY-ONE

I was lucky to have been befriended, "adopted" and/or mentored by some wonderful people in the film and literary worlds of the Hollywood community. Through Leonardo Bercovici's UCLA Extension Workshop in the Novel, I met the delightful Minnie Nathan, seventh wife of Robert Nathan, author of *A Portrait of Jenny* and *The Bishop's Wife*. Robert, a kind and gentle man of Henry's vintage, was considered the dean of literary Los Angeles. Minnie was writing a novel whose protagonist was based on psychiatrist Dr. Lawrence S. Kubie, head of the American Psychoanalytic Society at the time, whom I met through the Nathans, with whom I had a long correspondence on the subjects of LSD and Wilhelm Reich's medical orgonomy (of which I was a patient). Minnie often invited me to lunch at the Bel Air Hotel, one of her favorite haunts, where we would linger for extended hours of chit chat and laughter. She was such an enthusiastic supporter of mine, and went to such great lengths to praise me to all of her and Robert's many friends. Suddenly, without warning, Minnie was stricken with lung cancer which quickly metastasized to the brain. In just a few short weeks, she was gone at only 46 years of age. Robert, 75, lamented in a letter to me, "Oh, to be 74 again!" Robert's eighth wife was British actress Anna Lee, who played the matriarch on *General Hospital* for many years, and whose godfather was Sir Arthur Conan Doyle.

The Nathans entertained a great deal, and I was always a welcome guest at their wonderful affairs. It was they who introduced me to "the Writing Wallace" family – Sylvia and Irving and their talented offspring, David (Wallechinsky, who reverted to the original family name) and Amy Wallace. The Wallaces were splendid hosts renowned for their glittering parties, particularly on election eve, and smaller soirées throughout the year as well. Lucky to be on their guest list even for intimate gatherings, through them, I met everyone from Carlos Castaneda to Norman Lear.

To bring Henry to our Sunday *Life* shoot, Lee Merrin picked him up and drove him to the Wallaces' at 108 South Bristol Circle, Brentwood. Here, Lee was immediately at home, being on familiar ground since she handled all Irving's books as well as Sylvia's, and in fact, the entire Wallace family's literary output. Knowing well the layout of the Wallace abode, Lee immediately headed for the bar, not for a drink, but to surreptitiously place a tape recorder behind it out of view.

Author of such mega bestselling page turners as *The Chapman Report*, about human sexuality; *The Prize*, a fictional behind-the-scenes account of the Nobel Prize; *The Man*, about a black man becoming president of the United States; *The Word*, about the discovery of a new gospel; *The Fan, The Celestial Bed, The Seven Minutes* and others, as well as the phenomenal nonfiction *The Book of Lists*, Irving was ever the jovial, genial, outgoing host who made everybody feel right at home. The phrase *"mi casa es su casa"* must have been coined with the Wallaces in mind. Irving Wallace was one of the kindest, most thoughtful, selfless and generous persons I have ever known. Without being asked, he was always poised to help, volunteering to write letters and make phone calls to his important literary, press and Hollywood connections in praise of other writers.

Henry and Irving took to each other instantly. The three of us engaged in a several hours' long discussion on literature, sex, obscenity, art, music, contemporary mores, mysticism, memories, personal experiences, philosophical ideas, and much more. Irving smoked his pipe, which he was seldom without, and Henry smoked his eternal cigarettes, while Lee taped the entire afternoon's fascinating conversation.

Irving was known for his carefully researched novels. He said his method of writing consisted of reading all you could on the subject, interviewing experts, and traveling to the sites where the story took place to guarantee authenticity and get a feel for the background. At the present time, the four members of the Wallace family were working on *The Book of Lists*. Henry was invited to contribute, which he did.

We talked about Irving's latest novel, *The Seven Minutes*, published by Simon & Schuster, with the esteemed Michael Korda as his prestigious editor. Irving said, "The book concerns the effects of pornography and freedom of speech. It deals with a fictional obscenity trial of a banned book titled *The Seven Minutes*, which purported to be the thoughts in a woman's mind during seven minutes of sexual intercourse."

"Hmmm.... hmmm," Henry said, "a wonderful idea."

"It's a book about a book that was supposedly written in the

1930s by a fictional writer, J. J. Janeway, which is known as one of the most banned and obscene books of all time, criticized as the most disgusting piece of pornography ever written."

"Yas, yaz, I can appreciate that, a book that details the thoughts and passions that a woman experiences ..."

"Exactly, during the seven minutes from the commencement of intercourse to orgasm."

"I congratulate you on your inventiveness. Without reading a word of it, I congratulate you for having come up with this intriguing idea."

Irving said, "The book presents arguments for both sides of the debate."

"What's to debate?" Henry asked, chuckling. "There's something to argue about?"

"Well," Irving said, "the book is read by a minor who is so aroused that he rapes a woman and is accused of rape. The fictional book within the book is condemned not only for obscenity, but for having driven a nice, clean cut college boy from a good family to brutal rape and murder."

Lee put in, "The book is set for a film. Irving has sold the screen rights."

The film version of *The Seven Minutes*, filmed shortly after our get-together, was directed by Russ Meyer. Appearing in lead roles were John Carradine, Tom Selleck, Yvonne DeCarlo, and Russ Meyer's wife, Edy Williams. Edy had been my roommate for seven weeks in Hawaii on the movie *I Sailed to Tahiti with an All Girl Crew*, starring the gorgeous Gardner McKay, in which I played a wily French saboteur. Edy subsequently became a permanent fixture at the Cannes Film Festival, every year turning up in one more revealing outfit than the next.

Irving continued, "Taking a stand in the face of incredible odds, the main character risks his personal and professional life to defend the controversial banned book. Overnight, the trial becomes a battleground where censors and anti-censors meet in open combat."

"Hmmm.... hmmm," Henry said. "I see tremendous conflict possibilities here, in a manner of speaking."

"Exactly. The prosecution contends the Janeway book is immoral, filthy and dangerous to society, while the defense side says the book is a masterpiece, it's literature, it's art not made for monetary purpose but with social importance. So the characters are caught up in dramatic conflict over sexual freedom, perversion, nudity, obscenity, censorship, and human rights."

"This is excellent," Henry said. "Controversial and timely, to be sure. But I must confess being unfamiliar with your books. I've never read what you write. I do know that somehow you managed to write these novels in a sexual vein and not be condemned for it. How did you pull that off?"

"Ah, that isn't precisely so," Irving said. "Truth is, I've been branded a hack who writes semi-porn just to make money. I can identify with the experiences you've had, Henry, as I've been criticized for the same reasons you have, and for the same reasons my fictional character J.J. Janeway was."

"We're unfortunate prisoners of the Zeitgeist," Henry said, shaking his head. "America has that Puritan strain. And there's also a strain running through western culture that we can blame the Church for."

"Well, I'm not so sure I'm tainted with that, being Jewish," Irving said.

"Of course you're tainted," Henry countered. "We all are. We can't escape it. It bores into our soul, though we try our best to fight it, doncha know. Religion, in its desire to control, created fear, shame, and guilt not merely for its adherents, but for one and all."

"Fear, shame, guilt – doesn't that stem from original sin?"

"In part, yes – and we can thank organized religion for making it worse, you might say."

"The opposite of shame and guilt is taking hold right now," Irving pointed out. "Licentiousness may be better than abstinence, but it's not the answer either."

"Love is the answer; it's something we all seek. I certainly have always sought it throughout my entire life," Henry said.

"And now Jeanne is undergoing a similar experience that both of us went through," Irving said. "How can we advise Jeanne? How can we help our young writer? What advice would you give her, Henry?"

"Well, according to what your mutual publicity woman says ... hmmm ... hmmm ... Lee over there at the bar, that is ... Jeanne seems to be holding her own. Lee was reading me some of the favorable reviews of Jeanne's book just before."

"Yes, I've seen them all. Jeanne's got the attention of the *New York Times, Playboy, the Saturday Review, Publisher's Weekly*, and all the rest, which is to her credit, and there are some excellent quotes to be culled from them, to be sure, but at the same time, she's had her share of snide and dismissive remarks and put downs as well."

"Undeservedly, to be sure."

"Yes, but par for the course. Even *Screw* magazine took a swipe at her," Irving said.

"Well, screw them, if I may speak boldly," Henry retorted. "As I see it, these critics are a bunch of frustrated would be writers who only wish they had published books, books they either can't find time to write but think they could, or books they did write that were rejected by publishers."

The conversation turned to writers who had inspired us all, starting with Nobel Prize winner Hermann Hesse. Everyone had read and loved *Steppenwolf, Siddhartha, Journey to the East, The Glass Bead Game (Magister Ludi), Narcissus and Goldmund*, "each of which explores an individual's search for authenticity, self-knowledge and spirituality in the quest for enlightenment theme," Henry said. Henry liked writers who reached into the unconscious, portraying instincts of the heart, the gut, the soul, he said.

"Nietzsche was a heavy influence on Hesse's novels," Irving said.

"As were Buddhism, Schopenhauer, and theosophy, all of which stimulated his interest in India," Henry added. "And he received continued support from Romain Rolland, the French writer, who, like Hesse, also won the Nobel Prize."

"Hesse's wife's schizophrenia brought him in touch with Jung, which undoubtedly also influenced his work."

"He wrote nothing after *The Glass Bead Game* some twenty years ago," Henry said. "Spent most of his time pursuing his interest in watercolors, that and doing his correspondence. I marvel at his daily output being in excess of 150 pages."

"Maybe he felt he'd said it all by *The Glass Bead Game*," Irving suggested.

Henry said, "The current Hesse boom in the United States was helped a great deal by Timothy Leary, isn't that right? Hesse has become the most widely read and most translated European author of the 20th century."

"Hesse is a great favorite of my children, too," Irving said.

"The younger generation reveres him," Henry agreed. "I would love to be able to write books like *Siddartha* and *Narcissus and Golamud*, wouldn't you?"

"Definitely. By the way, Henry, you and I share another favorite writer in common," Irving said, "Isaac Bashevis Singer."

"Wonderful!" Henry exclaimed. "Fabulous writer."

"I'm glad to see he's so frequently published in *Playboy* and *Esquire*," Irving added. "I have a particular empathy with Singer; we have roots in common. Both our families are of Polish origin."

"Ah, yes," Henry said. "Singer saw the writing on the wall and emigrated to America before the holocaust. When he first settled in New York, he worked as a columnist for a Yiddish newspaper, ya know. He later claimed, after the war was over, that although the Jews of Poland had died, something—call it their spirit or whatever—is still somewhere in the universe."

"I relate to that;" Irving said. "It's a mystical feeling, and there's truth to it."

"Singer's treatment of the bizarre and the grotesque, his themes of witchcraft, mystery and legend are inspiring to me," Henry said, "particularly as contrasted with his ironic consciousness."

"My children pointed out to me that Singer has been a vegetarian for most of his life," Irving said.

"Yes," Henry said, "he feels that the ingestion of meat is a denial of all ideals and religions. He asks, how can we speak of justice if we take an innocent creature and shed its blood? When asked if he had become a vegetarian for health reasons, he replied: 'I did it for the health of the chickens.' I love that line."

"That's a thought my children relate to," Irving said. In fact, the Wallace's vegetarian son David and his fiancée Flora were near daily diners at Yogi Bajan's Golden Temple of Cosmic Consciousness, located on Third Street, one of the premier vegan places in L.A., and one of my favorite restaurants as well.

"The younger generation is definitely tuned into these ideas," Henry said, "certainly more so than our generation has ever been. Singer wrote that in relation to animals, all people are Nazis; he says for animals, it is an eternal Treblinka."

Another favorite writer in common was Knut Hamsun, of whom Henry said, "You may have heard that it was Hamsun's novel

*Hunge*r that inspired me to take the bull by the horns and write *Tropic of Cancer*."

"I believe I did read that," Irving replied. "Hamsun's writing has inspired me too, though there's an aspect of him that has always disturbed me."

"Sure, sure, his antisemitism. There's no getting away from it: that disturbs everyone."

"Hamsun even excused the Nazi concentration camps, saying the world should understand that the Nazis had good reason to establish them! He met with Hitler in person, he welcomed the German occupation of Norway and gave his Nobel Prize as a gift to the Nazi propaganda minister, Joseph Goebbels. After Hitler committed suicide, he sent a telegram of condolence to the German people. He published an obituary in which he described Hitler as a preacher of the gospel of justice for all nations, and declared, 'I am not worthy to speak his name out loud.'"

"All true, regrettably," Henry acknowledged. "Hamsun was an advocate of German culture, a lifelong opponent of British imperialism. He had an intense dislike of both the English and the United States. A great believer in Aryan supremacy, he wrote, 'the Germans are fighting for us all, and will crush the English tyranny over us.' His Anglophobia was extreme, to be sure. He championed the collaborationist Quisling. He was a fascist and a racist who called blacks in America 'a people without a history, without traditions, without a brain.'"

"In the end, Hamsun turned from a national idol into one of the most loathed men in the country. In court, he was found guilty and fined, yet he refused to apologize."

Henry said, "He was a great writer, but he had severe ego problems. He claimed to have outwritten Dostoyevsky and killed off Ibsen's social realism for good. He hated and envied Ibsen. He once invited Ibsen to a lecture in order to insult him. He was known to be abusive to his wife and children."

"Unfortunately, he was a soul brother of Ezra Pound and Céline," Irving said. "France eventually caved on Céline. Knut Hamsun was luckier than Pound, in one sense, because Norway went easy on her genius son."

"One can see why. After all, there are not that many revered Scandanavian literary figures – Strindberg, Ibsen, Sigrid Undset, Isak

Dinesen and Hamsun comprise the select group who became internationally known," Henry said.

"While America reviled Pound, our country has so many famous authors, so Pound was not indispensable to our culture," Irving suggested.

"And France – well, perhaps that's a bit more complicated." Henry said. "France has so many outstanding literary figures, and..."

"What about Jean Luchaire?" I put in. "Céline got off easy, but they shot and killed Luchaire."

"France was suffering from guilt and shame from its easy surrender to the Germans. Regarding Luchaire, they acted reflexively, in my opinion. In another time, he might have been spared," Henry said.

"But why forgive Céline and not Luchaire?"

"These two were not in the same league. Luchaire was a journalist, perceived as an opportunist who sold out to the Vichy government. He controlled the press, he had enormous influence," Henry said. "Céline was in no such category, and in his favor, he was a cultural icon."

Irving said, "From what I know of the situation, Luchaire had always been a pacifist, a champion of Franco-German relations, although he was not one of those pure race proponents, he was not an antisemite like Hamsun, Céline and Pound."

Henry said, "I think there's a common character problem with Pound, Céline, and Hamsun expressing their views instead of keeping quiet on them. The problem is a question of judgment. These fellows all should have known better – we wish they had. If only their self-censorship faculty had been working instead of their ego. If only a guardian angel could have tapped them on the shoulder and said do not go in this direction. Stop, hold your tongue, say no more."

"I agree. They should have stepped back, asked themselves why am I even thinking of broadcasting such hateful material?" Irving echoed. "But sadly, they made mistakes that invited serious consequences for them."

"Theirs was a stubborn refusal to acknowledge certain conventions, society's minimal requirements of discretion. They went too far, doncha know," Henry said. "I myself am considered an iconoclast, a breaker of barriers, if you will. But I have never stepped over the line. These aforesaid gentlemen did. And didn't think it mattered."

"They were unable to discern ahead of time the serious effect their actions would have. Take Arthur Miller's reaction to Ezra Pound: Miller considers him worse than Hitler. He even said, 'In his wildest moments of human vilification, Hitler never approached Ezra ... he knew all America's weaknesses and he played them as expertly as Goebbels ever did.'"

"Some things are unforgivable in the eyes of public opinion," Henry said.

Gurdjieff came up briefly. Henry said, "As Jeanne knows, I have my differences with Gurdjieff, but he did get some things right, in my opinion. I believe he was correct when he made that remark about sex being mainly based on type and polarity."

"Do you think that might be another way of saying chemistry?" Irving suggested. "Meaning sex is best when the chemistry's there?"

"Yes, but I think it's deeper and more exact than just chemistry, so to speak."

Our conversation continued until almost dinnertime, when Henry had to leave for a previous engagement, presumably dinner.

Where is a copy of the priceless transcript of that Sunday afternoon in which Henry, Irving and I shared thoughts on every manner of subject? I have looked all over for the typed copy Lee gave me years back, but have yet to find it. I could have sworn I came across it several months ago, but maybe it was just my imagination or wishful thinking. I'm not sure how many more boxes and file cabinets Lee has to look through in her garage, but I still have about fifty unopened boxes in Florida and a couple dozen more in California. So I continue to be hopeful the transcript will eventually turn up.

As Henry said, "You never know what life has in store next, something that could change the whole picture. Life is full of surprises." I like to think of the Miller /Wallace / Rejaunier transcript in that light, that one of these days, I will be surprised to find it, and even more surprised by its wonderful, illuminating contents.

Stories and pictures of Henry, Irving and me from that memorable Sunday afternoon were published not only in *Life* magazine in a four page spread entitled "What It Takes To Be a Lady

Author Anymore," but in the San *Francisco Chronicle and Examiner*, *Parade* and *Pageant* magazines, as well as in several other media outlets throughout the world.

AFTERWORD

Being in the company of Henry Miller was a rare treat.

Henry never sought to dominate a conversation, although he was the natural center of attention with his incisive mind and quick wit, his wonderful stories, his incredible storehouse of knowledge. At the same time, he was deferential to others, respectfully honoring everyone, going out of his way to include them and draw them out. Any supportive anecdote he could find in praise of another person, he would make sure everyone heard it: "Noreen is studying French literature, and doing splendidly;" "Joe plays a very special role in Dean Martin's new picture;" "Jeanne is appearing in an episode of *Mr. Ed* on TV this coming week that I hear is hilarious. Be sure to watch it!" Henry was no egotist; he was a very modest man. As has been said before and by many, it was nearly impossible to mention anything Henry didn't know something about. If by some wild stretch of the imagination you might hit on a topic Henry wasn't on intimate terms with, he could always ask the most probing, pointed questions, and had the knack of drawing others into a lively discussion, propelled by his endless curiosity.

Today, years after our encounters, I appreciate the richness Henry added to my life even more than I did at the time. I could only wish Henry and I had been born closer together, instead of more than four decades apart; I'm sure our relationship would have taken on a very intriguing texture had we been in a romantic relationship. Is there more to say about Henry? Yes, there is. Henry and I had many conversations not included in this book, particularly those concerning material covered (from a different perspective) in my book *Planes of the Heavenworld*, about my decades long studies with a remarkable spiritual teacher in Pasadena. Additionally, there were thoughts shared with Henry about a fascinating group with whom, for several years, I spent Saturdays, pertaining to the JFK assassination. There are additional memories and notes to look through, blurry pages written in longhand on both sides of the paper with ball point pen, the ink which in time has spread into oily pools, making the writing difficult to read. And I could still get lucky and find that elusive transcript. So with handwriting to decipher, mysteries to solve, and memories to plumb, could there be another Henry book in me?

Perhaps. Time will tell.

Unfortunately, the *Life* transcript is not the only memento of Henry I lost. I had a small collection of brief, prized letters from Henry. I kept them in a table drawer along with my letters from Anaïs Nin. The table was moved to the terrace to make room for new bookshelves I had installed in the apartment, plus an elaborate floor to ceiling cat tree purchased for my two calicos. The woman who lived upstairs, an elderly busybody who was always complaining to the landlord about everything in sight, insisted the table was an eyesore that offended her sensibilities every time she looked out her window and saw it on my terrace below. Finally, I was badgered by the landlord into agreeing to have him remove the table to accommodate the woman upstairs. Sam, the Polish landlord, barely spoke English, so perhaps didn't understand when I specified my availability. He jumped the gun, came to my apartment at a time when I wasn't home, let himself in and disposed of the table, despite having been given the specific timeframe when I would be there to supervise. I had certainly planned on rescuing the letters, but alas, it was too late.

I had the two autographed lithographs Henry gave me framed and hung them on my apartment wall. When I moved back to New York, I stored them, along with some 150 boxes of other items, in my friend Louise Cabral's storage area under her house in Agoura Hills. Later, when I returned to claim my belongings, the Henry Miller lithographs were missing, apparently stolen, my guess is by exterminators. Fortunately, I do have photos of the lithographs, although the inscriptions are unreadable.

So many who appear in these pages, persons who played important roles in my life, are no longer with us. RIP: Henry and Anaïs, Dr. Siegel, Joe Grey, Nicky Blair, Irving and Sylvia Wallace, Minnie and Robert Nathan, Jacobina Caro, Leonardo Bercovici, Gene Shefrin, Norman Hickman, Charlie Fawcett, Kurt Frings, Sherman Fairchild, Maria Graciette, Mercedes Ospina, Sharon Tate, Eve Bruce, Judy Carrol, and others I have written about here and elsewhere, not the least of whom include beloved members of my family. So many of these fine people, though they no longer inhabit the Earth, remain an important part of me and always will. I think of them often and I miss them all. Friends, mentors, icons. Of which Henry Miller was a nonpareil standout.

Mercedes was right when she said Henry's greatest work of art was Henry himself. Henry the man and Henry the writer inspired not only succeeding generations of American and European intellectuals, but thousands of plain ordinary mortals, too. His legacy lives on.

As Henry affirmed, "You don't die, you reach a new level of being, a new vision." He often quoted the inscription on Allan Kardac's tomb in Père Lachaise: *'Naître, mourir, renaître encore, et progresser sans cesse, telle est la loi'* (To be born, to die, to be reborn again, and so to progress unceasingly, such is the law); he also quoted his much admired Swami Vivekananda: "Nature, body, mind go to death, not we. We neither go nor come... The man...is born and dies; but the Self we see as man is never born and never dies. It is the eternal and unchangeable Reality."

I was only a very small part Henry's world, but he was a huge part of mine.

FIN

ABOUT THE AUTHOR

Jeanne Rejaunier graduated from Vassar College, Poughkeepsie, New York, and did postgraduate studies at the Sorbonne, Paris, the Universities of Florence and Pisa, Italy, the Goetheschule, Rome, and at UCLA. While a student at Vassar, she began a career as a professional model, and subsequently became an actress in Manhattan, Hollywood and Europe, appearing on and off Broadway, in films and television, on magazine covers internationally and as the principal in dozens of network television commercials.

Jeanne achieved international success with the publication of her first novel, *The Beauty Trap*, which sold over one million copies and became Simon and Schuster's fourth best seller of the year, the film rights to which were purchased outright by Avco-Embassy. Jeanne has publicized her books in national and international tours on three continents in five languages. Her writing has been extolled in feature stories in *Life, Playboy, Mademoiselle, Seventeen, BusinessWeek, Fashion Weekly, Women's Wear, W, McCalls, American Homemaker, Parade, Let's Live, Marie-Claire, Epoca, Tempo, Sogno, Cine-Tipo,* the *New York Times,* the *Los Angeles Times,* and countless other publications.

In addition to *The Beauty Trap*, Jeanne published novels *Odalisque at the Spa, The Motion and the Act, Affair in Rome,* and *Mob Sisters*, as well as nonfiction titles *Planes of the Heavenworld, The 50 Best Careers in Modeling, Modeling From the Ground Up, The Video Jungle, Astrology and Your Sex Life, Astrology For Lovers, Japan's Hidden Face, The Complete Idiot's Guide to Food Allergy,* and *The Complete Idiot's Guide to Migraines and Other Headaches*.

Branching out as a filmmaker, Jeanne produced, directed, filmed, and edited the four hour documentary, *The Spirit of '56: Meetings with Remarkable Women*.

#####

CRITICS' REVIEWS - THE BEAUTY TRAP, BY JEANNE REJAUNIER

"Here is a novel that can't miss, crammed with all the ingredients that make a blockbuster." - **Publishers Weekly**

"A startling closeup of the world's most glamorous business, an intensely human story." - **The New York Times**

"Jeanne Rejaunier has concocted a sexpourri of life among the mannequins that's spiked with all the ingredients of a blockbuster bestseller."- **Playboy**

"A fascinating inside story of the most glamorous girls in the business, absorbing to read." - **California Stylist**

"A powerful novel that takes off like 47 howitzers." - **San Fernando Valley (CA) Magazine**

"New York's most sought after women find themselves having to make desperate decisions that will affect their very lives." - - **Wilmington (DE) News Journal**.

"The novel is rich in esoteric commercial lore about modeling...." - **Saturday Review**

"Possibly the most honest novel to appear by a female writer in the past decade."- **Literary Times**

"Crammed with all the ingredients of a blockbuster. ...Beasts in the Beauty Jungle... authentic, searing exposé." - **London Evening News**

"Ms. Rejaunier is most interesting when she goes behind the scenes in the modeling world." - **Detroit Free Press**

"If a male author had written *The Beauty Trap*, he'd be hanged by the thumbs." - **UPI**

######

ALSO BY JEANNE REJAUNIER

PLANES OF THE HEAVENWORLD
by JEANNE REJAUNIER.
Nonfiction.

In *Planes of the Heavenworld*, Author Jeanne Rejaunier examines life between two worlds, showing how our physical existence on Earth and the invisible realms beyond our planet are intricately interconnected, and how the possibility of visiting the Planes of the Heavenworld in our sleep at night prepares us for the Afterlife and enriches our present lives in the here and now.

MODELING FROM THE GROUND UP
by JEANNE REJAUNIER
Nonfiction

The huge multi-billion dollar modeling industry attracts thousands of hopefuls every year. Not all models are gorgeous supermodels or handsome male hunks. Armed with a good set of professional photos, enough ambition and an understanding of how the modeling profession works, almost anyone can model. Former international model Jeanne Rejaunier tells what you need to know to begin a successful career in modeling.

THE 50 BEST CAREERS IN MODELING
by JEANNE REJAUNIER
Nonfiction.

In *The 50 Best Careers in Modeling*, bestselling author Jeanne Rejaunier shows how you can give yourself a competitive edge by learning about the best job areas a modeling career offers, no matter what your age, sex or type, whether you're aiming for a career in front of or behind the camera, and whether you are a beginner or an established player.

ODALISQUE AT THE SPA
by JEANNE REJAUNIER.
Fiction.

Two self-made billionaires, both at crossroads in their lives, **meet** at the elegant five star Brenners Park Hotel and Spa in the resort town of Baden-Baden in Germany's romantic Black Forest, seeking initiation into the hidden secrets of ecstatic lovemaking through a clandestine organization of women, the Odalisques. One magical night with an Odalisque changes a man's life forever. *Odalisque at the Spa* explores the unusual journey of two men's search for meaning and authenticity, and the never-ending human longing for "something more."

AFFAIR IN ROME
by JEANNE REJAUNIER
Fiction.

Tania Jordan's husband, world famous author Leo Jordan, is researching political terrorism in Italy when he is blown to bits. When Tania embarks on an urgent mission to Rome to locate Leo's final manuscript and millions hidden in his secret bank accounts, she has no idea that danger awaits, nor that she will meet the love of her life in the devastating, charismatic terrorist leader Eros Falcone.

THE BEAUTY TRAP
by JEANNE REJAUNIER
Fiction.

The Beauty Trap, a revised reissue of the globally publicized international bestseller by Jeanne Rejaunier, tells the inside story of the modeling industry, the beautiful faces, the fabulous bodies and how they are used by their agents, their clients, and their lovers. Rejaunier, a former model herself, strips away the dazzling clothes and false eyelashes to reveal the grime behind the glitter.

THE MOTION AND THE ACT
by JEANNE REJAUNIER
Fiction.

In this ebook edition of her international bestseller The Motion and the Act, Author Jeanne Rejaunier writes of the interweaving lives of California seekers, introducing the reader to the strange and varied ways in which four fascinating, distinctly different characters search – intensely, passionately, desperately – for meaning in their lives, in their work, and in their sexual experiences.

MOB SISTERS
by JEANNE REJAUNIER
Fiction.

The inside story of the world's first all-female Mafia. Kristin Cates, a member of the La Femmina Woman's Mafia has disappeared, leaving behind an explosive manuscript documenting the true story of this powerful group of international lady mobsters. Kristin reveals the story of four charismatic women who rule a world class multi-billion dollar empire, their secrets, crimes and torrid love affairs.

All books are available in print and on eBook platforms - for all computers, tablets, eReaders and smart phones.

######

COMING SOON FROM JEANNE REJAUNIER

Fiction

All That Glitters
The Zoetron Revelation
Secrets of an Odalisque

Nonfiction

Fifty Shades of Success in Modeling
Astrology For Lovers (new edition)
The Afterlife in the Here and Now
Everything You Ever Wanted to Know About Heaven

#####

WATCH JEANNE REJAUNIER ACTING PERFORMANCES

http://www.imdb.com/video/hulu/vi3259105305?ref_=tt_pv_vi_1 - McHale's Navy

http://www.youtube.com/watch?v=JsEjcTs4zjM - Combat!

https://www.youtube.com/watch?feature=player_embedded&v=FJtpwsiHAcI - Mr. Ed

http://www.youtube.com/watch?v=g6WQ3mIkNsY - Burke's Law

http://www.run4.us/carpellacollection.htm - Run For Your Life

PLANES OF THE HEAVENWORLD, by JEANNE REJAUNIER
Chapter Six - The Isle of Segregation, The Mirror of Life, Registration

Violet asked, "Mary, would you say something more on the Isle of Segregation?"

"After the seven days' rest, the disincarnate goes into that Isle of Segregation, where they are apart from everyone else, alone with the teachers. There are one or two People of Light along with the teachers, and the disincarnate talks over the life he has just departed from with them. They talk over their past, their future, their options. They analyze all the facts as to how they have led their lives, how they have failed and what they've gained, what still needs to be worked on, and how it might best be accomplished."

"Would that be mostly regarding their character, their mistakes and flaws, their lack of understanding, how and where they fell short in the way they treated others in life, particularly their loved ones?" Frank, a slim, grey-haired physicist wearing bifocals asked. Frank was the only man in the room who did not wear a coat and tie.

"That certainly, and an acknowledgment of their positive traits and achievements as well, and how these were forwarded and realized in life. But yes, there is certainly emphasis on how the person failed to measure up to the ideals he came into the world to express. It's quite a problem to go through Segregation and not feel awfully wounded."

"Would you say that after the delights of Restland, Segregation might come as a shock?" Sylvia asked.

"It depends on soul level, on the state of the individual soul, Sylvia," Mary said. "One thing about Restland - it rather picks people up. When they leave Restland, they're quite happy. It's like you know you have to go to another place, and you expect it to be even better than the last – Restland was so nice, so pleasant, that the next place will be a step up, you believe. I suppose there's been that atmosphere of promise that maybe wasn't intended, but people are easily caught that way when approaching Segregation. Yet they do realize Segregation is a necessary move in their ongoing. Most people accept it and sincerely want the understanding that Segregation affords."

John, Katie's husband, Grace's son-in-law, said, "I'm thinking that a line in the New Testament, in First Corinthians, could be applicable for what occurs in Segregation: 'For now I see through a glass darkly, but then, face to face.' To me, it makes sense that because in life there is so much we don't understand, when we get to a specific part of the Other Side and look in the mirrors – those Mirrors of Life right after Segregation – it will be revealed to us and we will understand."

Sandra said, "Mary, I believe you once said that they – that is, the discarnates – find when they progress to the Plane they've earned, where they belong, say the 6th Plane, that it's even harder to accept than it was down there in the first Restland."

"That's so."

"Why is it so?"

"Because they realize they have more privileges now, and more is expected of them."

"And they're concerned they might not be up to the task?"

"That's right."

"Would the soul who'd been in Restland seven days and then goes on to their Examination, wouldn't they finish whatever tests they had to do before they go on to the Plane they've earned, where they really belong?" Eleanor asked.

"Yes, they get up there to the Rhythmic Centers and go up to the Examining Field for Fourteen Tests before they start going on to other Planes," Mary replied.

"If I may backtrack a bit," Fred said, "I'd like to ask what does the word 'registration' have to do with the activity in this area?"

"After Segregation, you have your Mirror of Life; then comes the Registration and the tests. Then from there - remember you are getting over to the Rhythmic Centers, Powerhouses, over into this Area of Christ Consciousness."

"What is the purpose of the Seven Tests of Registration?" Ed von Gehr's wife Helen asked. Helen exemplified the description of a "busy bee." She spoke in breathless, excited tones and always seemed to be in a hurry. To class, she usually wore circular skirted cocktail dresses that made rustling sounds when she moved, which was frequently. She was short of stature with taffy colored ringlets and an ample bosom, and played both piano and organ with jewel encrusted fingers and wrists dangling with a series of clanking gold bangles.

"Those are places of cleansing and learning," Mary said. "What's emphasized here are pride and humility, selflessness, compassion, motivation and purpose, compatibility, and justice. Those seven steeps —Tests of Registration – are as if they were special talents that we're offered. And they seem to be golden talents. Turn them to the Other Side, and the reality of what they are is quite astonishing. We feel we should have known what they are in the first place."

"It's like a surprise?"

"Usually. Turn them over on the Other Side and you see something else - you were not prepared for what you see and are not at all eager to see. In other words, what you see next is the opposite of what you originally saw – or thought you saw. You have these golden talents, say, like latent talents, and you see their opposite, which is how you expressed a golden talent negatively - failed to express the golden talent. And you realize how you could have done things differently and perhaps lived a totally different life. In speaking back to me, a number of people said, 'The seven talents were the hardest to get by - it seems almost as if they were unjust.' But ultimately, you take your seven talents and you go on with them.

"I went past this Mirror of Life, and I don't think any of you want to miss it. Now you've just gotten along, passed seven tests without fear. I haven't known anyone to tell me they had any fear of this next bit. The seven tests are so awfully difficult, and when you can pass them, you know there are tests all the way up. If you don't pass them, you just stay till you do. You're well taken care of - you go to your own accounting, wherever you have earned the right to be, and you have to keep coming back until you've gone through in the proper way."

Miriam said, "You were referring to the Mirror of Life."

Mary said, "This Mirror of Life is one of the most interesting things. You even see your childhood and the ugly little things you've done when you were growing up. And you never doubt that you've done any of these things when once you see it in the Mirror of Life. You see the little girl or little boy you were. You see the ugly little traits you had – the lies, the selfishness, the unkindness to your friends and family when you should have known better. You are responsible for everything from the age of seven on.

"There's a continual movie as you watch. This just goes through like a moving picture; you see your own tendency to take what you want and cover what you don't want."

"You mean what you don't want to accept of what you've done in your lifetime? What you've been in denial over, or what you were avoiding in life?" Pat, a sixty-something retired nurse from Van Nuys, asked.

"Everything. You see your first lie, you know your first confession, your first apology, your first resolution, your promise to do better next time, your next failure to live up to your promises. Most people have the same things to go through. It's astonishing, but it's all written there in the mirror of your own life. As you stand there, from the time you enter these Planes or these years in school that you have lived, everything is there. There are just as many things you did well. It's odd how many wonderful things you've done.

"But when you step away from that mirror, you don't remember those. There's no memory of what you've done that was right. It's what you haven't done that you remember."

"And yet you see your positives as well?" Bill asked.

"They're shown to you. You do see all the right things you've done – it's just as real as if you lived the life today. But you don't remember them later. You only remember what you have not done, what you neglected."

"And what type of wrongs do you see?"

"Sneaky little things, very often. The ways in which we attempted to deceive ourselves and were dishonest about our motives."

"What is the reaction of the discarnate when confronting the wrong things, the things that have held them back that still need correcting?" Willard asked.

"Sometimes they're quite sheepish about it. One man, when telling me about his experience with the Mirror of Life, said, 'Only God could plan a scheme like this that will really show you up.'"

"I thought we were shown our credits, and accepted them," Barbara said.

"That is so, at Registration, after you have seen the Mirror of Life."

Sylvia, whose father was deceased and who received messages from him asked, "Is everyone who goes over there following death more or less pushed up through the Segregation? My dad said he was with his mother and they lived in a little house together. I wondered does that mean he has gone through Segregation?"

"He's gone through Segregation or he wouldn't be with his mother."

"He also said he was going to rest there awhile before he went on and faced certain problems."

"There is that privilege too. A mother can ask for the granting of some child to come to her for a certain period. That would be after they had both gone through Segregation. Segregation is absolutely necessary. It's a sort of entrance to the next testing."

"Please explain the fourteen tests in the Examining Field at Segregation," Sandra said.

"The fourteen tests are just deliberation tests. We're taking up the rhythmic centers of the body. Then you are taking up the balances of why you had this trait - this is where the first recognition of the unfinishing comes in. If you accept it - and you don't have to accept it there any more than here - but if you do, you can see that right through your life these certain traits have shown up. Many times it is the negation, something that you just will not recognize or that you believe isn't worth recognizing.

"Many Christian Scientists suffer the most when they go over, because always through their lives, they tell me they've been able to see (and my brother was one) they had failed to recognize certain responsibilities which were theirs - the recognition of sickness in the body, in a number of cases, would have saved a life; they would have finished out a life they should have, accomplishing what they were sent here to accomplish."

Sandra spoke: "My dad's parents, my paternal grandparents, of whom I have no memory because they died when I was a baby, were Christian Scientists who both experienced early deaths because of their refusal to seek medical help, or as you said, failure to recognize sickness that needed attention. Not only they, but their practitioner, who was their sister-in-law, same thing happened to her. She died in her early 50's, and I've always thought these three family deaths could have been delayed — all three people could have lived another 20 or more years, finished work they could have accomplished in this lifetime. I'm not saying this in any way against Christian Science, only that in some people, it could create a blind spot. And I guess my question is, will these people, in a future life, have to overcome their tendency of denial?"

"We all have to overcome our blind spots, the areas we don't want to acknowledge, in which we're in denial," Mary replied. "Facing reality squarely is one of the things that's required of us in the physical, and one of the chief stumbling blocks we all experience in life."

"Who does the examining there?" Andrew asked.

"That would be the sponsors who sponsored you into the world, the teachers that have helped you, that you might call your guardian angel, and someone that is always from a very high Plane. People have said to me they come from the 100th Plane or more. You feel almost alone with yourself, yet these people are about you and support you. They aren't teachers but really see into your soul. You do appreciate the very gentleness of them."

"Does the soul on trial there try to alibi and explain away the things they don't want to acknowledge that appear in the Mirror of Life?" Barbara asked.

"Remember, you're not up before a judge, no one is judging you but yourself, you're judging yourself entirely. No, you never defend yourself. There's something about coming face to face with what you see in those mirrors. You first exclaim, almost in horror, 'I didn't think I was a bit like that.' You initially want to disavow this could possibly be you, but you recognize very quickly that the mirrors don't lie. You see it, you recognize it, so you accept it."

Linda said, "And these higher beings ask you fourteen questions. These questions that are asked – what type of questions do they ask you?"

"The questions vary according to the type of person, the advantages he had in cultural and educational values. They vary in sense of how much religious training they've had, and the tolerance they've had toward other people. But these tests are fourteen different questions that you must answer. Many people answer them satisfactorily enough that they go on, and their ongoing is easier than for others."

"Why would it be easier for some than others?"

"They have already faced certain things here on earth, certain hardships, yet in spite of the lot they endured, they realized the only way to live was to live close to their true God-center. That is what won them the easy test. That doesn't mean that man can live on an island, because, as they say, no man is an island. Man must take his responsibilities and live up to them."

"After death, if you fail the various tests, then you go backwards to wait to repeat them? Is that right?" Andrew asked.

"If you fail, you would repeat the tests when you decide to repeat them. After that, you go onward to a Plane where you've earned the right, and continue to progress at the pace you choose."

"When you still have tests to pass, is it possible to go on up to another Plane?"

"You go up to stay only when you're ready. You may visit a higher Plane briefly for a certain purpose, go where you haven't earned yet, but you won't have the privileges of a developed person there. You will come back and take those tests. Tests may be taken on the next Plane; there are Segregational tests all the way through. You go to the record of your life – one by one you overcome what is for you to overcome."

"When a soul has the opportunity to come back to Earth to live another life, would there be some certain level of Plane that they would advance to before they could come back again?" Clara asked.

"The only thing I know that has been given me that I have the right to share is the fact that in the state of reincarnation, I have been told no soul of any grade of understanding that had a number of lives before, but what requests to come back and undo. Their last life did not meet their expectations, nor the requirements of that Plane of the Heavenworld. They have to come back and want to come back and overcome whatever was wrong in the life before. None of us are free from wrong going, we have all grown through experience."

########

CONNECT WITH AUTHOR JEANNE REJAUNIER ONLINE

Nearly 200 of Jeanne's videos can be seen on YouTube:
http://www.youtube.com/user/jrej?feature=mhee.

Worldwide publicity from Jeanne's books, including her bestselling novel about the modeling business, *The Beauty Trap; The Motion and the Act*, about California New Agers in search of perfect sex; *Affair in Rome*, and several of her nonfiction titles can be viewed at:
http://www.youtube.com/watch?v=PyxXbu24s04&list=UUEq7ATRVTR8sfBbQmBk3w3Q&index=14&feature=plcp:

and at:
http://www.youtube.com/watch?v=N9NCObTQArU&list=UUEq7ATRVTR8sfBbQmBk3w3Q&index=17&feature=plcp

Additional Rejaunier writing is found on Jeanne's blog:
http://www.jarcollect.blogspot.com.

Connect with Jeanne on Facebook:
http://www.facebook.com/profile.php?id=1171012552

and at: http://www.facebook.com/BooksByJeanneRejaunier

Connect with Jeanne on Google +:
https://plus.google.com/u/0/photos/104645427544174014108/albums

Connect with Jeanne on Amazon Author Central:
http://www.amazon.com/-/e/B001K7XL12

#######

JEANNE REJAUNIER

MY SUNDAYS WITH HENRY MILLER

Manufactured by Amazon.ca
Bolton, ON